The Complete Guide to Tax Havens

by Adam Starchild

Published by
International Law and Taxation Publishers
London

The Complete Guide to Tax Havens

by Adam Starchild

Copyright © 2000 by Adam Starchild
ISBN 1-893713-10-5

Published by
International Law and Taxation Publishers
London

Contents

OF MORALITY AND

PATRIOTISM

This book will introduce you to a highly effective method of tax reduction. But who really wants to reduce his tax burden?

This question may seem stupidly naive. Who doesn't want to keep more of what's his? But this sort of answer, derived from the cynical "everyone is selfish" notion, is not what we are looking for.

Tax reduction as outlined in this book requires considerable initiative, alertness, determination, and dedication. Not that it doesn't pay. Sad to say, the net gain from each hour dedicated to developing a tax reduction strategy is almost sure to be higher than the net gain from an hour of productive employment. Thanks to "progressive" taxation, this goes double for someone in a relatively high tax bracket.

There is also a psychological dimension to tax reduction that must not be neglected. Many people derive a "clean" feeling from making a living through their work, but feel that there is something "dirty" about "scheming" to reduce their taxes.

Heavy taxes, whether used to provide luxury for a ruling elite or to support welfare schemes, always have the effect of penalizing individual initiative and productivity, reducing investment capital and thus the resources required for economic growth, reducing the standard of living, and forcing individuals to hide things, both activities and incomes, from the government and from one another.

Heavy taxation is, therefore, a danger to the future of any country. If more and more people would consciously and systematically act to reduce their individual tax burdens, they would not only improve their own lot, they would make a tremendous contribution to their country and the safety and freedom of the world. It is hoped that this book will make at least some small contribution to such a fight for individual liberty and national survival.

TAX REDUCTION: IS IT LEGAL?

Tax lawyers and accountants usually like to stress the distinction between two seemingly similar methods of tax reduction: tax avoidance and tax evasion. It is important to understand this distinction, as well as to realize the limitations of its applicability to the ideas and information present in this book. At first glance, the distinction seems quite obvious. Tax avoidance is using whatever legal means are available to minimize a tax burden; tax evasion is the use of illegal means to the same end.

Using the services of an accountant, classifying certain verifiable expenses as "business expenses" with an acceptable, or seemingly acceptable, justification to reduce the taxable net income from one's business or profession is legal. Even if the taxman does not accept the validity of these deductions, and even, if worse comes to worse, all compromise attempts fail, the businessman doesn't have to fear being indicted for a criminal offense. The worst that can happen is that he will have to pay the tax he believed he didn't have to pay. This is tax avoidance.

On the other hand, willfully failing to report part of his income on his tax return or failing to comply with other reporting requirements is acting illegally. This is tax evasion.

Lawyers and accountants will explain, most sternly, that while they can help one to the best of their abilities to avoid taxes legally, by using all possible accounting tricks and legal loopholes, they will have nothing to do with tax evasion schemes. They cannot be accomplices to a crime; it could destroy them professionally (not to mention the possibility of going to prison), and anyway, they are law-abiding citizens. Thus, it would seem that the distinction between avoidance and evasion is very important.

However, once one looks into the matter, one will discover that the distinction is far from clearcut. Vagueness, ambiguity, and holes in the law make it unclear just what and how one is legally obliged to report.

The law, one's strategy, and a host of other factors may entail so much uncertainty that a harsh legal decision against the tax avoider could become unlikely. The defendant's lawyer may be convinced that his client is a genuine tax **avoider**, albeit a slightly clumsy one; the government's lawyer may claim that he is an **evader**; the judge may reach an in-between verdict; the appeals courts may reverse the trial judge; and so on. Thus, the government may decide that the whole matter will cost more than what the government stands to gain and try to compromise out of court, or even drop the whole thing. On the other hand, it might try to make an example of the avoider/ evader, going all out to force a new precedent and thus cow potential tax dodgers, and so on. Anything can happen given the crazy tax laws of most countries, bureaucratic and political imperatives, and the imponderables of human nature. But even a clearcut, legal tax avoidance could be fought in court by the government and become, Wonderland-like, tax evasion.

What must be borne in mind is that in practice there is a continuum between easy-to-discover tax avoidance, provable tax avoidance, and punishable tax avoidance. What one is faced with is a set of probabilities. One's fate does not depend on hard and fast rules and facts, but on circumstantially determined chance. Some things one might do have very unclear legal status, and one may play for time, using complexity and good professional advice to guarantee oneself almost complete safety.

While, for obvious reasons, it would be most unwise to tell a legal counselor or accountant flat out that one plans tax evasion, this does not mean that it is not possible to discuss with them possibilities that are legally dubious. Tax **avoidance** terminology must be used, a language in which everything involved can be fully understood by all parties but that in no way smacks of criminal intent. The most important distinction to bear in mind is that between tax reduction methods that can lead one to court and prison and those that protect one from such consequences as well as protecting one's money from the taxman.

The legal distinction between **avoidance** and **evasion** is the key here. If pushed, one may admit that one is involved in tax planning for tax avoidance purposes — strictly within the letter of the law — and that one abhors tax evasion as much as the next guy. There is no simple legal classification applicable to most approaches.

Put simply, in tax matters, one should steer clear of stupid actions that will surely result in indictment and conviction for tax evasion. If a person has "black" money in a foreign bank account in his own name and this is proved in court, he's had it — and deserves it.

The Caribbean tax havens in particular, and all tax havens to a growing extent, are waiving secrecy in many cases. The justification is always that it is for a criminal investigation. However, the United States calls almost everything criminal, and uses that as the basis to demand, and get, the information it wants. Any "conspiracy" which involves the United States in any way is grounds for such an investigation — overpricing goods sold to an American company, diverting commissions on American business, having a friend who is suspected of knowing a drug dealer — any of these can be enough.

Being an alien is not sufficient reason to think that the U.S. may not be interested in one's assets. Conspiracy can involve any dealings of a foreigner with the United States, or with an American citizen or company. One need not have **ever** been in the United States to be guilty of a major crime in America. In fact most of the alleged drug dealers that the United States wants to extradite from Colombia have never been in the U.S. — the U.S. government charges that they headed conspiracies that intended to distribute narcotics in the United States. This is not a comment upon their guilt or innocence, but simply an example of how the United States' view of its jurisdiction works. It is equally possible for a person who has never been in the United States to be guilty of conspiring to assist a U.S. taxpayer in tax fraud, simply by sending normal and legitimate commissions to a European bank on behalf of the taxpayer.

Switzerland has now introduced "money laundering" legislation, making it a crime to assist "money launderers." Anyone who knowingly hinders the identification or confiscation of assets from a crime will face a prison term of up to five years and a fine up to one million Swiss francs.

The law aims to curb the handling of drug money and any funds derived from criminal offenses including securities fraud (and maybe deposed dictators), but it stops short of changing the principles of Swiss banking secrecy. It remains illegal for a bank or company to pass on information about clients to a third party.

Someone who omits to verify the beneficial owner of assets which he accepts or transfers can be sent to jail for up to a year and fined if the assets turn out to be the proceeds of a crime. This covers Swiss lawyers as well as bankers.

Similar legislation was introduced in Luxembourg in 1989, but with higher fines and prison terms up to five years.

The Luxembourg banking community has been praised by U.S. narcotics authorities for its cooperation in seizing the funds of Panama's General Noriega and alleged Colombian drug baron Rodriguez Gacha. Luxembourg says it will only agree to help with investigations in criminal matters. It retains its banking secrecy laws and will not share information with other tax authorities unless they can prove there has been a crime. But remember, it is easy for a government to claim there has been a crime, and then once they get the bank information decide that you weren't a bank robber after all. Instead you were guilty of tax evasion.

Naive Fools Spend Time in Prison

One of the greatest problems of offshore privacy strategic planning is the naive fool who breaks laws without thinking through the consequences.

For example, as a consultant, I once had a call from a certified public accountant in a major American city, who said he had a number of clients who wanted to establish "secret" bank accounts in the Cayman Islands. He said his clients were paying all of their taxes, but were very concerned with secrecy, and wanted to be certain that the U.S. government would not learn about the accounts.

He became greatly offended when I explained to him that all of his clients were crooks. I explained in detail that no U.S. citizen (or resident) could have a "secret" bank account, because it is a felony to fail to immediately notify the government of the existence of the account. The penalties for such secrecy at that time were far worse than any possible tax offense — today the penalties have been increased so severely that no American should even contemplate such a violation. One bribed bank clerk (perhaps for a mere $100) in a so-called secrecy jurisdiction could put the client in prison for 10 to 15 years under new mandatory minimum sentencing laws. There are numerous legitimate ways that a U.S. citizen can make foreign investments without running afoul of these draconian laws, many of which are discussed in this report.

The most dangerous fools — to themselves as well as to everyone they deal with — are those persons who fail to understand the serious implications of their actions. They deal with lawyers, accountants, and/or bankers as if there was nothing legally wrong with their actions, and then seem startled when the family accountant or banker facing many years in prison testifies against them, because he was dragged into something he had no intention of being a part of. Or worse, they wind up blurting out their incriminating intentions to a lawyer or accountant who immediately notifies the authorities, frequently setting a trap for them. (Remember, lawyer-client confidentiality does not apply to stating an intention to commit a crime, and the lawyer is legally obligated to report it.) Many U.S. professionals today (perhaps fearing a possible set-up by authorities) venture on the side of caution and immediately report such approaches. This is no secret — it has been recorded in many, many court cases, but the naive clients continue to get convicted.

The penalties for most of the bank secrecy and money laundering crimes (money laundering includes moving unreported cash, even if you are the legal owner) are several times the penalty for armed bank robbery.

Most of these people would never consider committing a bank robbery, and if they were to plan such a crime they would choose their partners with extreme care, and full awareness of the consequences by all parties concerned. Yet they think nothing of committing financial crimes with far more serious penalties, and cavalierly involving others, as if it was a big joke and nothing to be seriously concerned about.

There are enough legal means to accomplish the same ends that nobody needs to commit these crimes — but if they wish to persist in doing so, they should at least face the reality of their acts and plan like a real criminal, choosing their associates with the same care they would use to choose a bank robbery partner. If you really want to be a criminal, then be one, but don't stagger around the offshore banking world like a drunk waterbuffalo.

If you want to gain a good understanding of how the U.S. government views tax havens, University Microfilms International, through its Books On Demand program, is now making available **Tax Havens and Their Uses by United States Taxpayers** by Richard Gordon. Frequently referred to as "The Gordon Report," this was a 1981 U.S. Treasury Department study prepared at the request of Congress. It gives considerable detail and examples of the uses of tax havens. It is available from University Microfilms for $67.30 softbound, or $73.30 hardbound. Out of print for over a decade, anyone interested in tax havens who has not studied the work will find much still useful information in it. Copies can be ordered through booksellers, or directly from University Microfilms International, 300 North Zeeb Road, Ann Arbor, Michigan 48106-1346; telephone 800-521-0600 or 313-761-4700. The UMI catalog number of the book is AU00435, and UMI accepts Visa or MasterCard.

As you read the following chapters, you should keep in mind that this is **not** a handbook, that I am **not** counseling any course of action. This is a source book, designed to provide information on tax havens, their nature, and their possible uses in tax planning. What the reader does with this information is strictly up to him.

One of the oft neglected areas of the investment of money in an offshore environment is what the actual investment scenario will be. Many times people enter a world in which they are unfamiliar and do not recognize the significant risks that can be made in investing in a world where issues of bonds, stocks, annuities, CDs, etc., are done in an unpredictable and unknown environment.

It is imperative that the investor be aware of the risks that they are taking and the market conditions they are entering. More times than not, what the less than professional investor should be doing is to seek professional and accredited money management. If one were to turn to established organizations, many times the unwieldy and unknown aspects of international investment would become easy and routine to deal with.

A decade or two ago, tax haven countries were used primarily by wealthy families setting up trusts for the grandchildren. As tax laws in various countries have changed, such simple solutions are generally no longer possible.

But today the same countries are being used, with the same trust and corporate forms, to provide asset protection. The tax neutrality of the tax haven countries is ideal for this purpose, since there is no additional tax complication for the person seeking asset protection. Thus the tax haven business has slowly evolved into the asset protection business.

It is far preferable to stay with jurisdictions where the asset protection features have evolved as a fundamental part of the law and the local social and political structure. The Swiss law protecting insurance policies from seizure has been in effect since 1908 — not to attract foreign business but because the Swiss wanted it to protect themselves. A Swiss court isn't going to look for excuses to carve exceptions out of the law.

Panama has been a corporate management center since it became a country, because that business was an integral part of the commercial center that developed around the Panama Canal.

Using offshore havens is an art, not a science, which means that you will find contradictions in this book. One of the things to bear in mind when studying an art is that taste plays a role. The offshore strategy that suits the needs, and prejudices, of one person may not suit those of another. It is not an exact science that can be replicated through experiments and demonstrations.

Most of these decisions are somewhat subjective, and depend upon your personality and your personal experience as much as they do on law. You have to go with the people, countries, and cultures that you feel comfortable with.

People frequently ask what is the best offshore haven, or what is the best country in which to open a bank account. There is no "best" answer — these things are very subjective, and depend upon what you want to do.

One of the major trends in tax havens is for "real" use of tax haven countries, instead of just using them for a place to register a company or trust that is actually managed elsewhere. This trend may have initially been driven by tax inspectors looking at tax haven operations with suspicion, and wondering why the investment decisions of an allegedly Cayman Islands company were being made in New York or London.

But as more and more pressure has forced tax haven users to honor the simple caveat of substance over form, they have learned that having the transactions actually occur in the tax haven jurisdiction, with real people making real decisions, is a pleasant and rewarding experience in itself. One can have one's money managed by an offshore investment management firm that is every bit as competent as one in New York or London, instead of pretending to be in the tax haven while making decisions elsewhere.

The same trend is applying to people actually taking up permanent or seasonal residence in tax haven countries, or opening real tax-free businesses. Whether it be consulting, computer programming, or import-export, the consumers of tax haven country services are learning that many haven countries today can offer real substance and value. Several of the new services I discuss later in this update are good examples of the kinds of services that one can now purchase in a tax haven.

Many people are realizing that they can actually operate their business from a tax haven. Computer programming, stock & commodities trading, consulting, import-export, and travel businesses are just a few of the many that are capable of being moved to a tax haven. For example, a securities trader who used to sit before his computer terminal in New York or London all day eventually realizes that he can do exactly the same kind of business, sitting before the same computer terminal, in the Bahamas or Malta. And the profit on each of his successful trades will be approximately double, because of the tax freedom gained from doing real business in a tax haven.

The growth of Mutual Legal Assistance Treaties and Tax Information Exchange Agreements is part of a pattern of growing attacks from all sides on secrecy and confidentiality in tax havens. Many consumers of tax haven services would be surprised to learn that many tax haven service providers do not consider these to be major issues. In many cases they feel that enforcement of such agreements tends to keep away the criminal elements and bring in the real business that is more suitable for long-term business relationships. Since banks and fund managers depend on maintaining a high reputation, they don't want dirty money, and are doing more investigation of who their clients are before accepting them.

One unfortunate consequence of this trend is that smaller and less stable countries are now trying to jump in on the "secrecy market" by offering tougher secrecy protection laws and no treaty relations with major countries.

As a practical matter, they also tend to lack any real commercial relations with the rest of the world. It has been suggested that all that is needed to set up a tax haven is a place above the water line at high tide and a telephone line. Some recent entrants are pretty close to making this old joke come true, with legislation copied from other jurisdictions and a press release announcing that they are open for business.

Many of the financial institutions in these lesser jurisdictions have turned out to be complete scams — there are still too many consumers who refuse to follow the simple dictum "if it sounds to good to be true, it probably is a fraud."

The demise of the European Union Bank in Antigua was a prime example of this in the past year. The bank had nothing to do with Europe (unless you count the unauthorized use of the name of a British lord on its stationery), and advertised secrecy and Internet banking services. It seems that few stopped to ask themselves how an unheard of bank could offer services that the bigger banks seemed to be incapable of providing. The answer of course was simple, the EUB only accepted deposits, not withdrawals, and nobody got any of their money back.

Other offshore scams abound — most of them unbelievable if the buyer would only give them 30 seconds thought before signing the check. Who for example can really believe that a bank, for a $495 fee, will grant a $5000 unsecured credit card to an anonymous customer? Yet variations of this scam have been very popular, and continue to sell well to the gullible. The bank needs to know its customer just as much as the customer needs to know the bank.

In a tax haven world of many sound, reputable, established organizations, there is no reason for any legitimate consumer of tax haven services to be dealing with the fringe elements of the business. Where money is going offshore, there needs to be equal consumer confidence in the **provider** and the **jurisdiction**.

WHAT ARE TAX HAVENS?

No investor can rely on the tax haven approach as an element of his tax-minimization strategy unless he has a full understanding of what tax havens are. It is also necessary to become thoroughly familiar with the ins and outs of the several kinds of tax havens available.

Simply stated, a tax haven is any country whose laws, regulations, traditions, and, in some cases, treaty arrangements make it possible for one to reduce his overall tax burden. This general definition, however, covers many types of tax havens, and it is important to understand their differences.

No-Tax Havens

These are countries that have no income, capital gains, or wealth (capital) taxes, and in which it is possible to incorporate and/or form a trust. The governments of these countries do earn some revenue from corporations; "no-tax" means that what is paid is independent of income derived through a company. These states may impose stamp duties on documents of incorporation, a small charge on the value of corporate shares, annual registration fees, etc.

No-Tax-on-Foreign-Income Havens

These countries do impose income taxes, both on individuals and corporations, but only on **locally derived** income. They exempt from tax any income earned from foreign sources that involve no local business activities apart from simple "housekeeping" matters.

For example, in such a haven there is often no tax on income derived from export of local manufactured goods.

The no-tax-on-foreign-income havens break down into two groups. There are those that allow a corporation to do business both internally and externally, taxing only the income coming from internal sources, and those that require a company to decide at the time of incorporation whether it will be one allowed to do local business, with the consequent tax liabilities, or one permitted to do only foreign business and thus be exempt from taxation. Again, it may seem that the latter approach is better — but the matter of "business justification" may be an important consideration.

Low-Tax Havens

These are countries that impose some taxes on all corporate income, wherever earned. However, most have double-taxation agreements with the United States that may reduce the withholding tax imposed on income derived from the U.S. by local corporations.

Special Tax Havens

These are countries that impose all or most of the usual taxes, but either allow special concessions to special types of companies or allow very special types of corporate organization, such as the very flexible corporate arrangements offered by Liechtenstein.

Even if one has already made up his mind about the structure of his tax-minimizing program, combining, say, a no-tax haven, a low-tax haven, and ultimate immigration, he still must know much more about each country under consideration before taking the plunge. It is not enough to know that X is a "tax haven"; it is not enough to know that one's lawyer likes its beaches. The tax minimizer must have both general knowledge about country X and specific knowledge about current political and social developments there: he certainly does not want to wake up one morning to a call advising that all his corporate assets have been confiscated by the new military government of X, or that no funds can be sent out of the country, or that the new corporate profits tax is 85 percent. Things like this rarely happen. But they do happen. The only insurance against them is comprehensive advance knowledge on the country or countries one plans to get involved in and keeping the information current. In particular, the following must be known:

Costs

A tax haven country usually derives substantial revenue from its "tax haven industry." This means there are charges that must be borne by any company chartered there: government fees (stamp duties, some form of stock-value charge) and non-government costs (legal fees, trust company charges, etc.).

In view of the fact that it may be necessary to have more than one tax haven company in more than one country to take care of things, these costs may weigh heavily in deliberations. Original incorporation costs are only the beginning. Usually, some sort of "legal presence" in the country of incorporation is required: an office with a sign bearing the company name, a local director or legal representative, etc. These services are available, but they cost, and in some places they cost more than in others. When deciding on tax-saving methods, the costs must be run against the tax savings. With relatively small amounts of investment funds, the tax haven approach may never be worthwhile. However, in view of the fact that the costs are essentially fixed, bearing no relation to the size of income involved, the larger the gross from investment, the less important are the expenses of using tax havens.

Flexibility of Corporate Structure

Some tax havens may require that stockholders' meetings be annual and local. This may require an annual visit to the haven. If keeping things "low-profile" is important, this could be a serious disadvantage. It also costs money and is a nuisance. There may be a requirement for "minimum paid-in capital" at the time of incorporation. This may, in some places, be got around through a local ad hoc loan from a local bank. In other places it may not, and the loan may be expensive. Another problem may be the required number of local corporate directors, or the need for more than one local shareholder, etc. Local firms are available to "ease" such official requirements on corporate structure by providing proxies, and such, but this involves extra expense.

Exchange Controls and Monetary Freedom

Since using a tax haven corporation usually involves a flow of funds in and out of the haven country, the issue of the freedom to conduct such exchanges is crucial. To what extent is one free to take money out of the country? If there are severe restrictions, the place is no haven. Similarly, are there any restrictions on converting foreign currency into local currency and vice versa? Are special permissions required for each exchange? General permission with reports on each exchange? General permission with no official control but with all exchanges restricted to officially approved agencies at fixed official ratios? Or is there a free money market? Can one deal as he pleases outside the country in foreign currency, keep an account in them locally, but be completely debarred from converting them to local currency? Can local currency generated by local business be converted to foreign currency? Detailed answers to these questions are very important.

Accessibility

Quick communication may be crucial to efficient utilization of a tax haven. Suppose it is necessary to instruct a haven company to make a quick stock purchase, but the haven lies in the other hemisphere, where it is after midnight. Suppose there is only one telephone in the building of the company agent, shared with seventy-five other offices, and it is usually out of order. Suppose cables are delivered only once a week, airmail is nonexistent, and surface mail takes eight months for a round trip. This is an extreme example, but in some cases it is not too far off the mark. These things must always be considered: Is there speedy, reliable telephone, telegraph, telex, and airmail communication? Is the place accessible by air, directly or indirectly? By sea? By land? If one can get there without too much difficulty, will the government let him in?

Professional Services

Tax haven activities involve many related professionals: lawyers, bankers, trust managers, accountants. Some tax havens may be too small or underdeveloped to have acceptable services. If there is but one local lawyer who is at the same time the country's only accountant and a barber in his free time (or perhaps the other way around), forget it.

Apart from these obvious considerations, there are some subtler ones. Are all the local banks representatives of major American banks? It might be deceptively convenient to arrange everything through the Chase Manhattan Bank, relying on its local branch in the tax haven to handle money transfers and so on. Undeniably, Chase Manhattan is a good, reliable bank. Unfortunately, records of such arrangements are all too accessible to prying eyes. Especially if they are processed on a central computer in New York City.

With completely independent foreign banks, one has to be careful too. Some havens have very flimsy banking regulations. This may be good in general, but there's always the danger of a fly-by-night outfit. This is true of any professional service overseas. One should not go overboard with suspicion, but things must be carefully checked out in advance.

Language and Tradition

Tax haven business requires cross- cultural communication. This can be disrupted by language barriers and matters of legal tradition and practice.

Possibilities for Local Business Activities

Some tax havens may offer you positive business reasons for local investment quite apart from any tax considerations. Such reasons include special treatment, low labor costs, etc. Other havens may strictly forbid any "exempt" company from local business dealings.

Political and Social Stability

This is, needless to say, the most important consideration of all. It determines and affects all the rest. A country that is involved in a civil war, or that regularly changes governments "by bullet," or that has a strong socialist political faction is hardly to be trusted to keep investment assets secure. A political upheaval, or even a change in legislation introducing taxes or other restrictions on corporations or trusts, may take away everything. What are the indications of stability and instability? Clearly, there are no foolproof signs, but there are things that do help formation of an intelligent judgment.

History. A country that has had very moderate political, economic, racial, and social change over the years, where political and social violence are not common, can be deemed to possess a tradition of conservative peacefulness. A tradition is an almost tangible social force. It molds a people's way of thinking and acting, and it is a good predictor of stability.

There are, of course, more specifically segmented predictors of stability. A country that has never had any form of income taxation can be counted on to have a population that would be less than sanguine about the imposition of such taxation. This may apply even if there is some other form of political instability, say, regular military coups. Such coups could be totally irrelevant to any economic development, because economic legislation and public service may be unaffected by which general currently happens to occupy the presidential palace.

Population. A racially diverse population **may** mean racial tensions that could bring about some form of social or political upheaval. In some places, though, there is completely peaceful coexistence between racial groups.

Political-Economic Situation. There is a wide range of variables here. If a country has a one-house, popularly elected legislature and a very active socialist government, it will not remain a tax haven for long. If it has a government divided, say, between a governor general (representing the crowned head of the "mother country") and a locally elected two-house legislature, and there is little local political dissension, radically adverse legislation is not especially likely.

General poverty **may** be indicative of a potential for revolution, while stable prosperity is more promising. Trade union activity of any consequence may be indicative of a potential for socialism in the future. A government with strong motivations for "progress" may be a mixed blessing. Such a regime may encourage overseas investors and at the same time increase welfare budgets and thereby create a future need for heavy taxes. Universities with politically active leftist student bodies are bad signs.

Prospects for Foreign Invasion and War. These are slighter for an isolated island country than a continental country, but in the latter case, things to consider are: Which continent? Which neighbors? It is quite unlikely for Liechtenstein to be invaded by Germany, Italy, or France. But what are the prospects for Israel or Jordan?

In my survey of tax havens, I have screened out those countries that superficially could be classified as tax havens. I will not elaborate on the Hungarian "competition" to Swiss numbered bank accounts. I will also pass in relative silence over Israel's claim to be a tax haven for certain foreign investors. Whatever might be the attractions of its specific tax laws pertaining to such investors, a country that has gone through five wars in thirty years, that has had an inflation rate of more than 100 percent and heavy exchange controls, where devaluation happens monthly, trade unions are rampant, and racial tensions are explosive, is not a reliable haven of any sort.

I have selected only countries that possess some credible stability and that can really compete on the tax haven market. Each has its own specific advantages and disadvantages. It is up to the individual investor to decide which are best suited to his needs and circumstances.

THE ROLE OF TAX HAVENS

IN TAX PLANNING

This is not an exhaustive handbook of tax avoidance methods. Rather, it is designed to bring to the reader's attention a specific method of tax avoidance that can be used in combination with other, more conventional methods, not as an alternative to them.

To understand the precise role of tax havens, it is important to distinguish two basic sorts of income: (1) return on labor and (2) return on capital. The first kind of return is what one gets from his **work**: salary, wages, fees for professional services, and the like. The second kind of return relates, basically, to the return from **investments**: dividends on shares of stock; interest on bank deposits, loans and bonds; rental income; royalties on patents.

It is the second kind of income, income from an investment portfolio, that tax havens are useful for. If one does nothing about it, this income is treated for tax purposes in essentially the same fashion as salary and wages. If the resulting tax bracket is reasonably high, investment returns are "punished" much more severely than work-originated income since it is difficult to apply to it tax-saving measures related to concessions, allowable deductions, etc.

There are ways other than the use of tax havens to defend this investment income against heavy taxes. All of them involve a common principle: reduction of the applicable tax bracket through legal alienation of income. For example, if an executive's salary is $25,000 a year and his gross return on investments is $5,000, the extra $5,000 is taxed, if considered a part of his income, at the rates applicable to income in the $25,000 to $30,000 range. If, however, he gives his wife the stock, and she has no further income, she is taxed according to the much lower rates that apply to an annual income of $5,000 (assuming they file separately). There may be an initial tax penalty in the form of a gift tax on the stock transfer. It is a matter of calculation to find out the most economical way of making such a change of ownership. On the other hand, the transfer could save estate taxes and probate expenses when the husband dies. The precise calculation is complex and may involve such hard-to-measure considerations as the relative likelihood of a divorce somewhere down the road.

But what we are interested in here is the principle of **alienation**: transferring to some different legal person income that would have otherwise gone to the alienator, thereby making use of the fact that the other legal person is subject to lower tax rates.

Why did I use the term **legal person**? One's wife is both a legal and a real person, of course. She is a legal person, with personal assets and responsibilities, because she is a human being. But the same principle is illustrated by another method of alienating income: incorporation.

A corporation is as much a legal person as a human being. It has separate assets, separate liabilities, separate income, and separate tax burdens. Thus, if a businessman (1) incorporates his business; (2) hires himself as a corporate employee with a modest salary; (3) deducts all conceivable business expenses — including, of course, his salary and those he may pay to members of his family — (4) pays corporate income tax on the company's net profit at a flat rate that should be less than he would have had to pay had the income been his personally; (5) takes the net profit after tax and pays himself out of it the minimally allowable dividend (there are, usually, some legal requirements that some minimum percentage of the net profit of a corporation after taxes has to be distributed as dividends); (6) makes his wife, daughter, son **et al.** stockholders (taking into account the gift tax) and pays them dividends as well, thus taking advantage of their lower tax brackets; and (7) reinvests the rest of the profits in the growth of the company, he should be considerably better off in the tax department.

Needless to say, this is not a sufficiently detailed "how-to" plan, but it illustrates the point. Taxes are lower on the combined income derived from salary (or salaries) and dividends than the incorporator would have paid if the net profit all around were his personal income. Also, by reinvesting corporate profits that have never been part of personal income, he increases the value of his company and, thus, the value of his holdings in it. Later on, if he sells the stock, the profit from the sale is a capital gain. The tax rates on capital gains are usually much lower than regular income tax rates on comparable income. Thus, the principle used here is **alienation of income for reduction of applicable tax rates through lowering of applicable tax brackets**.

The kind of arrangements outlined above are probably well known to the reader from his own experience. He may very likely have used similar methods himself. There are, as yet, no tax havens involved. Observe, however, that two specific features of the tax system **are** involved, each giving rise to a distinct tax-minimizing principle: (1) Taxes are imposed on **net** income. This gives rise to the principle of **maximizing** deductible expenses and thus **minimizing** recorded, taxable net income. (2) Taxes are levied "progressively," with increasing rates on higher income brackets. This gives rise to the principle of alienating income to legal entities whose applicable brackets are lower than those of the alienator. These entities may be real people with little or no other income, or corporations, whose applicable tax rates may be lower than the incorporator's.

These two principles are, essentially, the same as those involved in tax planning when tax havens are used. If our income tax system imposed taxes on **gross** income at a flat rate, these two principles would not apply, and taxes could not be minimized. If, indeed, the tax rate were reasonably low, there would be little motivation for such action. However, even with a uniform rate on all gross incomes, these two principles could still help to reduce taxes through tax havens in a fashion not available here at home. This is because tax havens introduce a third principle, that of the free market.

Different countries have different tax policies and laws, and one can, in principle, alienate part of his investment income to a business entity in another country. Thus, to give a very simplistic example — one that does not take into account all the complications that we will have to consider later in our discussion — if an investor incorporates in, say, Bermuda, which is a no-tax country, and vests his entire portfolio there, instead of paying, say his home country taxes of 50 percent of his investment income, he would pay nobody anything. He would thus be able to reinvest the **entire** yearly yield on his portfolio in more stock.

It is easy to see that over twenty years there is a big difference between reinvesting gross dividends and after-tax dividends. Even if our hypothetical investor liquidates his company after forty years, "repatriates" the profits to his country, and pays taxes on them as a one-year income (which would put him in a very high bracket!), the multiplier effect of reinvesting "whole dollars" would still not be entirely wiped out.

Alternatively, when he decides to retire, he could immigrate to a friendly country that does not tax his income from abroad and start receiving dividends there from his no-tax-haven company, as well as any superannuation, pension, social security, etc., due from his home country. Another possibility for him would be to leave his stock in a foreign trust (which we will discuss in detail below) with his family members as beneficiaries, thereby avoiding inheritance taxes.

Obviously, the foregoing case is a huge oversimplification. We will deal with the qualifications and complexities later, as well as the extra costs they incur. If things **were** so simple, tax revenues would have dried up years ago. Nonetheless, many have found the effort and study required to learn how to use the tax haven road to riches well worth it indeed.

Offshore Reinvoicing for Exporters and Importers

Reinvoicing is the establishment of a tax haven corporation to act as an intermediary between an exporter and his customers. The profits of this intermediary corporation and the exporter allow the accumulation of some or all profits on transactions to be accrued to the offshore corporation. It should be noticed that a similar structure can be utilized by an importer.

An exporter corporation sells $1,000,000 of exports to France normally every year. Assuming cost of goods sold and operating expenses are $600,000. The exporter corporation earns $400,000 on its sales before taxes. Taxes will average say $160,000 thus reducing net profits to $240,000.

The exporter establishes a tax haven corporation to act as intermediary. The exporter corporation sell its products to the tax haven corporation on paper for say $600,000. The tax haven corporation in turn sells the goods to the French client for $1,000.000. The tax haven corporation, thus earns $400,000. Since there are no taxes, $400,000 is the net income after taxes. The exporting corporation shows no profit. ($600,000 gross sales less $600,000 cost of goods sold).

The $400,000 in tax free income is then deposited in a bank account or other investment instrument in London, New York, Miami,

Nassau, or Panama according to the wishes of the exporter. The account is under the control of the exporter.

The basic process of reinvoicing saved the exporting corporation say $160,000 in taxes less a small reinvoicing charge.

The intermediary corporation is formed in a country that has no taxes on import-export transaction. For example, the British Virgin Islands, Cayman Islands, and Panama have no income taxes on reinvoicing transactions.

To provide anonymity, the nominee officers and directors are provided by a management firm who manage the company. Bearer shares are issued and delivered to the owner as proof of ownership.

The management company can establish the account with any financial institution in any major financial center in the world. For example, many reinvoicing clients have established bank accounts in New York, Miami, Channel Islands, Bahamas, Cayman Islands, etc.

The beneficial owner of the intermediary company provides instructions on a regular basis by telephone, telex, facsimile, courier, or airmail.

The profits can be immediately released as instructed by the owner or alternatively they can be accumulated offshore say with a major international bank where interest on deposit accounts is not subject to tax.

The merchandise can be sent directly to the exporter's client. The only functions performed in the reinvoicing country are the preparation and dispatch of the new invoice and the management of the banking operations.

Once the offshore company has been established, the management company will arrange for a post office box, telex, telephone, and facsimile service available for use by the offshore company. The management company will then begin reinvoicing.

The set up costs are generally less than one would think which includes letterhead, telephone, telex, facsimile, mail service, as well as a tax haven corporation.

Tax Havens and Tourism

The use of a foreign corporation domiciled in any one of the famous company tax havens such as Switzerland, Panama, the Bahamas, or Bermuda (among others, can enhance the profitability of any international business, and especially a travel or tourism enterprise.

Many European and American companies are expanding and diversifying overseas as a means of growth and as a hedge against economic ups and downs in their country of origin. By incorporating a tax haven operation to accumulate tax-free income, accomplishment of multi-national objectives is accelerated. A travel or freight operation can be established in a tax haven to be used as a conduit for international sales activity and financing. Such operations can accumulate trade discounts, commissions, advertising allowances, etc., completely tax-free while the parent or associated company can assume tax deductions by absorbing administrative and selling costs.

Most offshore companies can defer any tax until the profits are repatriated to the investor's home country. These are generally companies actively engaged in the conduct of a local business. In the travel business, such a definition is especially easy to meet. A retailer, or group of retailers, could set up their own travel wholesale operation in a convenient tax haven, such as Bermuda, and put all of their European business through it. The profits of the Bermuda firm would accumulate tax-free, and could be invested in other foreign operations.

In addition, a great many countries offer tax holidays of 5 to 20 years for new hotel construction, often including smaller hotels down to as few as ten rooms. A travel company or group of companies could easily invest some of their foreign profits in such a venture, continuing to build for tax-free profits. Among countries offering such incentives for hotel construction are Morocco, Jamaica, Tunisia, the Dominican Republic, Panama, most of the British-associated islands of the Caribbean, the French West Indies, and many, many more. Such concessions usually include an exemption from customs duties on building materials and fixtures.

Most developed countries do tax the current income of certain types of corporations controlled by their residents, such as leasing companies, and other financial enterprises dealing the parent company. But this concept of a controlled foreign corporation applies usually to passive or tax-haven type corporations, not to active businesses. But even for a passive business, a joint venture with foreign partners on a 50-50 basis will allow the income to accumulate tax-free since the company is not controlled by nationals of either country. If you are leasing aircraft, coaches, or whatever, consider a joint venture with your foreign partner whereby you set up a jointly owned company to receive some of the income. You will both profit by it, and have a tax-free pool of funds to invest together in other ventures. Such profits will not be taxed in the country of either partner until they are repatriated, since they are not controlled by either country's citizen.

The cruise ship operators have long been able to use Panama and Liberia, but they are about the only segment of the travel industry which has shown any understanding of the advantages of tax havens.

Many businessmen looking for tax haven opportunities would envy the daily opportunities open to the travel industry, and yet the travel industry rarely uses these opportunities — or even understands them.

PUTTING TAX HAVENS TO WORK

Tax havens offer a possibility for tax savings that cannot be matched by any other approach to tax avoidance. However, the precise use of tax havens depends very much on one's particular circumstances, objects, and concerns.

The use of tax haven corporations requires expenditures for both incorporation and corporate maintenance. Very roughly, $2,000 a year (including the year of incorporation) per company is what can be expected. An investor must have investment capital on the order of $50,000 to consider using a tax haven. And since most "foolproof" tax haven plans require at least a double-tier combination to take full advantage of haven benefits, at least two corporations are necessary, doubling the sum to be put in. Only when investible savings total at least $100,000 can one get lucratively involved in tax havens on a full-scale basis. Five years of work and saving may bring a person into this investment class, but even if he is not yet there, it is worth starting today to plan for the future.

Another point that must be considered is what is to be done with the proceeds from tax haven investments. Will it pay for luxurious pleasure trips? Will it underwrite retirement in comfort and security? Or will it be left to loved ones? In the latter case, a tax haven trust may allow one to transfer his estate to his family with all the benefits of money growth in a haven and without the burden of inheritance taxes.

These points indicate that whether and how one should get involved in tax havens depends upon his investment capital and his personal plans concerning the earnings from it. To come to a sound conclusion, one must compute, with the aid of an accountant and a tax advisor, the tax liabilities and expenses he would have to meet for the forthcoming years, based on the best available estimates, and then run these figures against estimated tax savings and extra costs incurred by the use of tax havens. And he must make up his mind **now**, not later. A later change of mind could cost a pretty penny.

Another consideration is the effect that tax havens have on the nature of investments. Clearly, an investor must change his perspective concerning his investments when considering the use of havens. To firmly delineate the nature of this change, let us make some distinctions between investment orientations.

Pure Business

This is the attitude the taxman wants an investor-businessman to have. It means that he is expected to plan his investment (and life) with the central objective of making a maximum gross profit — and to pay the maximum taxes attached to such success. A more reasonable man will utilize the services of an accountant to minimize the tax penalty, but tax considerations are not supposed to affect any business decision. They may affect accounting and bookkeeping, directed at keeping a very good record of all deductible expenses, but not how or where one does business. This is the attitude one may have to feign if his tax haven corporation comes under unsympathetic scrutiny. Thus it pays to have a sound "pure business" reason for setting up shop in a far-off land.

Pure Tax Planning

This may be the attitude of somebody who keeps his income so low as to be untaxable or who immigrates to a no-tax country. Here the motivation is the exact reverse of "pure business": This person does not want maximum profit; he wants minimum taxes. Some tax rebels are ideologically motivated to do just that. They forget about how much money they have in their pockets and concentrate on how they can fend off the government pickpockets.

Net-Profit Planning

This attitude is not based on the desire to make the treasury richer, nor on the desire to make it poorer. It is based on the objective of maximizing the money left over after the taxman extracts his cut. In other words, gross profits concern the net-profit planner only insofar as he needs them, for accounting purposes, to calculate tax rates and net profits. And the government concerns him only as a kind of undesired creditor whose share in the profits is to be minimized. His net profits are not monies that his accountant classifies as such; they are monies he can use to achieve his own life purposes, to do with as he pleases. Whether they are on the books as "business expenses" or "salary" or "rent on the company car," or what have you, is a matter that concerns the net- profit planner only to the extent that there is always the possibility that the government might decide that what he has classified as business expenses were actually personal expenses.

This approach underlies everything offered in this book. The principles and ideas herein are for people who want to increase their purchasing power, the money they can use as they wish. The legal or accounting label for the money — whether one "owns" it or merely controls it—matters little. Similarly, the view on capital taken here is that only a fool would maximize the amount of capital he **owns**, in the

31

sense of having direct, personal legal title to it. What should be of primary interest is the capital one can control, dispense with as he sees fit, whatever or whoever has formal title to it.

Contemporary attitudes and politics have transformed ownership and profits into "social sins" and tax liabilities. Therefore, the tax minimizer should seek control and usable assets available in such forms that avoid these strictures. This line of thinking is important in trying to assess whether or not to use the simplest form of tax haven: the offshore fund.

Offshore Funds

At first sight, an offshore fund is the ideal means of utilizing the advantages of tax havens without falling prey to their disadvantages. An offshore fund is an internationally financed corporation based in a tax haven. It operates by selling stock to the public, and it invests the monies for the stockholders in a manner that, ideally, gets maximum possible "gearing," doubling the invested funds as quickly as possible. The profits are reinvested in turn, and since the offshore fund is based in a haven, it pays no taxes on its profits and can reinvest whole dollars.

Such a setup gives these apparent advantages: (1) An investor can enjoy the benefits of a haven without incurring the costs of creating his own company. (2) He can "forget" about the troubles of deciding how best to invest his money. By buying a share of an offshore fund, he is buying the services of professional investment managers who will optimally invest his money for him. (3) Offshore funds do not usually pay dividends because they reinvest all profits. This means that personal income tax liability is not increased. (4) The investor's personal means of claiming his share of the fund's profits when he wants to is to sell his shares in the fund. If the fund does well, its stock will go up, and the investor will have a gross capital gain. This is taxable in many countries, but usually at a rate much lower than regular income. (There are ways of eliminating or reducing capital gains taxes, but even if these are ignored, the investor has still saved taxes by allowing them to be deferred over the years and by using the leverage of reinvestment of whole dollars through the fund.) (5) Tax haven offshore funds are free of government regulations imposed on domestic investment companies. Domestic companies are required to invest in ways sufficiently "conservative" that the "small investor's" money will not be risked on "chancy" ventures. But an offshore fund can take advantage of a "risky investment" to give the maximum return in a short time. A competent offshore fund manager should be attentive to the security of money entrusted to him because he depends on his reputation to stay in business. Thus, one can expect considerable security coupled with a very quick rate of increase in the value of his investment. The prospects for a high and speedy rate of return are enhanced by the fact that most tax havens are not only non-tax countries but highly free enterprise countries, where substantial decisions of corporate executives are not hampered by regulations and red tape.

Thus, offshore funds should, in principle, couple both gross-profit benefits, coming from cleverly calculated "speculative" investment utilizing the whole range of possibilities of the world economy, and net-profit benefits, avoiding the trouble and expense of finding an accountant and a lawyer to help with incorporation, the fees associated with incorporation, the burden of managing one's own investment, etc. Further, such funds do not require the relatively large amounts of capital needed to take advantage of other approaches.

All in all, offshore funds seem to offer the full benefits of tax havens at a bargain price — the ideal get-rich-quick-with-small-cost-no-worries scheme. However, while all of these advantages are real, they all hinge on one crucial factor: the honesty and competence of the individuals who run the offshore fund. Government regulations on investment companies do restrict the profitability and capital growth of such companies, but they also guarantee some sort of minimal security to the investor. They serve to screen out, however inefficiently, the straight-out crooks and the impractical dreamers who are frequently taken in by the crooks. In other words, whenever one transfers management of his own investment portfolio to an investment manager, either directly or by buying shares in an investment fund, he must be on the lookout for crooks, fools, and the lethal combination of the two. Any get-rich- quick scheme, whether or not initially viable and valid, attracts the scam artists and the dreamers, and together they generate a fantasy industry that all too quickly turns into a nightmare for the unwary investor.

Offshore funds are completely unregulated. One's only security is his own verification of the personal integrity and professional competence of the people running the fund he buys into. There are no shortcuts to verifying such information. Even what seems to be on paper, even "verified" paper, a very large and promising fund can be large because many fools, manipulated by very clever crooks, goaded by other fools, or both, have bought lots of stock. What looks good in a bright, shiny, beautifully produced prospectus may turn out to be an elaborate fraud not worth the paper on which the slick presentation is printed. If one cannot verify beyond a reasonable doubt the ethical and professional credentials of the people running the show, he should not put his money into it. Period.

To emphasize this point from another angle, one may be motivated by ideological considerations. There are many libertarians and conservatives who consider antitax measures to be of primary ideological significance, over and above the money remaining in their pockets. Some clever manipulators, aware that an ideologically motivated person may easily and blindly trust someone who behaves and talks as if he were similarly motivated, will offer "fantastic investment possibilities" laced with the appropriate ideological buzz words. The ideologically motivated "investor" would feel safe with, say, "a fellow libertarian." He could not be deceitful or stupid. He would certainly protect one's investment and handle it with great care and wisdom. Anyone who approaches his investment decisions this way should not be surprised to find himself on the short end of the stick — if indeed there is a stick. There's a con artist out there for every sucker. Beware.

Before investing in an offshore fund, an investor **must** study the track records of the fund and the people running it. How many years has the fund existed? How has its stock behaved? What kind of profits has it made? What investments has it made, and how many of them were considered risky and then proved to be successful? How many were risky and wound up disasters? How many were prudent? As for the fund managers, what were they doing before they set up or took over the fund? How successful were they? What makes them personally reliable? What supports their claims that their investment judgment is sound?

All of these considerations may squelch any interest the reader may have had in offshore funds. This is not our intention. Rather, the purpose of raising these consideration is to make the reader aware of certain very important facts: (1) Whenever considering buying stock in **any** company — offshore fund, local investment company, or what have you — one should judge only by computing the probable net increase in net purchasing power resulting from the investment. Business advantages and profits and tax benefits should be computed together, not separately. An offshore fund should be evaluated as any other company, but in view of its special dependence on the personal qualities of those running it, a little bit more carefully. (2) It is a fallacy to think in general-category terms about offshore funds. While they share some general characteristics, they vary enormously, as do the persons running them. Specific companies and individuals must be evaluated, not the general concept.

Nonetheless, offshore funds still remain viable investment opportunities. Most of them offer privacy because they are registered in countries where even the shareholder register is not open to any official inspection. Combined with their investment potential, unhampered by regulation, and the fact that the only possible taxes are withholding taxes in the countries in which their investments are located, they offer, in principle, a good hunting ground. But one must hunt very carefully, observing track records, individual and corporate, and disregarding vague though beautiful promises and propaganda.

Numbered Bank Accounts?

Investment in offshore funds is the lowest grade of possible involvement with tax havens. The next step "up" is putting money in confidential, or numbered, bank accounts. This is usually combined with out-and-out tax evasion. Needless to say, such a combination is illegal and very risky. Beware!

Incorporation

The next level of tax haven involvement requires that the investor incorporate in a tax haven or establish a trust in one. Trusts are good if the money is intended not for oneself but for his loved ones. If, however, the objective is to advantage oneself rather than his heirs, what is needed is a corporation. This opens up a very wide range of possibilities. We will discuss some basic and important ones, but not the whole range of opportunities; that would require a volume in itself.

The simplest possibility, and the one that most investors are likely to be interested in, is a holding company. A holding company is a company that is not directly involved in trade or production; rather, it deals in investments in other companies. It makes it possible to direct funds into investments that produce passive income — rent, dividends, royalties, interest on bonds and deposits, etc. The advantage in transferring one's investment portfolio to a tax haven corporation (whether a holding company or some other variety of investment company) is that the income derived from these investments will not be taxed as part of personal income.

However, there are different kinds of tax liabilities to be dealt with in transferring a portfolio to a haven company. It is these three kinds of liabilities that make the use of a haven a more sophisticated operation than just a simple act of creating a company in a haven and transferring investments to it.

The first of these is **withholding tax**. This liability exists in most high-tax countries. If the source of the income is in such a country, the withholding tax may be 30 or 35 percent. Clearly, since a holding company has no real costs of operation (apart from fairly low maintenance costs), this means that the no-tax corporation brings income down into a 30 percent bracket — quite an improvement from British or Swedish rates, but not a total remedy.

One way to improve on this is to use a low-tax, double- taxation-agreement haven for incorporation. In this case, the agreement would usually serve to reduce the withholding tax to 15 percent, and then the low local haven tax would be imposed on the remaining 85 percent after allowable deductions. Even this can sometimes be improved on if a second company in a no-tax haven is involved.

This two-company setup might work this way: If Company A is established in a low-tax, double-taxation-agreement haven and derives income from the U.S. (or Great Britain or Canada, for example), and if Company B is in a no-tax haven, Company A could, in principle, lease some property from B and pay rent to it. Since the lease agreement is, in effect, between the investor (under the guise of Company A) and himself (under the guise of Company B), he can make it rather expensive for A to get the lease. A could even be in the "unfortunate" position of having all its gross profit (85 percent of the U.S.-source revenue) paid out as expenses to cover the very uneconomical lease with greedy B. Such a maneuver is legally chancy because the parties involved are within "an arm's length" of each other, but let us say it works. The money reaches B. There is usually no withholding tax between the country of A and that of B, and there are no local taxes on B. Thus, U.S. withholding tax has been reduced to 15 percent (or even 5 percent in some cases), local taxes have been reduced or canceled out, and the tax rate has become about 15 percent.

The above outlined approach is at best quasilegal. It involves concealment of information that, had it been available to the U.S., may have made the investor's calculated tax burden greater. But it seems to be within the **letter** of the law, though perhaps barely so.

A more complex (and more secure) version of this approach might have Company B formed by a local trust company in B's haven country and its shares "owned" by nominees who have private contracts with the investor, valid under the laws of the land of B, to the effect that they will vote in stockholders' meetings of B as the investor instructs. The investor then instructs the nominees to decide that B will never distribute dividends and that it will reinvest all its profits, or that it will cover all his expenses as an "honored guest" when he visits the land of B, or what have you. In this case, the investor is technically neither directly nor indirectly a stockholder of B. The company is owned and run by local citizens of the land of B, who happen to have a private local contract with the investor concerning their actions as stockholders in B.

Is this all fully legal? It is very hard to say. The "evasion/avoidance" distinction is more than a little vague and open to interpretation. The IRS could claim that the investor indirectly exerted control over Company B, though this would likely require a very strong case to prove the investor's control over the nominees' voting behavior at stockholders' meetings. It is possible that the whole affair might be construed by U.S. courts to be a case of foreign "corruption" outside the judicial authority of the United States—and then again, maybe not. Such things are very "iffy," and although the chances of this kind of arrangement coming to light are quite slim, the potential penalties are grave. The worries associated with it may well not be worth the potential gain. It all depends on the peculiarities and particular circumstances of the individual investor.

We have already indicated that a double-tier corporate arrangement **seems** to escape the first requirement. This is open to question, however, because a court could interpret **control** in a "liberal" sense, extending it to mean indirect methods of control.

Another kind of tax liability one must consider is that which his heirs might have to pay if he operates only with corporations. Even if he merely owns the stock of a corporation that merely owns the stock of another corporation that makes, accumulates, reinvests, and increases tax-free profits, there is something in his title (stock) potentially subject to estate taxes, inheritance duties, and so on.

Trusts

The answer to this problem could be a tax haven trust. This will be developed more fully in chapter five. For now, here are the highlights of this approach: (1) The investor establishes his trust **now**, thereby alienating the property from his estate. (2) He uses all legal means of transferring his assets to the trust without incurring gift

39

taxes. (3) He transfers assets directly to the foreign trust only if they constitute property on which all due income taxes have been paid. (4) He guarantees that the trustee is not of his residence country, the trust deed is legalized outside his residence country, and all trust assets are located outside the U.S. The trust deed should be irrevocable, otherwise his government may consider the arrangement to be a trust.

Trusts can reduce the tax load on one's heirs. A trust holding the shares of a tax haven corporation that accumulates profits tax-free can avert all estate duties and the like. A trust combined with a double-tier corporate arrangement using a low-tax, double-taxation-agreement haven and a no-tax haven, as described above, can provide some immunity against withholding tax, estate tax, death tax, and probate. Needless to say, such arrangements are costly. However, if appreciable savings over many years are involved, the cost may be more than justified.

Thus far, we have discussed methods that might be used to avoid tax liabilities on a portfolio of investments. This is in line with our basic premise that the major use of tax havens should not be to defend against taxes on primary income — that accruing to one from his work — but against taxes on secondary income from investments. This is on the assumption that most people do not wish to change their basic life plan and lifestyle in order to reduce taxes, but merely to reduce the tax burden on an already established life pattern.

However, tax considerations and business considerations are really inseparable, once the basic departure point is the maximization of money one can use, and not gross profit or minimal taxes. Tax havens open up certain possibilities not only for better general investment (offshore funds) or tax-secured investment (foreign holding companies and/or trusts). They also offer active possibilities for moneymaking as bases for international trade and production that are not only untaxed but relatively unregulated and uncontrolled. The legal basis for such activities is quite the same as that discussed above with respect to transferring an investment portfolio to a tax haven corporation, trust, or a multitiered combination of more than one tax haven legal entity. And the specific possibilities are rather large.

The first of these is financial activities. One can establish a finance company, or even a bank, in some havens, alone or with partners. In some havens, the local regulations on finance companies and banks are surprisingly lax. Most people believe that only a Rockefeller can consider starting a bank. Yet, in certain havens, this is possible with relatively limited funds.

Finance companies are usually even easier to establish than banks. Nice profits are possible in the international money market, especially those connected with currency exchange deals, utilizing the day-to-day fluctuations, as well as the differences in relative values of currencies from place to place. Clearly, this is no mere pastime involvement; it may become a thrilling full-time activity.

Another enterprise, requiring substantial capital, is a haven-based insurance company, to insure one's own business. This is called a "captive" insurance company. Because this is something few people can do, we will indicate the advantage of such a company only in passing. The premiums a business pays to an insurance company are tax-deductible expenses in the business and net **profit** in the haven locality where the insurance company is incorporated. The premiums may be, for the same kind of damages and other losses, less than what one would have to pay an outside company, which has to pay taxes on its income and so has to inflate its premiums. And a business can be insured against risks for which there are no actuarial (statistical) tables and for which ordinary insurers offer no coverage; this would provide a sound business reason for having a captive insurance company.

But back to more realistic possibilities. Manufacturing in a haven, using the low-wages, nonunion, no-regulations situation, and selling the product through another company in the U.S. or Europe, there would be taxes to be paid on profits from distribution of the product in the United States or Europe, but the profits as a manufacturer, accounted as export profits of the haven manufacturing company, would accumulate tax free. Of course, being a very hard-bargaining exporter and a very stupid importer would cause a majority of the total profits to be made by the haven manufacturing company. But high-tax country tax authorities look at deals between related parties very carefully these days (assuming they know of the relationship).

Thus, a haven corporation can be both a tool for reducing net taxable income as well as a basis for multinational operations. In some havens, the local government, eager for foreign investments, may even help by providing subsidies, privileges, low-interest loans, and more.

How about shipping? A shipping line based in Panama or Liberia, both noted tax havens, would be immune from most taxes if its ships stayed in international commerce, and would be free of the many complex and costly regulations concerning personnel imposed by other governments.

Another possibility, the last we will discuss but by no means the last one available, is to extend services (technical, managerial, engineering, architectural, scientific, and so on) through a haven corporation on an international basis outside one's home country. The haven company would be able to accumulate professional fees on a tax-free basis.

So tax haven involvement can range from the minimum of buying offshore funds through using haven corporate and trust entities to reduce taxes on investment returns and eliminate death duties to full-time involvement in international business activities. An investor's background, occupation, professional training and qualifications, interests, concerns, disposition, economic situation, etc., will determine what he does with tax havens. Only a cool and detailed inspection of the specific situation, with the aid of competent professional advice, can determine what precise approach should be followed.

This book does not offer a do-it-yourself kit of forms to finalize incorporation or trust formation abroad. Such a quicky deal is as dangerous as performing a kidney operation on your own wife by using a do-it-yourself surgical manual. The manual may be all right, but who in his right mind would risk it? In principle, a "Do-It-Yourself Tax Haven Manual" is possible; whatever expertise professionals have in the field could be formulated in precise and complete detail. However, such a book, if honestly and competently put together, would be gigantic, and would amount to a combination of relevant legal training, relevant accountancy training, and much detailed information about the tax and corporate laws of a multitude of countries. The time required for a layman to digest such a manual would be worth more than the price of good professional advice. Trying to avoid both such a detailed manual and the costs of professional advice, using a shortcut approach, would be cheaper in the short run — and much, much more costly in the long run.

Anyone interested in pursuing any of the possibilities presented here should definitely get in touch with the best professional advisors he can afford before going into action. It will mean risks, expense, and hard work, but properly done, it could be very much worth it.

TAX HAVEN CORPORATIONS AND TRUSTS

The essence of using tax havens for tax reduction purposes is the creation of legal entities that have these characteristics: (1) They are separate from their creator in a fashion guaranteeing that the income they derive from their assets cannot be considered part of his income. (2) They "reside" in countries where the tax situation is much better than in the investor's home country. (3) An investor can control them and their assets and income as he pleases, without either tax or debt liabilities.

Such business entities exemplify the basic idea of separating ownership and control. Once one's portfolio has been vested in such an entity, he no longer has title to it. But since he has title to stock in the company, he has the power to make decisions about the ways its assets are used.

There are two basic forms of such entities: the corporation and the trust. We will discuss both in turn, because all the countries that we will later consider as possible tax havens allow at least one form or the other; all of them allow corporations, and some allow trusts. (There are additional kinds of business entities available in Liechtenstein.) At this juncture, it is very important that the nature of corporations and trusts and all the related concepts defined by reference to them be clearly understood.

Corporations

Contrary to popular belief, corporations are not necessarily "big" companies, though there are some size characteristics that are relevant to the decision of whether or not to incorporate. Below a certain asset value, incorporation is usually not worthwhile.

But first, just what is a corporation? To understand this, it is important to reflect on the way the corporate form of business enterprise first came into being. The initial motivation for forming corporations had nothing to do with taxes; rather, it had to do with debts. If one is, say, a grocer who owns his own store, any loan he takes out to buy stock for his shelves is his **personal** loan, his personal debt. The security for the loan, the assets that can be taken away from him and sold to cover the loan and repay the debtor, is all the grocer's personal assets, everything he owns. If he fails to repay a loan taken out for business purposes, his debtors can claim his TV set, house, car — everything. This means that if one runs a business as a personal property, he has unlimited debt liability; the business' debts are its owner's debts.

Because of this, many persons felt the need to separate business from their personal lives and to defend their personal property from the adverse consequences of business mistakes and failures. The corporation was the answer. Incorporation was, in effect, a declaration like this: "If you give my business a loan, you should know in advance that, in case the business fails to repay you, you have recourse only to what the business owns, not what I personally own." In other words, the formation of a corporation is the creation of a new "legal person" insofar as liabilities are concerned. This legal person can assume its own debts and acquire its own assets. The assets may derive from the individual who establishes the corporation, and he then becomes liable for the debts of the company, but only to the extent of the assets expressly transferred to the corporation or committed to such a transfer. An act of government — the registration of the corporation — makes valid this "legal personification" and defends those with interests in the company from invasions of business debtors into their private lives.

At first glance, incorporation seems to be nothing but a legal trick to escape full responsibility for bad decisions. But it has fuller significance and justification when partnerships are concerned. If, say, one is a partner with his neighbor in a small, unincorporated repair shop, both partners are fully liable for the business' debts. If the neighbor runs off with all the company cash, his unfortunate partner would still be liable for all the debts incurred by the business.

Suppose one is a passive partner, having lent money to someone to open a shop saying, "I don't want to be a creditor, but a partner. Fifty percent of the profits will be mine after a salary for you is deducted from the profits." Sometime later it is discovered that the active partner has incurred debts beyond the value of the assets of the shop and his own personal property, leaving the passive partner — who had nothing to do with running the business — with the responsibility of covering the remaining debts out of his own pocket.

And what about many partners in an enterprise? There seems to be full business justification for becoming a partner with a very small percentage interest in a company, without any active participation in running it but with a percentage of the profit proportional to the original investment. But such an arrangement is quite unfeasible if one has full liability for the company's debts. Who would want to run the risk of having a $100 investment suddenly become a liability of $1 million as a consequence of someone else's blunders?

Since it seemed that economic growth required such investment partnerships, and since most people would be reluctant to take part in them if it involved unlimited liability for the partnership's debts, the idea of incorporation became widely accepted. It answered a need. Its essence was that instead of being a partner in the title of a business property (and thus a proportional direct owner of the business assets), one owned stock. Stocks are certificates of partial ownership in a corporation. The corporation is a legal person that owns its own assets and has its own liabilities. Owning the stock of the corporation does not mean owning its assets. The corporation has title to these. The stockholder has title to his stock.

The value of the stock may have been printed on it (par value); it might be, say, $20. This means only that this number was printed on the stock certificate, and that if one went through all the certificates ever issued in the name of the company, added up all the figures of par value printed on them, and got a total of $20,000 (the **authorized capital** of the company), the proportion of the ownership in the corporation represented by one share would be one-thousandth.

Par value is not necessarily what would be paid for the stock. In principle, a buyer could pay a "percentage" of, say, 10 percent of par. This would mean that he could pay $2 and owe the company $18. If everybody bought stock at the same percentage, this would mean that the corporation would start off with a **paid-up capital** of $2,000, 10 percent of its authorized capital. If tomorrow our example company got into heavy debt and declared bankruptcy, the liquidator, whether a private individual or the government, would inspect the company books and find that it has $2,000 of paid-up capital and that the stockholders owe the company $18,000. The stockholders' debt is the company's asset, and it has to be called in to pay off the corporation's debts. But the debtors cannot make claims against the stockholders beyond the amount they owe the company.

Some stock has no par value. In such cases, each certificate represents a part of the total ownership of the corporation equal to that represented by any other. Even so legal requirements for a minimum of authorized capital and, usually, paid-up capital apply everywhere. Clearly, such minima are necessary; nobody would give a loan to a corporation if there were no clue to at least its authorized capital.

A stockholder's percentage of ownership in a corporation equals the number of shares he holds divided by the total issued. The corporation may have a fixed authorized capital or, in some countries, a variable one. Say it can vary between $10,000 and $50,000. It may start, then, with 100 shares of $100 par value each. Each such share would then equal one percent control of the company. But then the company could expand its capital base by selling new shares up to the limit of $50,000. A $100 share would then represent only 0.2 percent control.

Another important distinction concerning shares of corporate stock is that between **registered** and **bearer** shares. A registered share has the name of its current owner printed on the certificate and in the official corporation record (the shareholders ledger). The record of registered shares is open to official inspection, and the owners of such stock are easily identified. A registered share thus has obvious drawbacks when privacy is important.

A bearer share belongs to whoever physically holds it; there is no name on it, and its sale is not logged anywhere. The sale of registered shares is always recorded and, depending on the corporation, may require the agreement of other shareholders. Bearer shares can be bought and sold in complete privacy without any third-party interference.

Bearer shares are not allowed in some tax havens. A major problem with bearer shares is that they can be stolen, and the owner has no means of proving ownership. In addition, unlike registered shares, which can be purchased at a percentage, bearer shares usually must be paid for in full.

It is possible to have the "best of both worlds" by buying registered shares at a percentage and having them registered in the name of a proxy. This reduces the capital requirements while at the same time providing privacy and security. A private contract can be arranged with the proxy that binds him to follow the real owner's instructions in all his actions as a stockholder. A proxy can be a real individual or an institution. Corporation A can hold stock in Corporation B, serving as a holding company. Holding companies are very popular because they can, if they are tax haven corporations, release their owners from registered ownership; they can be used to absorb and reinvest returns on the shares they hold without tax liabilities; and they can be established in many countries with very low local tax liabilities, even if there are heavy local taxes on other types of corporations.

This leads us to the issue of control of corporations in general, which is an important one. A corporation is a legal person; while being, in essence, a documentary fiction, it must simulate somehow the faculties and capacities of a real person. It must have the ability to evaluate its past actions and its present circumstances, to reach policy decisions in light of this information, to implement them in specific everyday decisions, and to commit itself contractually. A real person does all these things. A corporation must have a legal anatomy that allows it to simulate the psychological anatomy of a real person. This dictates the traditional structure and nature of a corporation.

The basic existence of a corporation usually derives from two documents, the **articles of incorporation** and the **articles of association** (by-laws). The articles of incorporation are prepared by the lawyer who represents the corporation. They must include certain information about the newly born pseudoperson: (1) **Its name** (including an indication of its status as a corporation such as "Inc." [incorporated], "Ltd." [limited], "Co." [company], or whatever else local conventions associate with corporate status). The name must not be the same as that of an already existing corporation and must not be misleading according to local conventions. Some countries, for instance, forbid companies to use their national names as part of a corporate name. (2) **Its registered address**. This is required to make possible communication with the corporation. (3) **Its objects and aims**. Usually these are stated broadly, but they must be so stated as not to allow any reason for suspicion that the corporation is formed to promote illegal or immoral aims. (4) **Its capitalization**. There is country-to-country variability concerning this requirement. It usually pertains to authorized capital, the paid-up capital, the nature of shares (par value, no par value, number, registered, bearer, premium, no premium). This stipulation is usually required to be backed up by some officially acceptable proof (such as a bank account record) that the minimum paid-up capital requirements have been met by cash or by assets whose provable value adds up to the minimum. (5) **A statement that the company is a limited liability organization**.

Apart from these general requirements, local laws differ. In some cases, names of persons associated with the corporation must also be mentioned, with their addresses: shareholders, ultimate-beneficiary share-owners (in the cases where shares are held by proxies), directors, officers. Other countries may require a specification of the span of time the corporation is supposed to exist before liquidation. Sometimes the articles of association are required to be a part of the articles of incorporation. The articles of incorporation are usually approved and confirmed by a government official, the "Registrar of Companies" or something comparable. Most often, but not always, an announcement of the formation of a new corporation is required to be published in some official government gazette.

The articles of association usually must also be submitted to the government registrar. These articles represent the basic terms of a corporation's structure and direction. There are variations from country to country on the requirements. In some places the local law is rigid and detailed; in others it indicates broad outlines and certain specific restrictions. Thus the law may require that each corporation have a board of directors and that at least one director reside in the country where incorporation takes place. However, the law may leave the number of directors open. This, of course, is a mere illustration.

Some uniform features of corporations, following from the essential nature of a corporation as a fictitious person that simulates a real person, are:

Stockholders' Meeting. This is the "ultimate authority" of the corporation. There is usually a requirement that it meet annually, and sometimes there is a requirement that it have a quorum of a certain percentage of the shares outstanding. In this meeting all stockholders are allowed to participate and, usually, to vote, with one vote per share. Sometimes, however, there are nonvoting shares, sold as such.

The annual meeting has to discuss and approve certain things by majority decision: (1) The business actions of the corporation in the preceding year as represented by its declared annual accounts of both profit and loss and its assets and liabilities. The correctness of these documents usually has to be certified by a separate body of auditors or accountants. Disapproval of such reports by the majority of the stockholders is similar to a parliamentary no-confidence vote. It is an expression of dissatisfaction with the management of the company. (2) Policy decisions on future business actions. Trends of possible company developments have to be approved, as well as the manner in which the net profit of the company (after deduction of both expenses and taxes) is to be divided. What dividend will the shareholders receive? How much will go for investment in company growth? How much will be kept in bank reserves? (3) Personnel decisions. Should the president, secretary, and treasurer be retained or replaced? Should the auditors continue to be the same? Are the directors satisfactory? (4) Constitutional issues. Should the articles of association be modified within the limit of the law? Should the quorum requirements be changed? The annual meeting is chaired by an elected chairman. His position is a distinct one in the company structure.

Board of Directors. While the annual meeting constitutes the "parliament" of the corporation, the articles of association also specify requirements for the "cabinet," the board of directors. How many directors? How are they appointed? How are they replaced? How many times do they meet? And so on. In general, the board is supposed to make decisions on the issues that are too specific for the general meeting to discuss but which are beyond the day-to-day responsibility of the company management.

Corporate officers. Another cabinetlike institution, sometimes part of the board of directors, is the group of corporate officers—the president, the secretary, the treasurer, etc. These individuals usually have the right to represent the company to third parties, to negotiate and make commitments in its name. This means they can put it into debt, and stipulations may be made as to whether they can do this separately or only in common. The local law may specify an annual minimum of officers' and directors' meetings, even sometimes demanding a specific location for them; it may stipulate whether the directors have to be at the meetings in person or whether they can be represented by proxies. The law may also (and usually does) require a corporation to keep records of proceedings and decisions in such meetings, a book of minutes that, in some places, must be open to public and/or official inspection.

Auditors. The last body usually required is the auditors, who are required to inspect the company's bookkeeping and verify the correctness of annual accounts. These are not usually employees or directors of the corporation but an outside firm.

The legal structure of a corporation is distinct, of course, from its operational structure. It may have branches, divisions, departments, etc., headed by managers or executives who may or may not be members of the board of directors and may act separately or collectively as the articles of association may specify explicitly or as the directors or officers dictate.

Now, this looks a formidable structure, and one may wonder if having so many employees may not cost more than the taxes to be minimized through incorporation. But all this vast structure need not be more than a tissue of technicalities if incorporation is accomplished in a tax haven. If the local law requires three initial incorporators, these can be supplied, for a reasonable fee, by the local law firm that handles the incorporation. These proxies can then either turn over their shares to the "real incorporator" after incorporation or continue to act on his behalf under a private contract. Similarly, the general meeting of stockholders can in some cases be no more than a meeting with the single majority stockholder in front of the bathroom mirror, with minutes duly recorded, of course. If this is not good enough for the local law, a real local annual stockholders' meeting can be arranged by the corporate legal representative in the haven, with proxies provided for moderate fees.

The same sort of arrangements can be made to cover all requirements for local corporate officers and the like. The "ultimate owner" can run the company as he pleases, with all the legally formidable structure and rituals carried out by proxies.

Returning to the essential aspects of corporations, it should be remembered that the corporate legal form came into being for business purposes, not tax purposes. Corporations were invented to encourage capital investment in the form of ownership with limited debt liability. Since corporations are legal persons, government approval is required to form them, and corporation laws, quite similar all over the world but with important place-to-place variations, have been enacted, establishing government control over the formation and operation of corporations. Moreover, since corporations, as legally acknowledged persons, make possible all kinds of sophisticated fraud, governments encourage their formation. This claim may seem strange, but nonetheless it is true. The existence of corporations enhances government's role of "defender of the innocent" against the "robber barons." Very complex corporation laws, requiring publication of annual corporate accounts and records, independent accounting, forbidding deals of "no less than arm's length" between two corporations with the same or virtually the same ownership of certain kinds, and so on, are justified by reference to the opportunities for corporate mischief.

On the other hand, corporations require special tax treatment, to avoid killing the goose that lays the golden egg. They cannot be taxed progressively, as individuals are, because the "justification" for progressive taxation of individuals does not apply. If an individual has a very large income, he is "too rich," and the soak-the-rich mentality of modern welfare statism makes progressive taxation popular. But even a huge corporation with large gross profits can be owned by thousands of "little men." Progressive corporate taxation would wipe out the little guys' profits — hardly a politically popular consequence — and would discourage investment in corporations. Consequently, with but two exceptions, corporate income taxes everywhere are assessed at flat rates, in most cases 40-50 percent of net profits. The exceptions are, of all places, Switzerland and Liechtenstein. In these two nations, corporate-tax brackets are determined by the ratio between profit and authorized capital. For example, $100,000 made on an authorized capital of $1 million, a 10 percent yield, would be taxed at a higher rate than the same dollar profit on an authorized capital of $10 million, a one percent yield.

The fact that corporate taxes are flat-rate taxes means that incorporation can be used to reduce tax burdens by alienating personal sources of income to a corporation. This may be a good idea, and it is a major reason for incorporation in a tax haven that has no or very low corporate taxes.

In sum, here is what a tax haven corporation can do for a shrewd investor: It can alienate returns on investments from personal income, and thus save them from crippling home country tax rates. Even if the investments are in a high tax country, a tax haven corporation can reduce the total tax on them, sometimes, with a proper setup, to as low as 5 percent. The profits can then be reinvested to grow in whole dollars. If these fast-growing savings are repatriated to the investor's home country as dividends or as capital gains on the liquidation of the corporation, the investor will have to pay his country's taxes. Shrewd investors live off the income from their work and keep reinvesting the tax haven profits abroad, to be tapped later upon retirement or to be passed on to heirs.

Concerning the matter of inheritance, if the money is returned to the investor's home country while the investor is still alive, there will be a tax penalty in the form of high income or capital gains taxes and, at the investor's death, estate taxes and probate duties. If the tax haven company survives the investor, its stock is part of his estate and is subject to estate taxes and probate in his country. In both cases, if the tax haven investment is principally intended to benefit heirs, a tax haven trust is called for.

Trusts

Like corporations, trusts were originally spawned by non-tax considerations. A careful father, suspicious of his frivolous and careless son, yet still affectionately concerned for his future, would decide not to bequeath the whole of his accumulated wealth directly to his son. Rather, he would set up a trust, a contract (the trust deed, or instrument) between himself (the trustor) and a trustee. The trustee would be somebody who could be counted on to responsibly manage and disburse the trust assets; he could be a personal friend, the family lawyer, or a professional trust company. The trustee would agree to manage the trust fund, or assets, which are thereby alienated from the founder's property and become a legally distinct entity, like a corporation, with its own assets and liabilities.

The trustee would invest the assets according to his own discretion within the limits of the provisions of the trust deed. He would then, after a period specified in the trust deed and in conformance with pertinent legal requirements, start paying the trust beneficiary (the son) a regular sum as specified in the trust deed. This payout might be subject to certain conditions laid down by the trustor: the son gets the money only if, say, he is married before he turns thirty, or only if he refrains from drinking cherry brandy, or what have you. The money distributed to the beneficiary would include both the return on the investment of the trust principal, the original sum constituting the assets of the trust, as well as, gradually, portions of the principal itself. The trust would be legally required to terminate at some point, when all funds, principal, and return on principal, have been distributed to the beneficiary, less, of course, management expenses incurred by the trustee.

As you can see, a trust serves a role similar to that of a will, with these additional advantages: (1) It can be separate from one's will and thereby maintain the secrecy of certain heirs who it would be socially inconvenient to acknowledge in a publicly read will. (2) It allows for the separation of some assets from one's property for inheritance purposes before death, and these assets are thereby immune to further business liabilities incurred by the trustor. This way, especially if the trust is **irrevocable** (the trustor being debarred under the trust deed from canceling it and reabsorbing the trust assets) and the trustor or his wife is not a beneficiary, money can be guaranteed to the trustor's loved ones without threat of loss through bankruptcy or other reverses. His creditors would have no access to the trust assets, since they would be separated from his estate. (3) It allows for competent professional management of the trust assets. (4) It allows the trustor to determine what aspects of the beneficiary's life he wants to encourage (or discourage) by allocating benefits for certain specified purposes. This contrasts with a will, which determines transfer of ownership, but which can establish no control over what is done with the transferred assets after the transfer is made. (5) It allows avoidance of laws that limit the right to decide how a legacy will be divided.

The major disadvantages of a trust are, of course, irrevocability and the chance of trustee abuse of trust assets. The latter can be avoided by careful formulation of the trust deed and careful trustee selection. In the case of professional trust companies, any temptation to abuse trustee powers is strongly moderated by the need to maintain a good professional reputation.

A minor disadvantage is that legal tradition generally requires that a trust have a fixed, or "upward-bounded," perpetuity period, at the end of which the trust assets must be completely disbursed to beneficiaries. The perpetuity period is variously defined in different countries.

It is important to understand that trusts are quite different from corporations. Usually, they need not be publicly recorded. A legal contract, combined with proper separation of the trust fund from the trustor's assets, establishes the trust. The contract, moreover, is peculiar in that (1) those who have rights to sue on the basis of it (the beneficiaries, who are entitled to sue the trustee if he violates the provisions of the trust deed in a manner that harms them) are not parties to the contract, (2) one party to the contract, the trustor, is usually debarred by law from any official right to intervene in the management of the trust, and (3) the trustee, who has full power to manage and distribute trust assets, cannot have any personal interest in the trust.

This peculiar legal structure, with the infinite possibilities for variation it allows, is a historical development in the common law tradition. Common law is peculiar in that it arose from a tradition of concrete cases, established in courts by reference to precedent rather than to statute law. It applies in the United Kingdom and its former colonies, including the United States and all Commonwealth countries. Only common law countries permit true trusts.

There exists another legal tradition, dating back to old Rome, revitalized and modernized by Napoleon in his Code Napoleon and accepted throughout continental Europe and in the new states that are former colonies of France, Germany, and others. This is the civil law tradition. It accepts as the basis for legal reasoning legal principles derived from explicit legislation. Precedent has a very limited role. While some civil law countries have enacted trust laws allowing the simulation of common law trusts within a civil law framework, it is generally advisable **not** to use such a simulacrum. It is generally the rich common law tradition that guarantees beneficiaries their rights under the provisions of a trust. An artificial trust law is unlikely to capture many of the undreamt of possibilities specific cases may pose, and a judge deprived of the support of the vast common law tradition may decide in a very arbitrary manner sanctioned by the schematic, underdeveloped, officially legislated law. There are many common law tax havens in which to settle a trust, so there is no need to consider the civil law havens for this purpose. (Liechtenstein, as we will discuss later, is an important exception to this general rule.)

But what do trusts have to do with taxes? To begin with, money given to a trust when the trustor is alive (a living trust) may be subject to a gift tax, but not to heavy estate taxes and probate duties. Thus, a living trust is superior to a testamentary trust, one that is established in a will, because the latter can be established only with funds already decimated by taxes and probate. Moreover, trust income is not usually taxable to the trustor. Nor is it taxable to the trustee, who derives no benefits from its growth (except his fees and expenses, which are tax deductible expenses of the trust). The beneficiaries, of course, cannot be taxed until they start receiving benefits. The trust itself is subject to a tax on its income. But a tax haven trust is not subject to this tax, and so can serve to reinvest its income tax-free, growing rapidly through whole-dollar investment. Thus, a tax haven trust can do for one's heirs what a tax haven corporation can do for oneself.

Tax haven trusts can be used in conjunction with haven corporations. Instead of owning a holding company that, in turn, holds stock and other investments, one can be a beneficiary of a trust established by a foreign holding company to hold its own stock. This and other double-tier structures are of huge importance when home-country tax provisions come into play.

Remember that trusts, unlike corporations, are almost never publicly advertised entities. No official confirmation of their creation has to be published anywhere. No audited accounts need reach anybody except the trustor and/or his beneficiaries. Such privacy allows one to decide, on the basis of whatever considerations he chooses to take into account, what information should be broadcast publicly.

The Limited Liability Company

The limited liability company (also called the LLC) is a form of business entity just now becoming popular in the United States and some tax haven jurisdictions, although it's been available in Germany, France, and many other countries for decades. Until its recent acceptance by a number of U.S. states, the business executive had three common choices when forming a business: the sole proprietorship, the corporation, or the partnership.

The LLC is a hybrid between the partnership and the corporation. It has all the flexibility of a partnership to define its own management structure, rules of procedure, voting rights, distribution of profits and a myriad of other details. The structure is created by a contract among all the parties. At the same time, if structured properly all the members and the management will enjoy limited liability typical of a corporation.

It is generally assumed that the combination of these two elements will be the reason most LLCs are formed, although there is a great deal of latitude with regard to the structure. Because it has partnership elements, in most jurisdictions that do not tax partnerships as entities but pass the tax liability through to the partners, the LLC is an attractive option.

The origin of the modern LLC laws allowing limited liability companies is in the German law of 1892 which created the GmbH (Gesellschaft mit beschranker Haftung). In the 60 years which followed, almost 20 countries adopted similar laws. In France, for example, the same type of company is known as the SARL (Societes de Responsabilite Limitee). In Central and South America it is known as the limitada.

In the U.S., the first state to adopt a modern limited liability company statute was Wyoming, on March 4, 1977. Florida followed in 1982 by enacting a similar statute. Now, most of states have either enacted similar laws or have legislation pending. It has become the most talked about and most imitated new business law in America. However, the Internal Revenue Service gave no assurance that such an entity could qualify to be treated as a partnership until September 2, 1988, when Revenue Ruling 88-76 was issued. It was the first Revenue Ruling from the IRS regarding LLCs. In February, 1993, the IRS issued four Revenue Rulings which describe the classification standards the IRS will apply to LLCs who desire partnership tax treatment.

Some lawyers predict that the LLC will steadily gain popularity as people become educated about its benefits until it will largely replace the partnership and the corporation as the preferred entity. The prediction may well be accurate, considering the popularity of the LLC in many European countries.

Now that most U.S. states have LLC laws, many tax haven countries are finding this an attractive piece of legislation to add to their offerings, opening up considerable opportunity for complex tax planning. There is a constant competition to vary the requirements, such as minimum number of members, so it may pay to shop around the jurisdictions for the precise structure you want.

Legislation was passed in Delaware in July, 1993, that now provides for Delaware corporations to convert their status to LLC by merging the old corporation into a new LLC. The LLC may take the same name as the corporation.

An LLC is taxed in substantially the same manner as a limited partnership (in most of those jurisdictions that have both limited partnerships and LLCs), without the following disadvantages that limited partnerships have with regard to liability:

1.   A limited partnership must have at least one general partner who is liable for debts of the partnership, while all of the

members of an LLC may be protected from such liability; and

2.   The participation of limited partners in the management of a limited partnership can result in a loss of limited liability protection, while such participation by members of an LLC will not have such effect, provided such management does not violate the applicable LLC statute.

Generally, each party to an LLC must agree to a contract with all the other members that will become the "constitution" of the company. This document may be called the "Company Agreement," "The Articles of Organization," "The Minutes of the First Meeting of Members", depending upon the jurisdiction.

Companies planning to operate their business in a jurisdiction that does not currently recognize LLCs should seriously consider the consequences of possibly losing their limitation on liability in that jurisdiction, before forming an LLC.

The corollary of this is that since the form is well recognized in a number of civil law countries, foreign investors may find it a useful vehicle for making investments in those countries, since the legal and tax status will be relatively clear. It is important to remember that in those countries to which the entity is new, this is a rapidly evolving area of law and it may be awhile before matters are fully settled.

In general sole owner companies cannot be LLCs, but some jurisdictions are now permitting such entitites. Traditionally a LLC must have two members or it automatically dissolves Of course, the second owner could be a children's trust or a family limited partnership holding 1%. And most jurisdictions have allowed two corporations, both owned by a single parent, to be members of a LLC.

Please remember that these are all generalizations, and the laws of many of the individual jurisdictions are still evolving, as is the treatment by the tax authorities of the jurisdictions that have to deal with these unfamiliar entities.

Some promoters sell LLCs to non-U.S. buyers by telling them that the LLCs are tax-free because the owners are taxed as partners, and that as non-resident aliens the owners would pay no U.S. tax on their share.

This information is not necessarily accurate, and may not be supported in future tax rulings or court cases.

If a partnership has income "effectively connected with a U.S. trade or business," the partnership must withhold 31% of the foreign partners' share of that income. The nonresident alien partners may treat such amount as a credit against the tax due for the year on their U.S. tax return.

Partnership income from U.S. sources that is **not** effectively connected with a U.S. trade or business is subject to withholding on distributions to nonresident alien partners at a 30% or lower treaty rate.

If all this wasn't enough, the U.S. estate tax applies to estates of nonresident aliens who own U.S. assets, at the same tax rates as those applied to U.S. citizens.

Another untested issue is whether being a partner may be deemed to be doing business in the U.S., and this may be a case where a bad case makes bad case law, depending exactly upon what the LLC in question is doing. One should assume that the U.S. will tend to look for ways to tax these entities rather than turn the U.S. into a tax haven.

The real value of an LLC in tax haven planning is when one needs an entity that is taxed differently than a corporation, but is clearly incorporated and has limited liability. In some complex tax haven plans, it may also be possible to use differing tax treatments — for example, the investor's home country may tax the LLC as a corporation while the host country taxes it as a partnership, or vice versa. Such schemes need very careful handholding by qualified professionals, but some multinational corporations are already using LLCs in this way.

Captive Insurance Companies

One of the hottest topic in board rooms today is whether or not to climb onto the captive insurance bandwagon, or if they are already participating, whether they should really venture into underwriting. Captives now number over 10,000. Many of these captives are located in Bermuda, Bahamas, British Virgin Islands, Cayman Islands, Guernsey, and the Netherlands Antilles. Several billion dollars in premiums flowed through Bermuda based companies last year alone. Of the U.S. Fortune 500 companies, over half have captives.

A captive insurance company is a company whose charter permits it to offer insurance to its parent or sister subsidiaries in return for premiums. Usually, this company is located offshore for tax reasons.

In almost every case, captives are started because of a general dissatisfaction with existing insurance coverage or costs. The advantages are in these areas: Insurance, Commercial, Financial, and Tax.

A captive can provide insurance for risks which may not be normally insurable For example, there is limited insurance available in the areas of strikes, product recall, patent suits, etc. Loss experience is based on the company's experience rather than being averaged with others that have less stringent controls and more prone to claims. Reduction of insurance costs is available as there is no sales force or overhead to pay for, no claims administration group, etc. Insurance company direct costs run around 20% to 50% compared to 5% for captives. Insurance income is earned on premiums, i.e., ceding commissions from reinsurance companies, inure to the captive rather than an outside insurance company.

The prime advantage is the ability to earn interest on capital and reserves, thus turning a cost center into a profit one. The development of insurance to enhance product acceptability is available. What would otherwise be a product warranty might be more attractive if packaged as a $100,000 insurance policy against damage by the product, when the manufacturer knows that claims will seldom if ever occur. The ability to be more flexible in the settlement of claims is possible; i.e., perhaps a company would wish to make a commercial judgement on a claim where an advisor or wholesaler might be held to be more/less liable under ordinary insurance proceedings. The ability to benefit from situations where evidence of insurance is more acceptable than a company guarantee or promise to pay; i.e., sick leave insurance for employees where a union wants a policy of state benefits.

Captives provide the opportunity of converting specific reserves to insurance costs at the parent level thus converting posttax reserves to pretax expenses. Examples would be reserves against product reliability or subsidiary debt, guarantees, etc. The ability to lower costs derived from the realistic evaluation of exposure (based on the insured's own experience) vis-a-vis existing premium/risk expenses is available.

In those countries with currency controls, the ability to transfer normally nonconvertible funds for exchange control purposes to a subsidiary as a genuine risk financing measure is generally available.

The improvement of cash flow is available using a captive in case of claims, the captive has use of funds until the claim is settled; in the case of reinsurance, premiums are paid quarterly in arrears instead of yearly in advance for normal insurance. Premium expense is generally deductible at the parent level, but income earned on investment at the captive level is not taxable. Special rules apply for U.S. and Canadian companies. The lack of regulation of investments at the captive level mean funds could, with prudence, be used to finance the needs of sister companies.

Premiums paid to a captive are generally deductible at the parent level (U.S. and Canadian companies require special planning, but remember the tax advantages are merely a bonus to the captive idea). Capital, reserves, and premiums are not taxed in most offshore locations. The success of a captive relies on good management not good luck. Top management must understand the longterm commitment to captive insurance. Bad risk assessment or a series of unlucky occurrences can cost a captive dearly in the early years. Annual premium costs alone are not criteria for establishing a captive. More importantly, a company needs a good spread of risks and low maximum loss potential.

Captive reserves may be invested in the money markets. Loans may be made to fund capital for the captive. Loans may be made to provide premiums which must be paid in advance. Loans for claims payments may be made where assets are temporarily not available in the captive or the captive is involved in legal action. New banking relationships are available with the captive. Direct access to reinsurance companies throughout the world, instead of having to deal with a local insurance carrier can be a major advantage. Added service may be offered to existing clients, such as a credit card or investment company offering free life insurance to its accountholders. Foreign exchange dealings are feasible; e.g., hedging tranasactions against premiums, claims, or reinsurance.

The Hybrid Company: A Unique Structure

Company law concepts in the Isle of Man derive from English company law, and can have interesting results. Since England never had a concept of a separate type of non-profit company (or corporation), societies were formed as ordinary companies, under the same laws as commercial enterprises. Their character was differentiated by having members who guaranteed the debts of the company. Each member's guarantee might only be a penny, a shilling, or a pound, just as shares in a U.S. corporation might only have a nominal value of a tenth of a cent.

Generally, a "guarantee" company and a company with shares were very separate entities, but there was nothing in the company laws that actually prevented the two concepts from being combined in the creation of a single company. Thus the hybrid company was born.

This is not just an exotic exercise in ancient company law — it has some highly relevant uses for the investor. Where a trust would be impossible, or too restrictive, a hybrid company may function as a quasi-trust, for example:

- for a person living in a civil law jurisdiction that does not recognize trusts
- where the trust law is too restrictive for the desired purpose of the entity
- for family foundations or charities
- for persons living in countries where forced heirship laws determine who must inherit upon the owner's death.

The hybrid structure can be used to separate the legal ownership of the assets from the beneficial interest in them. Since the concept of a company is universal, even in those countries which do not recognize trusts, the hybrid company can solve problems where either the owner or the property is in such a country.

The documentation for the company should be drafted by an expert to accomplish the individual results desired. A typical example would be a situation in which the shareholding members fund the company's share capital and provide the company with its assets. The company's Articles of Association (equivalent to Articles of Incorporation or charter in other countries) provide that the company's management and control rest entirely in the hands of the shareholding members, via the election of the directors. But the shareholding members are excluded from receiving any benefit. The guarantee members have severely restricted rights and cannot vote for the directors, but they alone are eligible to benefit from dividend payments and interest-free or interest-bearing loans. Many variations of these rights are possible, depending upon individual needs.

The hybrid company is particularly useful for asset protection, since the shareholding member of the company can retain control over the assets but is legally excluded from receiving any benefit from them (making him the equivalent of the settlor of a trust, and is therefore provided with a means of protecting assets from potential future creditors. The guarantee members are the approximate equivalent of the beneficiaries of a trust.

Just one of the infinite variations of structure than can be created is the possibility of making guarantee memberships non-transferable and with no value in the hands of the heirs or creditors of the guarantee member.

Because the guarantee members are legally guarantors, not shareholders, they are not required to disclose either a shareholding or a beneficial interest in a trust.

As I said at the beginning of this section, it is essential to use a qualified expert in this highly specialized area. My only recommendation is:

> Skye Fiduciary Services Limited
> Attn: New Clients Information
> 2 Water Street
> Ramsey, Isle of Man 1M8 1JP
> Great Britain
> Telephone: +44 1624 816117
> Fax: +44 1624 816645;
> Please mark fax "New Clients Information"

(As most of my readers will know, the Isle of Man is a very useful tax haven separate from Great Britain, but since most of the world's post offices won't know where it is, it is easier to humor them by including Great Britain in the address.)

Skye Fiduciary Services Limited are specialist consultants, designers of offshore and international fiduciary structures.

The chairman of the firm is Charles Cain, who was managing director of the second merchant bank to open on the Isle of Man, before he started his own business. He and his associates operate what I have no hesitation in calling the oldest and most experienced offshore corporate and trust management business in the Isle of Man.

In addition to hybrid companies, they can provide a full range of company management and trust management services. But it is their services in designing company and trust services that make them unique, and they can combine entities from several jurisdictions to create the most viable structure for the client. These can include trading companies, offshore family and charitable foundations, asset protection arrangements, and secure yet anonymous holding vehicles.

They also have the necessary expertise to ensure that offshore structures for U.S. persons precisely fit the required characterization under the Internal Revenue Code (and can develop tax efficient structures for those intending to immigrate to the U.S.).

SOME NOTES ABOUT TAXES

We have already said a lot about taxes in passing. In doing this it was assumed that the reader has at least some general familiarity with most of the concepts referred to. However, full utilization of the information in this book requires a firm grasp of the basics of taxation in one's home country and in the tax haven countries. We will not go into arcane technicalities; that is what accountants and tax lawyers are for. But informed decisions based on the recommendations of lawyers and accountants cannot be made without a solid command of the basics. So, to work.

The most familiar form of taxation is the income tax. In view of the fact that legal entities, those kinds of things that can have income, spend money, sign contracts, etc., and hence pay taxes, are of two kinds, human beings and corporations (including trusts), there are two kinds of income taxes: personal and corporate.

Personal income tax is what federal, state, and — all too often these days — local governments take from each of us as a percentage of our personal incomes. Its "skeleton" is a system of income brackets. These brackets establish varying rates of tax, varying percentages of taxpayer's income to be taxed away. The first $3,000, say, is not taxed at all. The next $1,000 is taxed 5 percent. Thus, only $50 must be paid on a $4,000 annual income, 5 percent of the fourth $1,000. Observe that while the percentage of the tax to total income is 1.25 percent, the tax bracket is 5 percent. Similarly, the fifth $1,000 may be taxed at a rate of 7 percent. Thus, on $5,000 the total tax would be $120, or 2.4 percent — much lower than the top tax bracket of 7 percent.

This concept of brackets is crucial to understanding what tax havens are all about because it makes clear what alienating income for tax bracket reduction means. If one divides an annual income of $5,000 between himself and his cat (somehow made into a respectable income-earning citizen by the tax computers), $3,000 to himself and $2,000 to Tabby, he effectively gets $5,000 tax-free, assuming the bracket structure in the above example. This is a saving that is much more appreciated by someone with an annual gross income of $30,000 or above, which may put him in the 40 percent tax bracket with $6,000 in taxes. Divided on paper between ten people, each getting $3,000, the bracket system implies no tax at all.

Personal income tax is based on **net** income. Net income is gross income less all expenses that can be claimed as necessary to produce the gross — or at least necessary to an **attempt** to create or increase it. Thus, to take a less than serious example, if one earns $30,000 as an undertaker and spends $10,000 on futile parties intended to convince people to commit suicide after signing wills entrusting the care and burial of their bodies to him, the $10,000 can be claimed as business expenses and so reduce his taxable income to $20,000. This means, of course, that the tax is also levied at a much lower rate (bracket). What constitutes a business expense depends, in large measure, on the imagination and experience of one's accountant and on adequate documentation — receipts, canceled checks, etc. This is important to remember for some tax haven applications. One may incorporate a tax haven company that can get funds from a high-tax country at a reduced tax rate, but which is locally taxable on its **net** income.

It is important to realize that personal income tax is only grossly determined by the brackets applicable to net income. There are further refinements, depending on the sources of income. In general, personal income derives from some or all of the following sources: wages, salary, fees for work or services; rent on property or real estate; dividends paid on investments; interest on bank deposits and corporate and government bonds; royalties on the use of patents or copyrights; and capital gains from the sale of property at a profit.

This breakdown of income sources is important for tax purposes. To begin with, capital gains are almost universally taxed separately on the basis of much more lenient scales and rates than those applying to ordinary income. Some countries do not tax capital gains at all. It is possible to channel investments in such a manner as to place all returns on the books as capital gains. Further, governments are not only interested in taking away part of our incomes as taxes. They are also interested in encouraging us to use what is left in "socially responsible" ways. Thus, they can reduce tax rates on income derived from interest paid on certain types of bonds or on certain dividends. Similarly, royalties may be taxed differently, depending on their source. In other words, the constitution of a taxpayer's income can make a big difference in his tax bill.

This means that, when making investment decisions, a businessman or investor should take into account tax rulings on the various tax rates applicable to income from different sources. For instance, if he gets dividends from stock he holds in a company, he is taxed twice, indirectly when the company is taxed on its net profit, and directly when he is taxed on his dividend income. The tax on dividends is inevitable, if the investor personally holds the stock. The tax on corporate profits may be eliminated if the stock is in a tax haven corporation or offshore fund, because a company operating outside the source country cannot be reached by the source country's tax authorities (with certain limited exceptions).

It is also important for our American readers to realize that they are citizens of the only major country in the world that taxes total **worldwide** income, regardless of where in the world a taxpayer may live. And it does so on top of whatever taxes he may pay to the government of the country in which he resides, unless that country has a double-taxation agreement with the U.S. In some cases, the United States is "generous" enough to allow the taxpayer to deduct the foreign taxes from his income for U.S. tax purposes.

But, the American reader may wonder, if I am living abroad what can the IRS do to me if I simply choose to ignore it and not pay U.S. taxes? For one thing, the U.S. government can ask the country in which you live to deport you on the criminal charge of tax evasion. For another, your American passport can be revoked. Neither seems a happy prospect, though some Americans have become "tax refugees."

There is much less to say about corporate income tax. It is a flat-rate tax, usually levied on the net income of a corporation, irrespective of its amount. Capital gains taxes may be different in come countries and states from taxes on income from other sources, and interest, dividends, rent, and royalties may all be taxed differently from straight business profit.

Other kinds of taxes to be concerned about, whether on the federal or state level, are estate, death, and probate. To protect loved ones after death, trusts as well as certain Liechtensteinian entities can serve very well. To avoid death taxes the simple way, by giving loved ones part of an estate while one is still living, is to reckon with gift taxes. Even so, the relative rates of gift taxes and estate taxes, especially when gifts are so divided as to be outside certain critical brackets, may make this approach worthwhile exploring. A trust, though, is generally the best solution.

Another sort of tax to be especially concerned about if one wishes to save money through tax havens is withholding tax. We have already referred to it, but it is important to clarify it in detail. Withholding tax is a tax deducted at the source from incomes generated in Country A by a legal entity residing in Country B and transferred from A to B. For example, if a businessman has a tax haven corporation, X, which owns stock in American Company Y, and American Company Y pays X $1,000 in dividends, Y must pay $300 of that (30 percent, the U.S. withholding rate) to the U.S. at the same time it makes remittance to X. X may be a genuine non-American residing in India or Belgium, but he is nonetheless subject to the withholding tax. Interest paid to non-Americans residing outside the U.S. ("nonresident aliens") on bank deposits in the United States is exempted from the U.S. withholding tax.

Withholding taxes are of importance whenever one has to consider the interaction between tax systems of different countries because he lives in Country A and derives income, directly or indirectly, from Country B. Thus, if one intends to receive dividends from his foreign corporation, or from **any** foreign corporation in which he has stock, the dividends may be reduced by the local withholding tax imposed by the country from which the funds are being sent.

Some people try to get around withholding taxes in a number of ways. One of these is to keep the dividends in a checking account in the country where the money originates and exchange a check on it with someone going there against a check on his deposit in the United States. This is usually illegal, and it may sometimes be illegal to have a foreign bank account. But, still, it is a gimmick that is hard to detect or prove without special and expensive detective work.

Suppose one doesn't want to take such risks. He may repatriate his dividends reduced by the local withholding tax. In this case, the following possibilities exist in principle: (1) The home country considers the dividends to be part of the gross income, regardless of what the gross sum of the dividend was. It therefore taxes the dividend again, by applying the relevant tax bracket after deduction of the foreign withholding tax. (2) The home country considers the gross dividend paid to be part of the gross income and deducts the tax withheld at the source from the total tax liability. (3) Some compromise between (1) and (2) occurs, in which the home country construes some part of the foreign withholding tax payment as a credit against the home country tax bill. (4) There is a double-taxation agreement between the foreign country and the home country consequent to which the foreign withholding tax deducted at the source is reduced and also credited against the total home country tax liability.

Double-taxation agreements are what to look for if one intends to invest in foreign stock from one's own country. They serve to reduce the foreign withholding tax and, at the same time, to cancel the double penalty of being taxed by both the home country and a foreign tax department. As such, these agreements have been introduced for "business" rather than tax reasons. They exist in order to encourage, or at least not discourage, investment in foreign companies. However, double-taxation agreements become of much greater tax-minimizing importance when considered from the point of view of a foreign corporation created for the purpose of investing in a high-tax country. Remittances to foreign corporations with such investments are normally subject to the full withholding tax on the gross. If a corporation is located in a completely no-tax haven, an investor manages to reduce his tax liability. This may be quite a saving, but he may wish to pay even less.

It is here that double-taxation agreements come into play. Of course, there are no double-taxation agreements with no-tax countries. But there are such agreements with a number of low-tax countries.

Suppose, for purposes of illustration, that a company's net income is what remains after a 15 percent treaty rate withholding tax has been deducted (85 percent of gross). The total tax on the gross would then be 27.75 percent, which is less than a typical 30 percent withholding. Clearly, the net income of a company can be reduced to much less than 85 percent of gross. And by using more than one company, the local tax can be virtually eliminated by eliminating the net profit of the local company. Moreover, certain approaches may allow reduction of the withholding tax to as low as 5 percent.

Thus, withholding tax is a curse that can be virtually neutralized by the careful exploitation of double-taxation agreements. But there is one fly in the ointment: more or less active cooperation between the tax departments of the governments involved. This is not as bad as it sounds, however, for there are plans that require nothing illegal, using only highly sophisticated, legal tax-avoidance techniques.

Let us wrap up this discussion of taxes with brief mention of a few less important, but still existent, taxes. Some countries levy annual land-value taxes. Others charge stamp duties, now almost universal taxes imposed on the value of certain officially registered documents (incorporation papers, bonds, bills of sale, IOUs, and even checks) and required for making these documents legally valid. Stamp duties must always be taken into account when dealing with a tax haven. Thus, even when we discuss no-tax havens, we do not mean places where nobody pays the government anything — more's the pity.

Now that we have the theory and practice of tax havens in hand, let us tour the best of these wonderful lands.

NO-TAX HAVENS: BALMY CLIMES FOR MONEY AND MAN

Over the last sixty years most people have come to accept taxes as a basic, inalienable part of life, a sort of necessary evil. There are, however, places where there are virtually no taxes. And, wonder of wonders, most of them have good governments, "good" in the Jeffersonian sense of governing little.

These no-tax countries share some basic similarities, which are important to anyone considering forming a corporation or trust in one or another of them. These factors need to be kept in mind when forming a judgment about the likelihood of the governments of these countries violating their no-tax traditions.

All of the no-tax havens considered in this chapter are island, or archipelago, societies. Foreign invasion is most unlikely, and defense budgets are minimal to nonexistent. All have ethnically mixed populations, native peoples and white immigrants from Europe and America. They have almost no racial friction and are peaceful and nonviolent, so the "war against crime" as a major motive for taxation to support large government outlays for police activities is happily lacking.

Because of their multi-island geographies, all of these havens are free of strong central government. Where government officials have to use motorboats or even canoes to get around, their mobility is reduced and, correspondingly, so is their control. None of these countries share the European and American notions of technologically oriented living standards. The idea that someone is "socially underprivileged" because he does not have a late-model car would seem odd to a citizen of any one of these lands, and welfare policies are nonexistent and very unlikely to be introduced in the future.

Every one of these no-tax havens has a British colonial background and is a member of the British Commonwealth. While the present British government is a high tax government, these little Commonwealth countries still operate on the "imperialist tradition" of nineteenth century British colonial policy, which typically excluded all local taxation. Moreover, the legal tradition in all of these places is that of the common law uncorrupted by socialist legislation, and the official language is English.

Finally, all of these nations, in view of their restricted land areas, depend on tourism and foreign investment for economic success. The tax haven industry is an economic necessity for each of them, and any attempt to change this by future leftist governments is improbable to say the least.

All in all, the consideration of stability is very much in favor of these no-tax havens. They have been no-tax countries for many, many years, and they have both traditional and practical stakes in staying that way.

However, all these havens share a major disadvantage: It is very difficult to establish plausible business reasons for incorporating in them. The names Bahamas, Bermuda, and Cayman Islands are immediately suspect in the eyes of any tax collector. This means that a Bahamas, Bermuda, or Cayman Islands corporation would best be formed indirectly by a corporation in another haven.

A related reason for considering these havens only in terms of a double- or multi-tier arrangement is the fact that one might want to derive tax-free (or tax-reduced) income from high-tax country sources.

No-tax countries do not have double-taxation agreements, so a corporation located in one, if directly receiving income from high-tax sources, would be subject to the full withholding tax on gross profits. On the other hand, as a second company in a multi-tiered structure, not receiving income directly from the high-tax source but from another corporation in a low-tax double-taxation-agreement haven, such an outfit can be highly useful. And since these no-tax nations do not have double-taxation agreements, they have substantial privacy advantages, which are enhanced by local codes, official and unofficial, that derive from the healthy vested interest of local governments in cultivating the tax haven industry.

Before we discuss the specific no-tax countries in detail, a word about how their governments raise the little revenue they need to stay in business. The principal sources of government funds in these nations are stamp duties; legal fees, under various descriptions, payable for incorporation and legal maintenance of a company; and import duties. There are similar sources of government revenue peculiar to each of these countries (such as the "bicycle fee" in the Cayman Islands). We will mention these, to the extent that they are relevant, as we go along.

The Bahamas

This was one of the first tax havens. Geographically, it is an archipelago. It is composed of 700 islands and uncounted rocks and reefs, stretching from Haiti on the southeast to Florida on the northwest. It has a total land area of 5,400 square miles, scattered over 70,000 square miles of ocean.

The Bahamas are usually associated with pleasant tourism. Clearly, a country where the major means of transportation is boats sailing across vast stretches of tranquil ocean has its fascination. The pleasant climate is an extra consideration. The sun almost always shines; the temperature varies only slightly the year round, from an average minimum of seventy degrees Fahrenheit to an average maximum of eighty.

An archipelago like the Bahamas can only be organized politically and economically if there is some major island to serve as its center of trade and government. For the Bahamas, this is New Providence. It contains 50 percent of the total population and the capital, Nassau.

Economically, the Bahamas thrive on tourism, the tax haven industry, and the export of petroleum products, cement, rum, salt, and ocean products. It has no heavy industry, but the export trade is a good business reason for being there.

The Bahamas are highly accessible. Nassau can be reached by air from any major airport in the United States, and it is but thirty-five minutes flight-time from Miami. There are direct flights from London, Toronto, New York and other major cities.

Communications are no problem at all. The language is English, and airmail, telegraph, direct-dial telephone, and telex services are of the highest quality.

The Bahamas are a sovereign state within the British Commonwealth, independent since 1973. Commonwealth membership means that Her Majesty the Queen is head of state, and she is locally represented by the appointed governor general. This provides a measure of safety because the governors general have traditionally been very conservative. The legislature is bicameral, the upper house appointed by the governor general on the approval, recommendation, and joint agreement of the prime minister and the leader of the opposition, and the lower house popularly elected. The upper house can delay any legislation, though eventually it must approve it. The governor general can veto any legislation he deems inconsistent with the constitution.

However, there have been political snakes in the Bahamian paradise. The government has created problems both in the granting of work permits to aliens and in exchange-control matters. Both difficulties derived from programs of "Bahamization of the economy" and "social development." However, the same government has also put into force some programs of encouragement to foreign investors and tourism, so the situation is less ominous than some rumors would have it. Moreover, the government has repeatedly promised that it will not buck the no-tax tradition.

As noted above, the legal system of the Bahamas is grounded on the English common law. This tradition is implemented by a four-level court structure: local magistrates, magistrate courts for more serious matters, a supreme court, and a court of appeals. The ultimate court of appeals is that of the whole Commonwealth, the Queen's Privy Council.

Whatever professional services one might need — law firms, accountants, banks, finance companies, investment advisors, stockbrokers — are available in abundance. They are of an internationally high quality, too, based on a longstanding and thriving tax haven industry.

As for the tax laws, there are no personal income taxes, no corporate taxes, no profit taxes, no capital gains taxes, no estate or other death taxes. On the island of New Providence there is a tax on the value of improved land. A more serious qualification is the tax on local gambling casinos. After all, the government must get its share of this lucrative element of the tourist industry!

In accord with the general no-tax situation, there is no withholding tax of any kind. If one is a worrier, he can even incorporate in the Freeport area and get a thirty-five-year warranty against the imposition of any future tax, should one be imposed. The Bahamas are one among many tax havens that have such no-tax warranties. It is hard to say what the value of these is, if any, because a future government taking the extremely unlikely revolutionary course of introducing taxation may well refuse to respect such promises of preceding governments. Still, it is a nice touch.

The lack of any significant taxes in the Bahamas does not mean that anyone incorporating there will get off scot-free. After all, the local government does deserve something in return for providing a tax haven. Whatever one pays, however, will bear no relation to his profits. There will be stamp duties on the documents of corporate registration and an annual business-license fee. The rates are quite competitive with other tax havens.

What kind of business entities can one form in the Bahamas? How? At what cost?

There are two basic types of corporations: companies limited by shares, and companies limited by guarantee. Both types belong to the general kind of corporate entities discussed in part one, but there are certain differences. Companies limited by shares have a fixed, unmodifiable authorized capital. They cannot buy back their own stock. However, a shareholder's liability is limited to his stock. If the stock is fully paid-up and the company goes bankrupt, creditors have no recourse to any of the shareholders' personal assets.

Companies limited by guarantee can reduce their share capital by buying back their shares and canceling them. This means that they can present their creditors with an unpredictable security situation. The security for bonds, debentures, and other loans is, of course, the total authorized and real capital of the corporation. If it can be reduced after bonds have been issued or loans taken out, this means that the company is legally entitled to reduce the initial assets against which it took out loans. To protect debtors in such an instance, shareholders' personal guarantees for some extra sum beyond their own investment is legally introduced.

Offshore funds, with their typically expanding-contracting capital, are therefore incorporated in the Bahamas as companies limited by guarantee. Anyone who decides to participate in the tax haven industry through an offshore fund based in the Bahamas should read the "fine print" very carefully.

Incorporating in the Bahamas requires the services of a local lawyer, who will prepare and file a memorandum of association and articles of association. Both documents are standard, and the first includes the name of the company, the address of its local registered office, its general purpose and objects, a declaration that it has limited liability of the relevant sort, and the company's capitalization (total authorized capital, the number and kind of shares, etc.). The articles of association specify the number of corporate directors and regulations concerning annual directors' meetings. On the latter point, the directors can meet anywhere, not necessarily in the Bahamas. "Alternative directors" can stand in for the regular directors, and a circular, agreed to and signed by a majority of the directors, can have the same official standing as any decisions reached by a majority at a regular directors' meeting.

The local law firm handling incorporation will charge certain fees: the charges for preparing documentation; the costs of providing five local nominee shareholders (who will sign a "deed of trust" turning over their shares to a principal after incorporation); the costs of maintaining (according to longstanding, though unwritten, tradition) a local nominee director; and the cost of "office representation" in the Bahamas (a sign displaying the company name must be posted on the building in which the registered office is located). In addition, there are these statutory requirements that must be met: a register of directors, a register of shareholders, and a minute book must be maintained in the local office, and an annual return must be submitted to the Registrar of Companies, specifying shareholders, directors, officers, the address of the registered office, and amount of share capital.

As against government fees, which are fixed, there is some variation in the fees for the above services. On the average, initial incorporation costs run about $2,500. Of course, one can shop for the least expensive services and do a bit better.

Apart from the two basic forms companies described, which have always been part of the basic companies legislation, the Bahamas has created a new category called the international business company, with an annual government fee ranging from $100 to $1,000, depending upon the capitalization of the company. The Bahamian international business company needs only one director who need not be a shareholder, and can be corporate and non-resident in the country. Meetings of shareholders and directors may be held in any country, and bearer shares may be issued.

Companies incorporated under the Act must have at all times a Registered Office/Agent in the Bahamas. Documents such as the Memorandum and Articles of Association, Appointment/Resignation of Directors and Officers, Shares Register, and all Corporate Resolutions are required to be kept at the Registered Office.

The Bahamas common law tradition also provides for trusts, which can be arranged through local trust companies. No government fees are involved because a trust is a privately constituted entity that derives its existence from a trust deed and a trust fund, not from government registration. The local trust law allows a "Cuba clause," which means that if, by some strange course of events, the Bahamas becomes a "people's democracy," the trust would automatically revert to some other country where there is a "stand-by" trustee. The use of such a clause, of course, requires that the trust assets be outside the Bahamas.

Bermuda

Bermuda is similar to the Bahamas in many respects. Like the Bahamas, it is made up of islands, seven main ones, connected by bridges, and many small coral formations, accessible from the main ones by boat. It is situated about 600 miles east of Cape Hatteras, North Carolina, and so, like the Bahamas, it is close to the United States. Its land area, however, is much smaller, a mere 20.5 square miles, of which two were occupied by U.S. military bases. The former base areas have been turned over to the Bermuda government for development. The remaining area is densely populated. Understandably, land purchases in Bermuda are difficult, both legally and financially. This is reflected in office rentals and so on.

Bermuda is a tourist's delight. It has a very moderate climate and is warmed by the Gulf Stream. Its area is hilly, with beautiful banks of flowers and lovely rainbow-hued houses.

It is highly accessible. Daily flights connect it with any major city in the world; it is but two hours from New York. It is located at the crossroads of the shipping lanes between the United States, Canada, Europe, and South America. Direct-dial telephone, cable, telex, and airmail services are excellent.

There are few political differences between Bermuda and the Bahamas. Bermuda is a self-governing crown colony and so is not a fully independent Commonwealth member. It has a governor, appointed by the Queen. This official has larger responsibilities than his Bahamian counterpart. He handles foreign relations (in accordance with British policy), security, and police. All other affairs are monitored by the democratic institutions of the self-governing colony.

Despite foreign affairs and defense relations with Great Britain, there exist no governmental financial relations between the colony and the mother country. All Bermudian officials, including the governor, are paid out of local government revenues, and Great Britain gets no tax money from Bermuda. Thus, the high British taxes have no bearing on the tax situation in Bermuda. The self-governing nature of Bermuda means that any changes in the tax laws or other legislation cannot be imposed from without; they can only emerge from the local legislature.

The legal tradition in Bermuda derives from an ancient, pre-1612, British common law, modified by locally generated common law. The legal framework is three-tiered: magistrate courts, a supreme court, and a court of appeals. As in most Commonwealth countries, the ultimate court of appeals is the Queen's Privy Council in London.

The local currency, the Bermudian dollar, is on par with the U.S. dollar. As in the Bahamas, there are exchange controls on residents and resident companies.

Bermuda is similar to the Bahamas in having a large range of high quality professional services available. Very strict banking legislation has resulted in there being very few banks,.

The British tradition in Bermuda means that there are strong ties between accountants, lawyers, trust companies, and banks. Once one chooses his accountant, say, this gentlemen will "strongly recommend" the lawyer, trust company, and bank to be used, stressing that he is "accustomed" to working with them. This may seem a bit restrictive, but it guarantees good cooperation between firms that otherwise might not cooperate in one's best interests.

As in the Bahamas, local bank deposits have certain attractive features; the depositor can choose the currency, there is no withholding or other tax on interest, and he can have a joint account with his spouse allowing that he or she is to have immediate title to the assets in case of the other's death. If, though, both account holders die at the same time, any heirs will have access to the account only by reference to a properly executed will approved by a court, and the will will be a matter of public record.

As for taxes, there is no personal income tax, no corporation tax, no profits tax, no capital tax, no capital gains tax, no withholding tax, no inheritance tax. There are import duties and a 10 percent property levy on the rental value of houses and land. To take advantage of this happy situation, one can either incorporate or form a local trust.

Incorporation in Bermuda was made simpler in 1970. Previously, any incorporation required a special private legislative act. To incorporate one had to offer a petition to the local parliament through a legal representative. The legislature would then vote on the proposal and, eventually, approve it. This superceremonious method of incorporation still exists and must be used if any aspect of the structure, internal organization, or mode of operation of an intended company deviates from the pattern dictated by the General Corporation Law enacted in 1970. However, if the corporation is a "normal" one, incorporation can be accomplished without such legislative ceremonies by submitting the standard type of documents for the Registrar of Companies to approve.

There are two basic types of companies recognized by Bermudian corporate legislation, local companies and exempt companies. Local companies are those formed by Bermudians for purposes of internal trade or Bermuda-based international trade (import to and export from Bermuda). Such companies have a minimum percentage of local stock ownership, prescribed by law, are subject to strict exchange control, and have no guaranteed immunity against future taxes.

An exempt company is free of the first two restrictions above, and is given an official guarantee against the levying of future taxes for thirty years. However, an exempt company is restricted as follows: (1) It cannot buy, lease, or sell land, mortgages secured by land, or bonds and debentures secured by land without special permission. (2) It cannot buy shares of local companies. (3) It cannot locally sell whatever it produces without special ad hoc permission. These limitations narrow "business justification" possibilities for Bermudian incorporation, to say the least, and there is no way around them.

Incorporation in Bermuda is more difficult than in the Bahamas. Taking into account the various professional services that are needed for incorporation as well as the high government fees, both incorporation and annual maintenance run to $2,000-$2,500 a year depending on the specific services required.

In addition to the financial burdens, there is a "screening" of incorporation applications. A committee chaired by a member of Parliament examines bank references to eliminate Mafia types and such. This screening slows things up, and may take a month. In recent years this work has been delegated to the law firms and banks, subject to spot checking by the committee.

Bermudian trusts are much less costly. A stamp duty of 0.25 percent of the initial fund (plus the same percentage on any later increase in the fund) is the total governmental cost. A trust is not locally taxed on its profits, but if its beneficiaries are aliens, it cannot, in view of the land scarcity, invest in local real estate without special approval from the government — which turns a deaf ear to all such requests.

Even if the disadvantages noted above do not discourage a potential investor, the Bermudian political and social situation may. There is a policy of "Bermudization." There are problems with immigration and work permits for aliens; hiring a local office is difficult in view of the land restrictions; the distinction between local and alien companies is very strict. There has already been an attempt, defeated in Parliament, to introduce an income tax. Local companies pay a 5 percent "payroll tax," which means that on each $100 an employee gets, the company has to pay the government an extra $5. But this is a bad sign for a tax haven. (Remember, the U.S. income tax started at 5 percent.) There is also some racial tension between whites and blacks (60 percent of the population is black), although there is much public relations effort to deny that the tension exists.

Thus, given a choice between Bermuda and the Bahamas, the Bahamas may make the better bet. The only advantage Bermuda seems to have is the extra respectability conferred on Bermudian companies by the screening process.

The Cayman Islands

Like Bermuda and the Bahamas, the Caymans are — obviously — a collection of islands. There are three of them, located 475 miles south of Miami and 200 miles north of Montego Bay. Of the three, Grand Cayman, as its name implies, is the major one; it is there that both the capital and most business activities are located. Its area is significantly greater than that of the other two, seventy-six square miles, as against Cayman Brac's fourteen and Little Cayman's ten. Cayman Brac is east of Grand Cayman, and Little Cayman lies between the two larger islands.

This trio is rather hot. The only factor differentiating the tropical nature of the Caymans from West Africa is the trade winds, which cool them off — a little.

The Caymans are about five times larger than Bermuda and they are much less densely populated. Thus, the Bermudian "land sensitivity" reflected in harsh strictures on land purchases by foreigners and in high real estate costs has a very moderate counterpart in the Caymans.

Being a tax haven is for the Caymans, like Bermuda and the Bahamas, a tradition based on British rule. Here, however, the tradition is bolstered by a legend. In 1798 the islanders heroically saved from tragic death at sea a British royal prince and his mentor, an admiral, and King George III gratefully granted the islanders eternal tax exemption. Scholars may concern themselves with the authenticity of the legend, and its legal significance at present is dubious. But it is very significant as a predictor of the future; such a strong tax haven tradition would make it very difficult to introduce any sort of taxation.

Not that there is any special reason to worry about the Caymans. The Cayman Islands government is very keen on the tax haven industry, a major factor in local economic growth. Thus, the consideration of expected future stability favors the Caymans. It is important to see, therefore, whether they are inferior to their competition in other respects.

One can fly to the Caymans from Miami or Kingston, Jamaica. There are good airmail, telephone, telex, and cable services.

Politically, the Caymans are a Crown Colony by choice. In 1962, when Jamaica became independent of Great Britain and the Caymans were a dependency of Jamaica, the Caymans decided by national referendum against independence or a Jamaican connection and for the status of a Crown Colony. This indicates a rather unusual traditional conservatism in this era of "national independence" and the "fight against colonialistic imperialism," and it is a strong predictor of stability.

The local population is racially mixed, but mixed in the right way. There is a minority of pure Europeans (20 percent) and pure Africans (20 percent) and a racially mixed majority (60 percent). This indicates that racial tension, prejudice, segregation, and such, were never serious factors in the Caymans and are likely to become even less so. This, again, is important because leftist governments often come to power employing racial strife as a major crutch. Here leftists would not have much to lean on.

The government is headed by a governor, an appointee of the Queen. He heads the Executive Council, his cabinet. The council members are partially elected, partially appointed by the governor. There is a one-house legislature, the Legislative Assembly, elected by universal suffrage. Recent elections and day-to-day political life do not indicate any basic left-right polarization. The Caymans are a politically quiet place.

The law is British common law modified by local legislation. The court structure is similar to those of Bermuda and the Bahamas. Corporate legislation is modernized and efficient. Exchange controls are somewhat less strict than in Bermuda and the Bahamas. They involve major restrictions on local residents, but a "nonresident" company dealing outside the islands can be formed, eliminating all exchange-control considerations. The only restriction on such a company is that it cannot use the local currency.

A broad range of high quality legal, banking, accounting, finance, and trust services is available.

The **only** sources of government revenue are stamp and import duties. An automatic no-tax guarantee of twenty years is granted to nonresident exempted corporations, and there is a fifty-year guarantee to trusts. There is virtually no tax department.

Incorporation is quick and easy. A memorandum of association, involving three initial shareholders (which a legal representative can supply as proxies), is required. It has to specify the usual details: name of corporation, address of its local registered office, statement of purposes, statement that it has limited liability, and its capitalization (amount of authorized capital, division into shares, and par value of shares). On payment of a registration fee, the Registrar of Companies issues an immediate certificate of incorporation and files the memorandum. Maintenance of a corporation is quite reasonable. An annual fee is required, as are the standard office services, supplied by an agent for a modest fee. This same agent will also submit the required annual return to the government. This has nothing to do with finances. It merely specifies the name of the company, the address of the local registered office, the authorized capital, the issued capital (total par value of issued stock), and the names and addresses of the **nominal** shareholders. This annual return has to be accompanied by an annual fee.

Total costs of incorporation run about $2,500 — the only constant being the government fee, while the agent's fees vary. Annual maintenance averages about $1,500.

All of the above applies to an "ordinary" company. There are also exempt companies. The above mentioned twenty-year no-tax guarantee applies only to them. The fact that a company operates in trade outside the Caymans does not mean it has to be exempt. It is up to the incorporators to consider the relative advantages and disadvantages. An exempt company, apart from the twenty-year guarantee, can omit from its name the "Ltd." required of other companies, can issue shares without par value, can dispense with the formality of annual shareholder meetings, and can keep private with no representation in any official records, the names of shareholders.

Of course, all these benefits cost. Costs and annual maintenance run about 50 percent higher. Even with these fees, a Caymans exempt company costs about the same as a Bermudian nonresident company, and apart from the above advantages, it can also issue bearer shares, and there is no extra charge in the form of stamp duties on the transfer of shares.

Another advantage of an exempt company is the possibility of redeemable preference shares, which at the time of liquidation have priority over ordinary shares in being paid up by the company to the shareholder but which usually have no voting power. Such shares can be useful if one wants to finance his corporation not by taking out loans but by issuing new stock without at the same time compromising control of the company.

The reader may have wondered why articles of association were not mentioned above. The reason is that in the Caymans (as in most jurisdictions deriving their companies legislation from the older British companies' laws) there is a "Table A" that substitutes for these uniformly in a manner that creates only minor inconvenience. This table is not a curse of uniformity but a blessing of not worrying over what are usually irrelevant formalities. One can at any time offer articles of association, modifying Table A as he wishes, leaving the table to apply automatically to matters not mentioned in the modification. The table is thus a legal convention created to enhance convenience of local incorporation.

Of course, the common law tradition of the Caymans allows not only corporations but trusts. Trust companies galore compete to be of service. The trust deed requires a stamp duty and a nominal fee for official recording. However, total formation costs with an average trust company can be as low as $1,000, although they will usually run somewhat more. There are no undue limitations concerning either trust founders or beneficiaries, and, of course, no taxes on trust profits, which can accumulate and multiply nicely, enriched by whatever extra additions to its principal one may care to make. For an extra expense one can get the trust counterpart of an exempt corporation, the exempt trust. It has a fifty-year guarantee against future taxes, and its annual maintenance cost includes a yearly government fee. As against the exempt corporation, which offers a package of business advantages apart from the no-tax warranty, the exempt trust is worthwhile only for the real worrying types, who seriously believe that in the Caymans any form of tax on incomes of trusts with foreign founders, trustees, and, possibly, assets will be introduced.

The Caymans offer a large range of possible business activities. There is virtually no nationalistic spirit or land-scarcity anxiety, and bank privacy is strongly guarded. A governmental official who breaches bank privacy can expect heavy fines and a prison term.

Clearly, the Caymans are superior in virtually every respect — future no-tax security, costs, expediency of incorporation, flexibility of corporate structure, business opportunities, privacy, immigration, and prospects for land ownership. The very positive government interest in the tax haven industry is also a big plus.

As the Cayman Islands have grown significantly, it has become harder to find an independent company management service, as so many are now just divisions of big banks and institutions.

A Source of help in the Cayman Islands

Based in the Cayman Islands, Britannia Corporate Management Ltd. is licensed by the Government of the Cayman Islands to incorporate and manage Cayman Island registered companies. This function includes the provision of a registered office, corporate secretary, officers and directors, and undertaking the day-to-day management and administration of the company's affairs.

Britannia is licensed to manage a wide range of business activities including investment holding and trading companies (companies formed for buying and selling securities), real estate holding companies, patent holding companies, and life insurance holding companies.

They also manage invoicing and trading companies. Companies of this type are frequently created by import-export firms to invoice a product to the final buyer and allow the corporate earnings to be retained in the tax haven.

Under the Cayman Islands Mutual Funds Law, Britannia is able to provide the registered office, as well as the specialized management and administration functions associated with an offshore mutual fund.

The president of Britannia is Gary F. Oakley, a Canadian who has been a permanent resident of the Cayman Islands for over 17 years. He has an extensive background in offshore company and financial management.

For further information contact:

> Britannia Corporate Management Ltd.
> Attn: New Clients Information
> P. O. Box 1968
> Whitehall Estates, Grand Cayman
> Cayman Islands
> Fax: +1 345 949 0716,
> Pease mark fax "New Clients Information"

My Canadian readers will also be interested to know that Britannia also offers an offshore family estate planning structure specifically designed for Canadian residents. This family estate planning structure is not only within the provision of the Canadian Income Tax Act but also complies with the recently introduced offshore reporting rules.

Portfolio management in the Cayman Islands

For asset management and securities brokerage, Lines Overseas Management Services is one of the most respected businesses operating today. Notable is its independence from onshore influences. It does not have a parent company controlling it from a big country, and does not maintain subsidiaries. Lines Overseas Management clears its trades locally, leaving no paper trail on its client activities in New York, London, or elsewhere.

Rates on certificates of deposit and liquid accounts offered through Lines are generally higher than those available in other markets. The firm offers proprietary Visa Gold debit cards to access cash on deposit. Offshore asset managers are appointed to provide personalized service in the selection of investments in order to best meet specific client needs. These managers fully understand the investment and tax avoidance objectives of overseas customers.

Lines is clearly not for everyone, however. It only accepts accounts with US $250,000 minimums. One of its offshore asset managers has been widely recognized in best-selling books and periodicals. He is Scott Oliver, a British subject, who earlier helped to develop sophisticated trading systems for some of Wall Street's largest investment banks. Today, many American estate planning attorneys refer their wealthiest clients to Oliver for financial advice. He has broad familiarity and expertise not only with publicly-traded issues of all kinds, but has a strong track record in private placements.

For more information, contact the following:

> Mr. Scott Oliver
> Offshore Asset Manager
> Lines Overseas Management (Cayman) Ltd.
> P.O. Box 1159GT, Genesis Building
> Grand Cayman, Cayman Islands
> Mr. Oliver can be reached by telephone at
> +1 345 949-5808 or by fax at +1 345 949-1338

FOREIGN-SOURCE INCOME HAVENS: PROFITS ABROAD — TAX FREE

Bermuda, the Bahamas, and the Caymans provide natural and obvious no-tax alternatives to tax system of the industrialized countries. Most tax all income, regardless of its sources. The no-tax havens tax none of it.

There is a third possibility, countries that tax only income generated locally. If one lives and works in one of these places, the income from his work is taxed. However, if he lives there and derives income from abroad, or if he does not personally reside there but his legal "shadow" (a corporation or trust) does, then that foreign income is not locally taxable.

This illustrates an important distinction in taxing practices. Tax systems can be compared not only in terms of the types of taxes they impose, the proportions, or rates, they use to determine the amount of tax due, but also in terms of the sources of income that are considered taxable.

Countries that impose no taxes on foreign income are not always tax havens. Most Latin American countries tax only local income, but most of them are too politically and economically unstable to be worth even a passing thought. Moreover, governments that exclude foreign-source income from taxation are unlikely to face much political opposition if they decide to tax such income. The populations of such specialized havens are used to taxes. In other words, if there is any guarantee of the continuation of the practice of exempting foreign income from taxation, it lies in a sustained desire of governments to earn revenues from the tax haven industry in other ways. Unfortunately, such policies tend to be as fragile as the governments taking advantage of them. While the continuation of current policy can be reasonably expected in most no-tax havens because of the strong influence of tradition and simple individual self-interest. No such automatic projection of stability can be made in most no-tax-on-foreign-source-income countries, but there are some exceptions. Each of them merits attention because all offer the possibility of creating a local company, the bulk of whose investment is abroad and thus free from local taxation, but that is located in a country that does not possess a tax haven reputation. To be more specific, if one has a Hong Kong corporation, he may very well have some very good business (as opposed to tax) motivation for it: cheap local labor, excellent possibilities for international trade, etc. A Bermudian exempt company, however, instantly suggests tax avoidance to a suspicious mind.

Another general advantage of these havens is that their governments usually want foreign investment. In some of these countries, foreign investors get preferential treatment that may mean not only tax advantages, but subsidies, marketing privileges, etc. So let us look at these unusual lands.

Panama

Panama deserves first mention here because it is already so widely used by individuals and corporations as a base for their foreign operations. It is notable for the combination of tax and business advantages it offers despite the U.S. invasion a few years ago.

A major reason for the popularity of Panama is its location. It is the link between North and South America, and it includes the famous Panama Canal, connecting the Atlantic and the Pacific. Its total land area is 29,700 square miles. The majority of these people (60 percent) live off the land. The capital, Panama City, contains most of the urbanized population and most of the rest live in the other major city, Colon. Colon's significance, economically, derives from its freeport facilities, which we will discuss later.

A visitor to Panama is in no danger of freezing. The climate is tropical — hot, with heavy rains (50 inches a year on the Pacific side, 150 on the Atlantic). There is a dry season from mid-December through the end of April.

One can reach Panama more easily than virtually any other tax haven. Many airlines serve Panama. If sea travel is preferred, Panama has four excellent ports: Cristobal at the Atlantic end of the Canal, Balboa at the Pacific end, and Puerto Armuelles and Bahias de las Rouge.

Telecommunication is extremely efficient because Panama is an international crossroads of trade. There is direct telephone service via satellite and very reliable telex, cable, and airmail.

Politically, Panama is a republic. It has a democratic election system that every six years is supposed to produce a turnover in the unicameral legislature, the National Assembly, while the "chief of state," the president, and the vice president are supposed to be elected by the assembly. The chief of state is the chairman of the national cabinet and roughly corresponds to the prime minister in a parliamentary government. The National Assembly has the job of examining and approving or disapproving legislation drafted by a national legislative commission. Prior to the American invasion, Panama was a typical Latin American dictatorship run by whoever happened to be in charge of the National Guard (army), with all the republican and democratic trappings as mere window dressing. However, the military leaders — even the leftists — never seemed to tinker with the tax and corporation laws. There is a kind of economic freedom absolutely unaffected by political turnover. The rulers seemed to have the good sense not to slay the goose that lays the golden eggs.

Another indication of the considerable independence and stability of economic policy is the structure of the Panamanian civil service and government. We are used to a public bureaucracy in which each department is headed by a political appointee to a ministerial/secretarial position. In Panama a variety of governmental functions are handled by purely bureaucratic agencies with no political honchos. Electricity and hydraulic resources, national telecommunications, tourism, social security, all these functions are handled by a semiautonomous official institute, which is not under any cabinet minister.

Spanish is the official language, but English is very widely used. Most professionals and businessmen speak English.

A very pleasing feature of Panama is the absolute monetary freedom. The local Balboa is on par with the U.S. dollar and exchanges freely with it. All paper money is American. The lack of exchange controls implies that the government cannot regulate the money supply, and there is no central bank. Add to this banking legislation comparable to that of the Switzerland of old: numbered accounts in the currency the account holder designates and tight secrecy laws.

The central position of Panama in inter-American as well as transoceanic trade means that its professional services — banking, accountancy, legal, brokerage — are of the highest quality and intensely competitive. There are many banks, both local and international. Name any major international banking organization and it has a branch in Panama.

There are many Panamanian management companies that can handle local corporate creation and management in all necessary aspects. They play a role analogous to that of Bahamian and other trust companies, and they even offer trust services. (However, in view of the fact that Panama is a civil law country, trusts, though legally possible, are best avoided.) They will handle anything and everything: incorporation, registration of assets, provision of all required nominee officers and directors to cover the various requirements of corporation law, etc. They will even conduct feasibility studies on the advisability of alternative possible investments.

Panama taxes locally generated income and exempts from tax all income generated abroad. This policy has existed since the country was founded in 1903, good reason to believe that the policy is too well entrenched to be changed with ease. The income tax on the local income of residents is progressive to 46 percent. If one is in the country less than six months in a year and generates local income, he is not exempted from tax altogether or even allowed to "spread" his income over the whole year. Rather, he pays taxes on a pro rata basis; the ratio of Panamanian residence duration to a full year is the basis for calculation. Thus, Panama is not ideal for an immigrant tax-refugee. (A curious feature of local tax laws is that tax evasion creates liability for fines but not for a prison term.)

On the bright side, all income generated by movement of commodities that never pass through Panama (even though they may be invoiced in Panama and managed from a Panamanian office) is completely exempt from taxation. Thus, there are good business reasons — "business motivation" — for setting up a Panama-based corporation. Moreover, if dividends are paid to stockholders residing outside Panama, no withholding tax applies, provided the profit underlying the dividends is all derived from sources external to Panama. Similarly, if one inherits property owned by a Panamanian corporation (by inheriting the stock) and the assets themselves are outside Panama, no inheritance taxes apply.

Even if the assets are in Panama, inheritance taxation is quite liberal when compared to the United States. Inheritance taxes are calculated after the estate is divided between the various heirs. The first $30,000 is exempt from tax (this means that if an estate of $150,000 were divided equally among five heirs, each would inherit $30,000 tax-free); close relatives are taxed much less than more distant relatives; and tax rates are only 80 percent of their officially stated ratio because of an automatic 20 percent deduction of tax liability.

The fact that overseas operations based in Panama are not taxed, together with easily demonstrated business motivation for Panamanian operations, the free exchange of currencies, and the economically strategic position of the country account for the 35,000 corporations, mostly foreign, that are registered in Panama — more than in any other tax haven. This large corporate presence is, in itself, the strongest guarantee of future preservation of the tax-free-foreign-income policy. Any change of this policy would scare off most of the 35,000 companies, terminate the flow of money they feed into the Panamanian economy and the government treasury, and thus would be a vast net loss. The free market situation in the international tax haven industry, following from the existence of many alternative havens all competing for patronage, should keep Panama very much "in line."

Panama's principal claim to fame as a haven for foreign companies is based on the shipping industry. Like Liberia, Panama offers special advantages for ship owners who elect to fly its flag as a "flag of convenience." The cost of ship registration in Panama is low. Even if a shipping company regularly imports and exports from and to Panama, none of its income or profits (or the salaries of its crews, for that matter) are subject to any Panamanian tax. Moreover, Panama's maritime labor regulations are liberal.

Let us now review Panamanian corporate law. Fortunately, it is based on the Delaware laws of 1927 (without amendments). As the reader may know, Delaware is the best U.S. state in which to incorporate because of its very advantageous corporation laws. In Panama incorporation requires two incorporators, who must execute the articles of incorporation before the Panamanian counterpart of a notary public. These two are usually nominees, employees of a local management company. The articles of incorporation are recorded at the public registry office, and the later costs of maintenance can be reduced to a $100 annual fee to a local legal representative. Nominee "incorporators," though nominally shareholders at the time of incorporation, will sign a deed of transfer returning their stock to their principal(s) after incorporation has been effected.

The articles of incorporation must include the usual details: (1) company name, with the standard designation for a corporate entity, (2) a statement, however general, of the objects of the corporation, (3) capitalization, specifying both the total amount of authorized capital (which determines the limit of the company's liabilities) and its division into shares with their respective par values (shares with no par value can be issued, but then the government assumes that each share has the nominal par value of $20 for the purpose of computing the registration tax) (4) specification of the nature of the shares— registered or bearer, common or preferred, voting or nonvoting, (5) names and addresses of at least three directors (usually nominees hired for an annual fee), (6) names and addresses of officers (again, nominees — who can be the same individuals serving as directors), (7) the duration of the corporation, which can be a specified limited period or "forever," (8) name and address of the local legal representative of the corporation, and (9) the domicile of the corporation (e.g., Panama City, Panama).

How costly is incorporation? Usually $800 to $1,000.

Annual corporate maintenance costs very little, about $100-$200. The low fees stem from the fact that the local legal representative has only to exist; he has no reports to file nor any other work to do.

Thus, neither incorporation nor company maintenance is very expensive in Panama. It is certainly much less expensive than the comparative action in Bermuda, the Bahamas, and even the Caymans. And one gets the same tax advantages for income generated outside the country. Moreover, there is further advantage to be enjoyed by Panamanian companies that deal exclusively outside Panama. They need keep no financial records locally, nor do they have to submit any annual financial reports with the local tax authorities. What has to be kept locally is a stock-register book for registered stock and a minute book for meetings of stockholders. The latter must be rubricated (for a special fee) by a local judge. It is also bound in such a way that the minutes must be entered manually; typed minutes cannot be filed in. This, though, is just an unimportant nuisance, not a serious consideration.

Another nuisance concerns stockholders' meetings. If not physically held in Panama, these have to be officially sanctioned by the Panamanian consul in the country where they are held and then registered in the minute book in Panama. Alternatively, they can be made official by the signature of the corporate secretary, the person whose name is recorded in the mercantile registry as the corporation's secretary. Again, this is merely a curiosity of some slight inconvenience, not a major problem.

If, however, a company does local business in Panama, it becomes subject to taxes on its locally generated income. In this case, a general ledger, a general journal, an inventory, and a balance sheet must be maintained. A commercial business license may also be needed. This could be bypassed by handling Panamanian business through a corporation domiciled in, say, the Cayman Islands. The Panamanian withholding tax is lower than the corporate income tax on locally operating companies.

In any event, if a Panamanian corporation is not in any way directly involved in domestic business activities in Panama, no annual report of **any kind** has to be made. Even interest generated locally on local bank deposits is free from any local tax or withholding. Thus, for a sum of about $1,000 for incorporation and $100-$200 a year in maintenance costs, a company can enjoy virtually complete business privacy — no reports, no books, no anything.

Another advantage of Panama, apart from its very private corporations, the low costs of annual maintenance, and the free exchange of currencies, is the Colon Free Zone. Located at the Atlantic entrance to Panama and accessible by air and sea from every corner of the Western Hemisphere, it is very active economically, with an annual trade volume of about $950 million. It has attracted international companies from the United States, Japan, and Europe. Its freedom of trade involves complete exemption from duties on merchandise imported into it, packed, labeled and/or assembled in it, and reshipped from it. Moreover, no commercial licenses are needed.

How to use the freeport facilities depends on the size of the commercial operations one intends to conduct from them. Land can be leased there, and warehouse or other facilities can be built on it. The usual lease is for twenty years and is renewable. Warehouse space can be leased too. Finally, local warehouses are also available for fees based on the value of the total merchandise stored. Clearly, the leasing of space and construction of warehouses for hire is a lucrative business possibility in the Free Zone.

Unfortunately, the freeport, although duty-free, is not totally tax-free. Merchandise that physically passes through the Colon area and is subject to some form of local processing — repacking, labeling, etc. — is taxed by the Panamanian government. The tax rates, however, are extremely low. They are based on a 1954 income tax law, under which corporate income tax was but 30 percent on net profit. Add to this a 90 percent "tax discount" applicable in the Colon Free Zone, and the result is a negligible 3 percent tax on net profit from all merchandise that physically passes through Colon not later sold in Panama. (Standard taxes apply to all Free Zone goods resold in Panama.)

In 1995, Panama passed legislation enabling the creation of private foundations, similar to those which may be formed in Liechtenstein, but at far less cost. This new form of entity is likely to become extremely popular with people who need a situation in which they are not the legal owner of the assets controlled by their private foundation.

Summing up, Panama has an impressive array of advantages over its competition: (1) No exchange controls, no federal reserve or central bank, complete monetary freedom. (2) No taxes and no required financial or other annual reports by corporations doing business exclusively outside Panama. (3) Relatively low incorporation and annual maintenance costs, with a rich array of professional services to take care of everything. (4) The possibility of safeguarding privacy with both bearer shares and numbered bank accounts in the currency of the depositor's choice, with tax-free interest. (5) The possibility of dabbling in the shipping industry with minimal governmental costs, costs that are a low function of tonnage and are unrelated to profits. (6) The prospects of doing business through the Colon Free Zone, duty-free and almost tax-free. (7) A tradition of being a tax haven, bolstered by the local presence of many tax haven corporations, creating a virtual knockout argument for any future government tempted to impose taxes on foreign income. (8) The ease of supplying a business justification for a Panamanian corporation should the need arise.

Of course, Panama is not perfect. As with the no-tax havens we dealt with in chapter seven, it is not a good location for a holding company holding high-tax country stock. Panama has no double-taxation agreement with any country. However, in a multihaven arrangement of the sort already discussed, Panama could compete with a pure no-tax haven, even the Caymans.

Cyprus

Cyprus is an island country in the Eastern Mediterranean. It was formerly a British colony, but since 1960 it has been independent. It is a member of the United Nations, the Council of Europe and the Commonwealth, and has established a relationship with the European Union that will eventually lead to a full customs union (although not to full membership in the European Union). It maintains politically and economically viable relations with the Arab nations, as well as considerable trade with Eastern European countries. Its ties to Britain and Greece are close. The fact that the northern portion of the island, after an invasion by Turkish forces twenty years ago, has declared independence as the Turkish Republic of Northern Cyprus, is not thought unfavorable to its tax haven uses.

The majority of the Cypriot population is Greek, with a few Turks and other nationalities making up a minority of the population. The national languages are Greek and Turkish, but English is widely used, especially in the legal and business communities. Communications are excellent, and it is a popular tourist destination.

As a result of its relationship with Great Britain, Cyprus is a common law country with its companies laws patterned after Britain's. The costs for organizing and maintaining a Cyprus company are based on Cyprus internal costs that are quite low.

Cyprus is popular for shipping companies, and there are two ways of using Cyprus for other companies. One is the Cyprus-registered company, which if owned by non-residents and dealing only with foreign business, pays tax at 10 percent of the normal corporate tax rate, which means currently an income tax of 4.25 percent for the company. The other method is the branch office of a foreign company, which pays no Cypriot income tax.

The branch cannot use the Cyprus double-taxation agreements, although the Cyprus registered company can, because the latter is a resident of Cyprus.

For Cyprus tax purposes, the offshore company may be a holding company, a finance company, an investment company, an insurance company, a management company — many types of companies.

Cyprus has tax treaties with the United Kingdom, Denmark, Sweden, Ireland, Norway, Greece, Germany, Hungary, Italy, France, Russia, Romania, the United States, Canada, and Bulgaria.

Foreign employees of an offshore company, who are employed in Cyprus, pay Cyprus income tax at half of the normal Cyprus tax rates.

Both the company and its employees can import duty-free motor vehicles, office equipment, and household effects (other than furniture).

Besides commercial shipping companies, Cyprus is popular for registering personal yachts. A Cyprus company is formed to own the yacht.

Malta

Malta has a tradition of being fiercely independent and neutral over a period of many centuries. An island strategically located in the western Mediterranean, it has historically been a staging post, trading point, supply center and a military and naval base. Today the former

British naval docks are a hub of commercial ship repair and shipbuilding activity, a thriving tourist industry has been developed and Malta has established itself as a profitable manufacturing base with a presence of over 130 international companies.

Since 1989 Malta has offered a wide range of tax and financial benefits to banks, insurance companies, insurance managers, fund managers, trading companies, holding and personal investment companies, pension funds, ship owners, and trusts.

An autonomous supervisory body, the Malta International Business Authority (MIBA) has been established "to balance the need for confidentiality with safeguards against abuse."

Malta is within easy reach of major European and Middle Eastern business centers, and is within the European time zone in line with Frankfurt, Milan, Paris and Zurich. By air Malta is 3 hours from London and Frankfurt, 2 hours from Paris and 1 hour from Rome. There are direct flights to 30 cities including Zurich, Brussels, Amsterdam, Athens, Cairo and Lagos.

It has a typically Mediterranean climate, with mild winters and sunny summers.

Malta is a sovereign European state with a democratic parliamentary system based on the British model. It is a member of the Commonwealth and its first self-governing constitution dates back to 1921. There is a total absence of cultural, religious, ethnic or racial problems.

Malta's judiciary is long-established and independent. Its laws are based on Roman law and the Napoleonic Codes, while more recent fiscal, company and shipping laws are based on English statute law.

The island has had an Association Agreement with the European Union since 1971. It has a large network of diplomatic ties, double taxation treaties, and commercial and investment protection agreements.

Trading companies are liable to only 5 percent tax. Non-trading companies are totally exempt from income tax. Trusts pay a small fixed annual tax in lieu of a registration fee. Trading companies are expected to have a physical and functional presence on the island. This follows from Malta's determination to establish itself as a reputable international financial and business center.

Non-trading companies may opt for non-disclosure of shareholders and directors, registration being possible in the name of local nominees. The law provides for the protection of this privacy in legal proceedings and includes special provisions to facilitate the transfer of shares in a non-trading company after death. Such companies need not have their accounts audited, nor need they file an annual return or a copy of their accounts with the government.

Non-trading companies include:

- Corporate and personal holding companies.
- Other companies which limit their activities to the ownership, management and administration of property of any kind, including assets held for the purposes of a pension, provident or similar fund (other fund and financial management operations being regarded as trading activity).
- Shipping companies which own and operate ships registered under any flag. The benefit of tax exemption applies equally to a holding company and to its subsidiaries, each of which may own one or more ships.

Malta also offers the possibility to owners of all types of vessels, from pleasure yachts to oil rigs, to register their ships under the Maltese flag. The registration and operation of Maltese ships is regulated by a Merchant Shipping Act which is based mainly on United Kingdom legislation. There are no restrictions as regards trading, sale and mortgaging of Maltese registered ships, or the nationality of the crew.

The offshore trust legislation closely follows United Kingdom law and, subject to the provisions of the relative act, allows the settler to determine the governing law of the trust.

No tax is chargeable on any dividend or interest paid by a trading company or a non-trading company. In fact, there are no withholding, capital gains or any other taxes.

No exchange control restrictions apply to offshore companies and trusts. They may have their accounts in any foreign currency or bank.

There is no customs duty on company property or on expatriate employees' personal belongings imported into Malta. Property held by a trust is also exempted from customs duty if imported into Malta. For a regional office, this gives Malta advantages similar to those offered by Greece, Jordan, and Tunisia, with the key difference being that those three countries offer the privilege only to branches of foreign companies, while Malta offers it to a locally incorporated company.

No stamp, death or gift taxes are levied in relation to offshore companies or trusts.

All rights, privileges and exemptions are guaranteed by law for a minimum period of 10 years.

Malta has double taxation treaties with all the major European countries, the United States, Canada, Australia, and others.

There is a readily available supply of qualified professionals in law, accounting, banking and insurance, among other fields. Many have considerable international experience and expertise. It is therefore no surprise that all major international accountancy firms are represented in the country.

The work force is highly educated, diligent and adaptable, with standards of performance comparable to those in other European centers, but at measurably lower costs.

The university is over 400 years old, and on a pro rata basis there are more graduates than in many European nations.

Malta is multi-lingual. Business is universally conducted in English. Italian and French are widely spoken. Maltese is of Semitic origin and akin to Arabic though written in Roman alphabet. Language is not a problem in Malta.

There is substantial investment in one of Europe's most advanced telecommunications systems. A full satellite direct dialing system will connect Malta with most parts of the world through a 2,000 port international exchange.

Housing standards are high. Quality office space, with all modern facilities, is available at reasonable cost, and first-class hotel accommodation is plentiful. For people who work or do business in Malta, facilities are on a par with any European city.

Malta's cultural heritage dates back to some time before 4,000 B.C., and its history has provided it with a varied but solid foundation. The Phoenicians, Carthagenians and the Romans; the Byzantines, Arabs and the Normans; the Knights of St. John; the French and the British; all have played a notable part in Malta's history. This gradual assimilation and cross-fertilization of cultures has created the exuberant and independent Malta of the late twentieth century with a unique cultural identity.

The Maltese have preserved their language and special characteristics for which they are well known: their overwhelming hospitality; a trading mentality developed since Phoenician times; diverse linguistic, professional and business skills; and a willingness and determination to provide quality service.

These attributes illustrate Malta's highly positive attitude towards business and life. Furthermore, living and working on the island holds many advantages. A European lifestyle at reasonable cost. International cuisine. A superb climate. Good leisure and educational facilities. A low crime rate. Historical and cultural environment. All in all, a friendly and relaxed lifestyle, yet fully equipped to meet the most demanding requirements of international business.

And an individual who receives a residence permit to work for an offshore company is not deemed to be a resident of Malta for income tax purposes, thus paying no individual income tax on income received from offshore companies. The same exemption applies to their dependents.

Malta has a residence program with special tax benefits. By obtaining a permanent residence permit in Malta, the holder and his dependents are entitled to a flat income tax rate of 15%, subject to a minimum annual liability of Lm 1,000 (after double taxation relief); exemption from death duty on the foreign estate of a deceased resident when this is inherited by the surviving spouse; and exemption from customs duty on one car and on used personal and household effects imported within six months of taking up residence.

Under the program an individual applying for a permanent residence permit must either own assets outside Malta worth at least Lm 150,000 or be entitled to an annual income of at least Lm 10,000.

The applicant will be required:

1. to purchase a residence in Malta at a cost of at least Lm 30,000 for a house or Lm 20,000 for a flat or to rent/lease a residence in Malta at not less than Lm 1,200 per annum;

2. to remit to Malta at least Lm 6,000 per annum, plus Lm 1,000 per annum per dependent.

3.   not to engage in a gainful occupation in Malta unless duly authorized.

Any unspent residue of capital brought into Malta and any income therefrom accumulated during the resident's stay, as well as proceeds from the sale of the resident's dwelling and/or other investments, may be repatriated without restrictions.

The Isle of Man

The Isle of Man, which is about 220 square miles in area, is located in the Irish Sea roughly 30 miles from the mainland of the United Kingdom. During the last several years the island's independent government has sought to promote favorable conditions to those who seek an operational base in a low-cost, low-tax environment, and have turned the island into an important international tax haven.

The Isle of Man is a dependency of the British Crown, yet it has never been part of the United Kingdom or its colonies. Its governmental origins date to Viking culture, and its own independent parliament, Tynwald, has existed for more than 1,000 years. While the island is tied closely to the United Kingdom, which insures the island's defense and presides over international affairs, Tynwald is responsible for all aspects of domestic legislation, including taxation. The legal system of the island is similar to that of the U.K., its currency is the pound sterling, and social and economic links with the U.K. are strong. The island maintains a special status within the European Union. It is excluded from the effects of the Treaty of Rome, other than those relating to the free trade of agriculture and industrial products within the EU. The island receives no revenue from the EU, and it does not contribute to EU funds. Most importantly, the island enjoys free trade with the EU, thereby enjoying many of the advantages of membership while retaining the freedom to develop as a low-tax area.

The island offers an excellent communications network, modern facilities, and a work force that is energetic and skilled. It is the home to over 30,000 companies, the largest contributor to the island's gross national product being the financial sector. Additionally, the island has the physical space and the infrastructure necessary to facilitate development of both service and manufacturing industries.

The government maintains a policy of encouraging 10,000 new residents before the end of the century, making the islands the only low-tax financial center in Europe that actively encourages new residents. Moreover, the government is accessible in regards to new projects. Decision-making is efficient, and work permits are easily and quickly available.

The government supports the development of the island's financial sector with much enthusiasm, yet maintains strict control over the sector through a Financial Supervision Commission and Insurance Commission that licenses banks, investment advisors and insurance companies. Such control assures the island integrity as an offshore financial center.

More than 50 licensed banks, including many international banks, are present on the island. Their services are comprehensive, discreet and confidential, comparing favorably with the banking sectors of Switzerland and Liechtenstein. In addition to banking, high-caliber legal, accounting, insurance and other financial services are available on the island.

Along with these many advantages, the Isle of Man offers an attractive tax structure. The major features are well worth noting:

- A flat income tax rate of 20 percent.
- No capital gains tax.
- No estate or inheritance taxes.
- Tax-free holidays for industry.

- Offshore tax is generally exempt.
- Value added tax at 15 percent.

Income tax is charged on all income arising on the island, and on worldwide income of island residents, companies, and trusts, subject to certain exemptions (as noted above and which will be discussed in more detail). Residency for individuals is determined by the time spent on the island in a particular fiscal year, typically April to April. (Non-resident individuals are subject to a tax at a flat rate of 20 percent of all income arising on the island which may be collected by withholding at source. This does not apply, however, to income from approved financial institutions on the island, or dividends from exempt companies, exempt insurance companies and registration companies.) For companies, whether incorporated on the island or not, residency is determined by the place of central management and control. For trusts, residency is established where the trust is managed.

Although resident companies pay income tax, they receive significant relief for capital expenditures on facilities and machinery. In addition, the following companies do not pay income tax:

- **Registration Companies**, which are companies that are incorporated but are not resident on the island. An annual registration duty of 450 pounds is payable.
- **Exempt Insurance Companies**, which are resident on the island but whose income is earned offshore.
- **Exempt Companies**, which are companies that are resident on the island in shipping, investment holding and commodity-dealing (and potentially other activities such as trademark, licensing and royalty). Such companies may qualify to be exempt from income tax on their offshore

income. An annual fee of 250 pounds is required to obtain exempt status.

- **Trading Companies.** Certain companies in the service or manufacturing sectors may be eligible for a tax-free holiday as an alternative to grants and incentives which typically are available for a period of five years.

In addition:

- Income from an island trust operated under laws similar to the trust laws of the U.K. will not be taxed if the beneficiaries are non-resident, and all of the income, except for certain income from approved financial institutions, is earned offshore.

Isle of Man resident and non-resident companies can engage in any activity worldwide, but exempt companies can only be used for insurance, shipping, property investment, investment holding, commodity dealing or the holding of patents, royalties, copyrights, licenses and trademarks. Certain activities including banking, insurance and investment advice require a government license. There is no requirement for disclosure of beneficial ownership of companies to the government and shelf companies are available. A company's share capital can be expressed in any currency and one can have various classes of share capital with differing rights.

Exempt and non-resident companies are not required to file their accounts with the government nor are they subjected to any withholding taxes. They pay a nominal fixed Exemption Fee or Duty each year. No exchange control exists in the island, and bank accounts can be maintained in any currency, funds being freely transferable internationally. Non-residents are not subject to tax on interest earned on deposits in licensed banks. No information regarding the returns of such persons are forwarded to the government so total privacy in banking matters is assured.

The island has no double tax treaties other than a 1955 treaty with the U.K. which only applies to resident companies or individuals. Under an agreement with the U.K., the island undertakes to impose value added taxes and customs duties (with a number of minor exceptions) as in the U.K.

Investors should be aware that the Isle of Man offers several investment vehicles, each providing its own advantages and opportunities:

Exempt Insurance Companies. The purpose of the Exempt Insurance Companies Act of 1981 was to encourage the development of the offshore insurance sector. Under the act, an insurance company may apply to be exempt from income tax on its profits earned offshore (or with other exempt insurance companies on the island) and on any dividends paid to non-resident shareholders, making the island attractive for captive insurance companies, reinsurance companies, and life assurance and pension companies. To obtain exempt status, several conditions must be satisfied:

- The company should have a sufficient cash paid-up capital.
- A solvency margin of at least 15 percent of the premiums should be maintained. This margin should be written in the previous financial year.
- The company's reinsurance support must be sufficient.
- The audited annual accounts and the quarterly management accounts should be submitted to the Financial Supervision Commission.
- A quorum of directors should be resident.

Trusts. The trust law of the island is based on similar legislation of the U.K. Trusts resident on the island that have non-resident beneficiaries will not pay island income tax on non-island income; there is no tax charge on any capital gains made by the trust. Thus it is possible to accumulate wealth without worry of taxes when later distributing assets to one's beneficiaries.

Exempt Companies. Companies involved in holding, investment, shipping, commodity dealing, patents, trademarks, licenses and royalties, may apply for exemption of island income tax. To qualify for exempt status, the company secretary and at least one director should be island residents. Further, no individual resident on the island should have any interest in the company. An annual fee of 250 pounds is required. If granted exempt status, a company's offshore income and dividends will be exempt from island income tax.

Shipping Companies. Ships may be registered with the Isle of Man Harbour Board. They will be subject to strict international safety codes and will fly the British merchant flag. Ships must be owned or managed by persons or companies resident on the island or some other U.K. dominion, but companies that qualify for exempt status (see above) do not pay income tax on their offshore income. To qualify for exempt status, ships concerned must satisfy an additional condition, which is that they do not operate from, or use, ports on the island regularly.

Non-Resident Companies. A company may be incorporated on the island, but remain non-resident. As such it will be exempt from income tax, though it will have to pay an annual non-resident duty. There is no requirement that non-resident companies file annual accounts or disclose the company's owners. Thus, a non-resident company could be used for protecting assets owned by an individual resident in another country. This may be desirable in several possible circumstances, for example, when assets are held in a politically unstable country, or when one wishes to protect assets from capital taxes imposed in the country in which they are situated. Non-resident companies may serve as trading entities with day-to-day administration taking place on the island, as long as central management and control of the company is stationed elsewhere.

Trading Companies. Various companies in the manufacturing and service sectors enjoy advantages because of the island's relationship with the EU, existence of a freeport, low costs and tax structure, and generous range of grants and incentives offered by the island's government.

Banks. Banks have benefitted from the general growth of the financial sector. As the island's government continues to encourage foreign investment, it is likely that the growth of the financial sector will continue, adding to the opportunities for banks. Operation of a bank on the Isle of Man requires a license issued by the Financial Supervision Commission. Licenses are granted only after specific conditions are met, including:

- The bank should have a sufficient cash paid-up share capital.
- To facilitate the accumulation of reserves, a sound distribution policy should be developed and maintained.
- Annual accounts and quarterly reports should be submitted to the Financial Supervision Commission for review.

Bearer Shares. Under provisions of The Companies Act of 1986, companies of the island may issue Bearer Shares.

Without question, the Isle of Man offers a variety of advantages for investors. The island possesses political stability, a modern infrastructure, good communications, a special relationship with the EU, established laws favorable to investors, and low direct taxes.

A Source of Help in the Isle of Man

Skye Fiduciary Services Limited are among the foremost experts in offshore planning. Under the direction of its chairman Charles Cain, formerly managing director of the second merchant bank to open in the Isle of Man, Skye Fiduciary is the most experienced offshore corporate and trust management business in the jurisdiction. Although Skye offers a full range of company and trust management services, their expertise in designing novel company structures to meet the needs of foreign clients is unique.

For further information, write the following:

> Skye Fiduciary Services Limited
> Attn: New Clients Department
> 2 Water Street
> Ramsey, Isle of Man 1M8 1JP
> United Kingdom
> Their telephone number is +44 1624 816117. Fax service is available at +44 1624 816645; direct communications to New Clients Information.

Jersey

The Island of Jersey is located in the English Channel off the northwest coast of France. Having an area of roughly 45 square miles, it is the largest of the Channel Islands, and has a population of 75,000. St. Helier is the center of the island's business activity.

Jersey, along with the other Channel Islands, is a possession of the English Crown, distinct however from colonial or overseas dependencies, which are possessions of the British government. The constitutional relationship between Jersey and the United Kingdom, therefore, is unique — the U.K. manages the island's external affairs, while the island government legislates domestic matters, including taxes and revenue. The Channel Islands were part of the Duchy of Normandy, so when William the Conqueror invaded Britain in 1066, they remained his as Duke of Normandy. Today they belong to the Queen in her role as Duchess of Normandy, not in her role as Queen of the United Kingdom.

The island has long been politically and economically stable. The political system is a conservative one; political parties do not exist and all elected officials are independents. Issues of controversy or social conflict are absent, and the island enjoys much respectability among the international community.

Although Jersey's economic policy over the years has focused on improving the lives of the island's populace, that policy has also made the island attractive to investors. The standard rate of income tax has remained unchanged at 20 percent since 1940. The currency of the island is the pound sterling, and while the States of Jersey issue their own currency notes, these are legal tender only within the island and are easily converted to sterling as necessary.

The island also maintains a special status with the EU, being exempt from many of the aspects of the Treaty of Rome. While the island is bound by the customs provisions of the Treaty, it retains its fiscal autonomy and constitutional rights.

Although French was the official language of Jersey until 1963, English is now used throughout the island. Most legislation that was passed before 1940 is in French, and French is still used exclusively for real estate transfers. However, English translations are available for the more important of the French laws and most legal firms employ staff who are fluent in French.

While there is no legislation on bank secrecy or secrecy of information, it is possible, through the use of a numbered account, to restrict the identification of an account holder to senior bank officers. It is felt that a legal duty exists to maintain secrecy, which arises out of the implied contract between professional advisors, for example, between banks and their clients. Only through law or by order of the Royal Court is information subject to disclosure. Exchange of information is provided for by two double tax agreements, one with the U.K. and one with Guernsey.

Investors who wish to form a company in Jersey enjoy several advantages. A company incorporated and controlled in Jersey pays income tax at a 20 percent rate. Although the formation of a company, for Jersey income tax purposes, requires a declaration of the beneficial ownership of shares, nominee shareholders are not disclosed to the Company Registry, and the name of the beneficial owner will not appear in any search.

To form a company in Jersey, the following is required:

- Approval of a company name. (Although this is normally available in 24 hours, it is advisable to submit at least three alternatives to insure a speedy process.)
- A minimum of three shareholders are required whose names will appear on the Annual Return, which is filed each January. Each shareholder must hold three shares. To shield the identity of the beneficial owner, nominees may be utilized.
- While no provision regulates the offices of director and secretary, it is usual to provide at least two directors.
- The company's registered office must be maintained on the island. Further, the statutory books of the company must be kept at the registered office and be open to public inspection. Although the annual general meeting must be

held in Jersey, it can be handled by proxy, provided the company maintains secretarial services on the island.

- Each January the company must file an Annual Return.
- While there is no need to appoint auditors, a company's articles typically provide for such appointments. Auditors do not have to be residents of the island.
- If a company must pay Jersey income tax, the accounts must be certified by an accountant approved by the Comptroller of Income Tax.

Amendments to the Income Tax Law, effective from 1989, add to Jersey's appeal as a possible tax haven.

One of the most significant provisions of these amendments is the creation of the "exempt company." An exempt company is treated as non-resident and thus gains considerable tax advantages.

An amendment to Article 123 of the Income Tax Law provides that from January 1, 1989, all companies incorporated on the island are to be regarded as resident. The place where a company holds its board meetings no longer has any relevance in the determination of the company's residence for tax purposes. As long as a company manages and controls its business on the island (i.e. if board meetings are held on the island), it is considered resident even if it was incorporated outside the island. One may assume that it follows that such companies must pay full income tax on their incomes, however, Article 123A allows for companies that meet certain conditions to be treated as non-resident. Such designated companies are exempt companies. The conditions for the granting of exempt status follow:

- Application for exempt status, along with the payment of the exempt company tax, which is 500 pounds, must be made within the necessary time period, not later than March

31 in the year of assessment. (A company incorporated in the year of assessment must make its application within three months of incorporation and annually thereafter. A foreign company that becomes resident in Jersey must make its application within three months of becoming resident and annually thereafter.)

- No Jersey resident has any interest in the company. (An exception here is a collective investment company, which, provided it is in corporate form, is entitled to become an exempt company upon payment of the tax of 500 pounds. Jersey residents may have a beneficial interest in such companies.)

- Satisfactory disclosure of beneficial ownership must be made to the Commercial Relations Department.

- No unpaid corporation tax or income tax is outstanding from assessments of previous years.

- If the company is an income tax company at the time of application, it must not have been an exempt company for any prior year of assessment. (Thus, a company is prohibited from switching to exempt status more than once in its lifetime, although the Comptroller has discretion in such matters.)

While no Jersey resident may hold any beneficial interest in a company applying for exempt status, unless the company is a collective investment fund, he or she may be a shareholder in, or a debenture holder of, a company that has a beneficial interest in an exempt company. To satisfy the Comptroller that he does not hold a beneficial interest in an exempt company, a resident will be required to file an

129

annual statement. In turn, the company will have to make known to the Commercial Relations Department its beneficial owners. Should a Jersey resident acquire a beneficial interest in an exempt company, the company is obligated to inform the Comptroller.

The exempt company enjoys various tax advantages. Because it is treated as non-resident, it is exempt from income tax on the profits of trade on the island, provided the trade is not conducted through an established place of business such as a building site, branch or factory. For example, the agents of an exempt company can meet on the island and conclude contracts without having to pay income tax on the profits. However, if the company produces or processes the goods detailed in that contract on the island, the profits attributable to that activity would be chargeable to Jersey income tax. Clerical functions, such as invoicing, in the Comptroller's view are not a part of the carrying on of trade and are not chargeable to income tax.

In addition, being non-resident means that a company pays no Jersey income tax on income derived outside the island. It pays no income tax on interest obtained from Jersey bank deposits, nor is required to deduct income tax from payments of interest or dividends (except in regards to collective investment funds). Furthermore, the company need not make a return of income (except of Jersey income other than bank deposit interest), and it is not required to file accounts (except in respect of trade carried on through an established place of business).

The tax law is favorable to non-resident directors of exempt companies as well. Directors are not liable to Jersey income tax for fees they receive from the company.

The Island of Jersey offers major tax advantages for investors, particularly those who establish companies and obtain exempt status.

Guernsey

The second largest of the Channel Islands, Guernsey is located in the English Channel off the northwest coast of France. St. Peter Port is the center of business activity on the island, which is approximately 25 square miles in area and has a population of 57,000.

Like the island of Jersey, Guernsey is a possession of the English Crown, but it retains its own government and legal system. Guernsey has the right to legislate on matters of domestic concern and taxation. Also, much like Jersey, the island enjoys a special relationship with the EU. Guernsey is bound by the customs aspects of the Treaty of Rome, which essentially provides a shield against imports, yet it retains its constitutional rights and fiscal autonomy. For example, Guernsey retains the right to levy value added tax.

Until the early 20th century, French was the language used in commercial and legal matters, however, English has replaced it and now is the official language of the island. Until recently, real estate transactions were required to be in French, and all legal firms maintain staff who are fluent in French. Translations of important laws and statutes written in French are available.

Guernsey has been stable economically and politically for hundreds of years. It has no political parties and the members of Guernsey's States of Deliberation, which is the island's legislative branch of government, are independents. Over the years the States has promoted policies that interfere with local enterprise as little as possible, resulting in a climate that is relatively free of control. Although British currency is used in Guernsey, English and local money circulates. In addition, Jersey currency circulates in Guernsey (and Guernsey money circulates in Jersey), and even French money is sometimes accepted and exchanged informally.

Along with a favorable tax structure, Guernsey offers other advantages to investors. Although no local legislation governs secrecy of information, English common law encourages banks and their personnel to maintain secrecy. There is also privilege against disclosure.

A company can be incorporated in Guernsey within seven working days. Detailed information is necessary, and "shelf" companies are not available. However, nominees can be used to preserve the identity of the beneficial owner. The company's registered office must be maintained within Guernsey, and notice of the registered office must be lodged at the company's registry within one month of incorporation. One can select any name for a proposed company, provided it does not include reference or allusions to the Crown, and is not in conflict with an existing company. A minimum of seven shareholders are required, each holding one share, and the shareholders may be nominees.

Guernsey law provides no statute regarding the officers of a company. Thus, a sole director might also be the beneficial owner of the shares as well as be the secretary. Details regarding the directors appear in the Annual Return that is filed every January, but here again nominees may be used. All persons who have agreed to be directors of a company must be lodged with the Company's Registry within three months of incorporation.

The Annual Return must be filed each January and requires a filing fee of 100 pounds. Failure to file the Annual Return will result in the company being taken off the register. Along with the Annual Return, it is also required that each year a company swear a Declaration as to its residence.

Guernsey tax laws are favorable to companies. A company that has its place of business and that carries out a major amount of its trade on the island pays local income tax at a rate of 20 percent on its profits. Companies may obtain non-resident status. A non-resident company is managed, controlled, and conducts its trade outside of Guernsey. Such companies are subject to corporation tax at the rate of 500 pounds per year, which is due each January. The corporation tax is payable in advance, the first payment being made at incorporation. The payment is then levied pro rata during the year of incorporation from the date of incorporation to December 31st.

Although perhaps not as well known as many of the other offshore havens, Guernsey offers significant advantages for investors, including stability, a comparatively free economic climate, and favorable tax laws for companies.

Gibraltar

Gibraltar, at the tip of southern Spain, is slightly less than 2½ square miles in area. Its population numbers about 30,000 and is composed of people of Italian, Genoese, Maltese, English, and Spanish descent. In addition, there is a small but important Jewish population, some Indian traders, and a significant group of Moroccan workers.

Gibraltar has been a colony of the British Crown since 1704, being formally ceded by Spain in 1713 in the Treaty of Utrecht. While its official language is English, most Gibraltarians are bilingual, speaking both English and Spanish. Gibraltar's Constitution gives legislative powers to the Governor, who is the representative of the Queen, and the House of Assembly. Although Gibraltar enjoys a substantial amount of self-government, it is a dependent territory and the formal assent of the Governor or the Crown is required for all legislation. The Governor is responsible for the conduct of foreign affairs, security and defense; ministers, who must answer to the House of Assembly, manage domestic concerns. The bedrock for legislation is English law. On to this base, laws relating to local circumstances are built.

Although Spain lays claim to Gibraltar, the British government insures the political stability of the jurisdiction. In the preamble to the Gibraltar Constitution Order, Britain has pledged that Gibraltar will remain part of the Crown until and unless an Act of Parliament provides otherwise. Moreover, it is stated that the Crown will never permit Gibraltar to pass under the sovereignty of another state without the democratically expressed wishes of the people of Gibraltar. In February of 1985 the border between Spain and Gibraltar was reopened, and the British and Spanish governments have agreed that there will be talks on sovereignty. However, the British have emphasized that the wishes of the people of Gibraltar are of greatest concern.

Gibraltar is part of the EU, having joined with the U.K. under the provisions relating to dependent territories. By concession it is excluded from the common external tariff, the common agricultural policy and the requirement to levy value added tax.

Gibraltar possesses the support systems needed by modern companies. With a new telephone system having come into operation in March, 1990, the jurisdiction boasts excellent telecommunications. Its postal facilities are good, and it has daily air service to Europe and the rest of the world. Its banking facilities are likewise good, and are expected to improve as Gibraltar continues to attract international banks. While Gibraltar issues its own currency, money of the United Kingdom is also considered to be legal tender.

Gibraltar is rapidly growing as an offshore center. Although it is a low-cost jurisdiction, it is a relatively high tax one. Its standard income tax rate for individuals is 30 percent with the tax rising to a maximum of 50 percent, while its income tax rate for resident companies is 35 percent. Still, Gibraltar offers three types of companies that provide important tax advantages.

The **non-resident company** is a company that is incorporated in Gibraltar but is centrally managed and controlled by directors who reside outside the jurisdiction. If such a company does not derive its income from within Gibraltar, it will be outside the scope of Gibraltarian income tax. Unlike other jurisdictions which charge an annual company registration tax or non-resident company duty, Gibraltar does not apply flat rate fees against non-resident companies.

A Gibraltar company may apply for **exempt status** in regard to Gibraltarian income tax. This is done after incorporation, and takes between 10 and 14 days, depending on the company and the details of the application. Once obtained, the company receives an Exemption Certificate that is valid for 25 years and which grants a full exemption from income tax and estate duty in Gibraltar. In return, the exempt company pays a flat annual duty. Along with requiring information about the beneficial owners, including a written reference from a professional and a statement on the proposed activities of the company, the authorities require that specific conditions be met before exempt status is granted:

- The company conducts trade and business in Gibraltar only with other exempt companies. (Exceptions are sometimes possible with the prior consent of the local authorities.)
- There are no changes in beneficial ownership, shareholders, or objectives for which the company was formed, unless the approval of Gibraltar authorities is obtained.
- The register of members is maintained in Gibraltar.
- No Gibraltarian or resident of Gibraltar holds any interest in any of the company's shares.
- The annual tax is paid in two equal installments by March 31st and September 30th of each year.

Exempt status is available to both resident companies, for which the annual fee is 225 pounds, and to non-resident companies, for which the fee is 200 pounds. The advantage for a resident company to obtain exempt status is that it is presumed not be resident elsewhere.

Qualifying companies were created in the Income Tax (Amendment) Ordinance 1983 for situations where the authorities of a foreign country require proof that a percentage of tax on profits has already been paid in Gibraltar. The tax rates for Gibraltar are 2 percent for income not remitted to Gibraltar and 17 percent for income remitted to Gibraltar. The conditions for obtaining a Certificate are essentially the same as for Exempt Company with the following: 1) a one-time only fee of 250 pounds is required; 2) a minimum paid-up share capital of 1,000 pounds; and 3) a deposit of 1,000 pounds must be lodged with the Government of Gibraltar as a guarantee toward future taxes.

Gibraltar is also attractive for company formation. A company must have a minimum of two shareholders and two directors, but the directors do not need to be shareholders. Although the details regarding shareholders and directors are listed on the public record, nominee services may be used to preserve the identity of beneficial owners. An Annual General Meeting of the Shareholders must be held in Gibraltar each year, however, other general meetings can be held outside Gibraltar. The accounts of the company must be submitted to the Annual General Meeting, however, these accounts are not filed at the Registry and are not available to the public. While no legal requirements exist for a company's accounts to be audited, an application for exempt status must be accompanied by a reference as to "residency" from an auditor registered under the Gibraltar Auditors Registration Ordinance.

A Gibraltar company must maintain its registered office in Gibraltar, from which the company can transact business with non-resident or similar companies. The statutory records of the company must also be maintained in Gibraltar, typically at the Registered Office. An Annual Return must be filed every January.

As Gibraltar is a common law jurisdiction and its courts follow the decisions of the English Courts, it is a favorable jurisdiction for the purpose of creating offshore trusts. In most cases, trusts do not have to be registered, an exception being charitable trusts. Where the beneficiary of the Gibraltarian trust is non-resident and the income is derived from outside Gibraltar, no Gibraltarian tax is payable in respect of the trust income.

Although its internal tax rates are high compared to many offshore havens, Gibraltar still offers several important advantages to investors, particularly in its favorable treatment of non-resident and tax exempt companies.

Gibraltar is looking more like a successful offshore finance center than ever before. It has a considerable amount of new office space and markedly improved telecommunications. For the past several years Gibraltar has been revamping its facilities and promoting itself as a tax efficient base serving EU banks and corporations. Gibraltar has equipped itself with digital fibre optics and a high quality development has sprung up on reclaimed land.

Hong Kong

Hong Kong is quite similar to Panama in many respects. It taxes only locally generated income. Its tax rates are extremely low by U.S. and even Panamanian standards. Its haven status is subsidiary to its role as an international business center, strategically located as "the gateway to the Orient" and as a station between the West and the vast markets of the speedily developing East.

Hong Kong also enjoys incredibly cheap labor, for it lies on the southeast coast of Communist China, bordering on the province of

Kwangtung. The population of Hong Kong is extremely dense, probably the most crowded in the world. Ninety-five percent are Chinese. This population makes for an extremely competitive and varied labor market, and no such ills as unions and their like are conceivable. In other words, quite apart from tax considerations, there are very good business reasons for setting up shop in Hong Kong.

Hong Kong's prominence as a trade and manufacturing center means that there are superb transportation and communication facilities. Major airlines connect Hong Kong by frequent flights to every major city in the world. Ships are also available to anywhere, and its airmail, telex, and international telephone and cable services are highly efficient, regular, and reliable.

The same superlatives apply to professional services of all kinds, and the fees for these services are kept very reasonable by vigorous competition.

English and Chinese are the official languages, and all official documentation is printed in both. Language presents no difficulty at all for a westerner.

The Hong Kong economy is very free enterprise oriented. There are no exchange controls, and the Hong Kong dollar circulates freely with all world currencies in a completely unregulated money market.

The legal system is based on British common law, modified by local law. The court system is British in structure. The treaty with China provides that Hong Kong will retain its separate legal and economic system for 50 years from the handover in 1997.

Hong Kong has preserved the nineteenth century spirit of free enterprise to an extent that is surprising in this day and age. Taxes are progressive, but these taxes apply only to locally generated income. There are no taxes on capital, gifts, or capital gains, and death duties, which apply to assets physically located in Hong Kong, are imposed in progressive brackets up to a maximum of 15 percent. There is no tax on dividends of local corporations. The official reason for this is that if the source of profit is local business, then the company has already been taxed on its profits and there is no justification for taxing the stockholders. As for foreign-source income, the idea of taxing this is unthinkable. A corollary of the happy lack of dividend taxes is no withholding tax on dividends. One can receive the profits of a Hong Kong corporation, dealing outside Hong Kong, in, say, Costa Rica without any Hong Kong tax liability of any kind.

Apart from the above taxes, government revenue in Hong Kong derives from duties on "luxury" commodities such as tobacco and alcohol, minor fees on imports and exports, and stamp duties. The latter apply to transfers of shares, promissory notes and bills of exchange, and mortgages and debentures.

Now, what about incorporation and trust formation in Hong Kong? As usual, articles of incorporation and association are required, and they must include the standard information. All these requirements are pure formalities, because nominees can be used for everything. In view of the labor situation in Hong Kong, $100 (U.S.) a year will cover a nominee director who is at the same time a registered shareholder as well as a company officer. There is no scarcity of law and trust firms to handle all the details.

Annual maintenance of a corporation involves annual auditing, signed by a chartered accountant, submitted to all shareholders, with a copy to the government. This is required because of the taxation of local income; all corporations must be audited to make certain that no such profits are concealed. A local representative can take care of the audit, keep the company seal, display the company name on a sign in his office, and do whatever else is necessary.

What are the costs? The government charges are very low. The initial expenses of incorporation, articles of association, and stock certificates, and the various uses of nominees can total as little as $500 (U.S.). Annual maintenance can be as low as $500. Bargains, to say the least.

Incorporation takes up to four weeks to accomplish. It can be done with complete privacy through nominee shareholders, for there is no legal requirement that ultimate beneficiary owners be disclosed.

The Hong Kong common law tradition also allows for trusts. The costs run about $1000 for trust formation and $500 a year to keep things running. A Hong Kong trust pays no taxes on overseas investments and can enjoy the advantages of the free currency market.

A popular Hong Kong combination is coupling a trust with holding companies. This may allow that the benefits to beneficiaries be deferred much beyond the legal period of allowed perpetuity for the trust, thus permitting a much greater growth of the initial investment. The way this works is to have the trust own the stock of holding companies. When the trust fully matures, the beneficiaries will receive the stock of the holding companies rather than money. The holding companies themselves may be so set up as to pay dividends only after many more additional years, using all the extra time to enhance growth by completely tax-free reinvestment of profits. Another beneficial aspect of Hong Kong trusts is that there are no stamp duties on the transfer of investments if they are outside Hong Kong, which makes a trust/holding company arrangement free of stamp duty to the trust beneficiaries. Finally, as in the Bahamas, the local trust law allows for a "Cuba clause," which means that a Hong Kong trust can be used with no worries about the political future of the region.

Just as Panama came out with flying colors as compared with even the Caymans, so Hong Kong, in certain ways, comes out with respect to Panama. There is business justification unlimited, at lower local tax and corporation costs and with similar privacy. On the other hand, the exclusion of bearer shares, the need for annual auditing, and the short time left until Chinese control in 1997 are negative factors.

The handover of the former British Crown Colony of Hong Kong to China is complete, and it is now called the Hong Kong Special Administrative Region, generally abbreviated to Hong Kong S.A.R., even on official documents.

As more than one local businessman has put it, "now that the politicians and journalists are gone (from covering the handover), we can get down to *business*." This attitude is typical of Hong Kong, still a true capitalist center. In fact, many of the wealthy who left to obtain second citizenships in Canada, Australia, and elsewhere, have now returned home to continue building their fortunes.

The major advantage of Hong Kong is simply that it is a real business center, not just a tax haven. One of the consequences of that is the ability to add value to services that are provided in only skeleton form in other tax havens. The reinvoicing business is a prime example. Most tax haven jurisdictions host a number of trading companies that do nothing more than reinvoicing. But one Hong Kong firm has now developed this traditional service into a "real" business mode, with an ability to arrange local trade financing. This is a healthy step away from traditional tax havenry into a true offshore **business** center.

ICS Trust Company Limited is part of the ICS International group of companies headquartered in Hong Kong. This highly successful entrepreneurial group was started by Elizabeth L. Thomson. Elizabeth describes herself as "a lawyer by profession" (2 law degrees, a member of 4 Law Societies internationally), "an entrepreneur by choice"! She has helped innumerable people start new enterprises in many parts of the globe and is well known in Hong Kong for her work with women entrepreneurs.

With a staff of 40 at ICS, every aspect of your business is covered — from deciding to incorporate, to obtaining financing from the bank, to managing your paper work including Letters of Credit, to investing your hard earned profits! ICS is truly a "one stop shop" for entrepreneurs.

Their clients range from multinational companies for whom they run Direct Import Programs worth millions of dollars to individuals who seek tax sheltering and estate planning on an international scale. As an entrepreneurial group, they attract many entrepreneurs as clients — business people who have grown their business to a level of maturity and profits that requires expansion into Asia for many diverse reasons.

Instead of just a paper thin traditional tax haven reinvoicing company, with ICS you can develop a real business in Hong Kong. With their extensive banking contacts, ICS professionals will "shop" for the best letter of credit facilities that Hong Kong's competitive banking scene can offer, likely better facilities than you can find at home. Depending upon the client, ICS can often arrange letter of credit banking facilities for clients with either a low or zero margin deposit, usually required by the opening bank. By freeing up your collateral and capital, they provide you with more purchasing power to increase sales and gain higher profits.

Most of these reinvoicing transactions are usually effected such that they are tax free in Hong Kong. There is no withholding tax on dividends so it is often possible to engage in international trade through a HK company and obtain dividends from that company tax free.

ICS will also work with international banks and factors in Hong Kong and overseas to arrange financing, secured primarily on the strength of purchase orders from your clients. Working with banks, factories, shipping companies and freight forwarders, ICS will structure a transaction to increase the likelihood of obtaining flexible, low cost facilities.

The goods do not need to go through HK for us to use a HK vehicle to pass title. Most of their clients ship from a third country direct to their own country.

Although the traditional Hong Kong focus is on firms who trade in goods, it is also possible to use these structures in cases where services are to be provided from overseas. For example, a firm could contract out a study to a company in Hong Kong. This Hong Kong company could then sub-contract out the work to a third party firm and the profit kept in Hong Kong, tax free.

If you import goods from Asia for sale to large chains, ICS can help you expand your credit facilities and increase your domestic sales by establishing and running a Direct Import Program for you. Combined with their international trade finance capabilities, the Direct Import Program is a powerful tool for generating more profits.

The primary goal of the Direct Import Program is to maximize your profits by making your customers perceive that they are buying "direct." This is achieved by:

- setting up a subsidiary company in Hong Kong
- getting your buyers to open their L/C or orders to this subsidiary
- liaising with suppliers to ensure goods are to specification.
- The Direct Import Program works because of two powerful reasons:
- The trend in the retail industry is for buyers to "buy direct" from the Orient. Having a subsidiary in Hong Kong which receives orders or L/Cs greatly enhances this perception.
- Large retail chains often can obtain freight and insurance at significant savings because of their economies of scale.

Selling FOB Asia can often result in a lower selling price for the importer but with the same profit.

ICS will set up and manage the subsidiary company for you, and prepare financing proposals for presentation to local banks. When everything is complete, goods are shipped directly from the Asian factory to the customer. The fact that you are now seen as an Asian supplier (and not the middleman) is often an important factor that clinches the deal. The added prestige of a Hong Kong office makes the customer think he or she is buying "direct" and therefore receiving the lowest price.

To get started, you should contact ICS with as much detail as possible about your business and its trading activities.

For further information, contact:

> Mr. Kishore K. Sakhrani
> Director
> ICS Trust (Asia) Limited
> Suite 605-6
> Nine Queen's Road, Central
> Hong Kong
> Telephone: +852 2854 4544
> Fax: +852 2543 5555

Puerto Rico

Puerto Rico is a United States-controlled tax haven in the enviable position of enjoying the advantages that an alliance with the U.S. can bring, but with an internal tax system that is separate and distinct from that of the U.S. Therefore, Puerto Rico has traditionally been able to offer substantial tax haven benefits to corporations. As a result of the Industrial Incentives Act, and various amendments, Puerto

Rico has become well known for the tax holidays granted to manufacturing and hotel investment firms. Of course, many countries offer such tax holidays for new enterprises, and that is not within the scope of this book. Certain locally based service corporations also can qualify under these incentive acts, usually receiving a 50% tax holiday for a period of years.

But for a regional headquarters, an inadvertent result of the unique political status of Puerto Rico has made it a popular base for regional offices covering Latin America, and many large American corporations use Puerto Rico for this purpose.

Puerto Rico is not a part of the U.S. for income tax purposes; therefore, for income tax purposes, it considers U.S. source income as foreign source income. A unique tax advantage becomes obvious. Puerto Rico does not tax foreign source income of a foreign company that has a branch in Puerto Rico. From this, we can readily see the tax saving potential of a tax haven corporation, formed in a jurisdiction such as Panama or the Cayman Islands, with a branch office registered under Puerto Rican corporate law.

The Puerto Rican branch could be used for the company's international business, and only the income actually earned in Puerto Rico would be subject to Puerto Rican taxation.

One large American manufacturer of air conditioners has used Puerto Rico in this way for many years. The Latin American sales subsidiary is incorporated in Panama, but actually operates from an office in San Juan, the capital of Puerto Rico. The sales representatives cover all of Latin America from the San Juan base, and the profits are entirely tax free.

Puerto Rico's access to the Latin American consumer market, together with its unique tax advantages, place the corporate office in a more enviable regional position than would be the case in Miami or other mainland headquarters. San Juan has become a major air transportation hub for the region, making travel between a San Juan base and both, North and South America extremely easy. It is about 2-1/2 hours flying time to Miami, and 3-1/2 hours to New York.

Mail-order companies, publishers, consultants, service firms, and many others who are looking to explore the Latin American market, should find a Puerto Rican-based enterprise to be profitable.

The Puerto Rican trade zones offer another business possibility. These trade zones, which are outside the U.S. Customs territory, rent such facilities as warehouse and assembly space. These are important assets for a company working into the Latin American market. Together with the export manufacturing exemption, available for ten years to a local manufacturing company, this provides a tax-free and duty-free base of operations within the jurisdiction of the United States. There is no other place in the territorial limits of the United States that provides such an advantageous base for the exporter.

Except for its income tax status, Puerto Rico is as much a part of the U.S. as is any state. This means that it is within the customs territory of the U.S., allowing equipment, supplies and goods to be transferred from the mainland without duties. Since Puerto Rico is part of the U.S., U.S. immigration laws apply to posting foreign personnel there, although for an American citizen a trip is no more restricted than a trip from one state to another.

Another extremely important consideration is that Puerto Rico is included in the U.S. postal system, with domestic postage rates applicable to mail between the U.S. and Puerto Rico.

Benefits from government aid programs such as employment training or loans from the Economic Development Administration and Small Business Administration that are available to the U.S. business, are equally available to Puerto Rican enterprises. Thus a Puerto Rican subsidiary or branch can apply for the various forms of assistance available under these federal government programs.

Some U.S. taxpayers find tax benefits by establishing residence in Puerto Rico. Provided that you are resident in Puerto Rico for the entire calendar year, you file a Puerto Rico tax return instead of a U.S. tax return. Puerto Rico taxes all income on a worldwide basis. You should check out the Puerto Rican tax situation before trying to qualify for this provision. You will be subject to Puerto Rican taxes, and Puerto Rico is not a tax haven. You might, in fact, find the country a tax liability, as its rates are now generally higher than in the U.S.

The one particularly interesting exception, however, is that dividends paid from a Puerto Rican company that has a tax holiday (such as the ten year exemption granted to new factories) is free of Puerto Rican tax. One U. S. couple owned a small manufacturing business in Puerto Rico. In the tenth year, they sold the business, but not the corporation, and paid a liquidating dividend from the corporation. Just before the tenth year, they established residence in Puerto Rico, and maintained it for the entire calendar year in which the liquidating dividend was paid. Total exemption from tax on the final payout!.

Since the dominant language and culture in Puerto Rico are Spanish, if you are immigrating to the U.S. from a Spanish-speaking country, you may find it preferable to make your base in Puerto Rico instead of the mainland, and have the tax advantages as well. In this case you could be continuously living on tax-free profits from the business. Salary payments would be subject to the Puerto Rican income tax rates, but dividends from the ongoing business would not be.

There are some older tax holiday laws on the books in Puerto Rico that are often overlooked. For example, a ten year exemption from tax for companies engaged in export of a locally made or assembled product. This is often a more useful exemption than some of the manufacturing exemptions which give only a partial exemption in urbanized areas.

Another way to play a different Puerto Rico tax angle is if you are entering the U.S. to operate your own business, and intend to eventually leave the U.S. A foreign corporation with a branch in Puerto Rico is only taxed on Puerto Rico source income. If you create a Panamanian corporation, open a branch for it in Puerto Rico, and accumulate the profits in the corporation, you can then take the money out of the corporation once you are no longer a U.S. (or Puerto Rican) taxpayer. In this situation you would be taxed on the salary you pay yourself out of the corporation, which you would keep as low as possible, and then let most of the money stay as profits.

Liberia

Liberia is one of the oldest tax havens, and perhaps somewhat unique for the simple fact that its has no infrastructure, and the tax haven clientele never goes there.

The civil war of recent years has not affected the use of Liberia as a tax haven, primarily because nobody goes there anyway. Liberia is in the business of registering corporations and ships. There are no other services offered. There is no infrastructure of local attorneys or accountants. All contact is carried out with Liberian correspondent offices in New York or Zurich.

The Republic of Liberia lies on the West African coast three hundred miles north of the Equator. Its three hundred and fifty mile pristine coastline stretches from Sierra Leone in the northwest to the Cote d'Ivoire in the southeast. No point in the interior is more than 170 miles from the Atlantic Ocean.

Almost half of Liberia is covered by verdant tropical rainforest. Six rivers have their headwaters in the mountains of Liberia.

The oldest republic in Africa, Liberia declared its independence in 1847.

The law of Liberia is based on the common law principles of the United States. Its government is modeled on the bicameral legislature, the judiciary and the executive branches of the United States government.

Liberia is a "grand-daddy" of corporate jurisdictions. The Liberian non-resident corporation has been in active international use since 1948. The Liberian Business Corporation Act, adopted in 1977, was modeled on the state corporate laws of Delaware and New York and expanded the original Liberian Corporation Law of 1948.

Not only is there in Liberian income tax on a Liberian corporation owned by non-residents of Liberia, but there is total secrecy simply because there is no requirement to file any information with the government — not even a list of directors. Presumably a lot of dubious business gets done through Liberian corporations, but one really has no way to know.

Costs for formation are in the $1000 range, and annual fees are around $350.

Any standard corporate suffix or its abbreviation (corporation, inc., limited, ltd., S.A., N.V., A/S, etc.) is acceptable. With this flexibility, a Liberian corporation can blend into the business environment in which its business is being conducted.

Existence can be obtained in one day. The only information needed is the corporate name, the authorized share capital, and the **number** (not names) of directors on the initial board. Privacy is maintained by the beneficial owner throughout the incorporation process and the corporate structure allows complete freedom of operation.

The same agents can provide ship registration services on behalf of the Liberian government.

Marshall Islands

The legislation of the Republic of the Marshall Islands is very similar to that of Liberia, although somewhat more recent.

The Marshall Islands are comprised of a group of coral atolls and islands in the South Pacific approximately 1900 miles southwest of Hawaii. Named for William Marshall, a British seacaptain and explorer, the Marshall Islands came under United States jurisdiction with the 1947 Trusteeship Agreement between the United Nations and the United States. Internally self-governing since 1950, the Republic of the Marshall Islands became an independent and sovereign nation in 1986. In early 1988, the Marshall Islands government initiated a ship registry program.

To expand this international maritime program, the 1990 Maritime Act was adopted by the Marshall Islands legislature, the Nitijela, on September 13, 1990. To introduce its non-resident corporate program, the Associations Law was also adopted with an effective date of September 13, 1990.

Directors, officers, stockholders, and incorporators may be of any nationality and may reside anywhere. Their meetings may be held in any location and directors, stockholders and the secretary may be corporate entities. Meetings of shareholders and directors may be held by proxy if desired or by any communication equipment that allows the parties to exchange ideas and viewpoints.

The corporation's executive office, where its recores are kept, may be located in any country.

Facsimile filings with government departments are permitted as long as the signature is legible. The typed name and title of the signatory is required. Corporate documents may be executed by a single officer or a person authorized to sign on behalf of the corporation. Execution may be under penalty of perjury without notarization so notarial fees are thereby avoided. Consularization is not required. A single executed copy of a corporate document is acceptable for filing.

Redomiciliation of a foreign corporation into the Marshall Islands is permitted.

The stock issue may be in the form of either registered shares, bearer shares, or both, depending upon individual needs.

The names of shareholders, directors, and officers need not be made part of the public record maintained by the Registrar of Corporations. However, the names of the officers and directors may be filed at any time after incorporation through voluntary filings should the beneficial owner desire it.

The registered agent in Majuro (the capital) is not required to report to the Government of the Marshall Islands regarding the activities of the non-resident domestic corporations it represents.

No specified minimum capital investment is required to commence corporate business but shares must be fully paid when issued. Funds of non-resident domestic Marshall Islands corporations are completely free from currency regulations and exchange control by the Marshall Islands. Shares may be with or without par value. If par value shares are authorized, the value may be expressed in the currency of any nation.

Using model forms of Articles of Incorporation, corporate existence is usually obtained within one business day. If an attorney drafts his own Articles, corporate existence can normally be obtained when the papers are received by the Registrar or the Deputy Registrar of Corporations. In either case, upon confirmation of the date of existence of the new corporation, it can be organized and transact business.

The cost of incorporation (including the first year agent's fee) is normally under US$1500, and annual maintenance under US$1000.

The name of the corporation may be written in any language employing English letters and characters, but the Articles and other papers or instruments must be in English. The name of the corporation may have as an ending word to indicate that it is a corporation any of the following: corporation, corp., company, co., limited, ltd., Societe Anonyme, S.A., Sociedad Anonima, Incorporated, Inc., Limitada, Ltda., A.G., Aktiengesellschaft, N.V., A/S, Societe par actions.

As with Liberia, the lack of any local services or infrastructure makes the Marshall Islands an incorporation haven rather than an operating tax haven.

The Marshall Islands also provides registration facilities for partnerships, limited partnerships, and unincorporated associations.

There is also ship registration legislation, including an active interest by the government in registering fishing boats as well as the usual ships. For a high seas, tax-free, fishing operation, this could be particularly useful.

Barbados

Barbados is a beautiful Caribbean island, a tropical paradise. It is the most easterly of the Eastern Caribbean islands and enjoys warm weather all year round. It is a popular tourist destination attracting thousands of tourists per year.

The economy is based on sugar, tourism, light manufacturing, data processing, and offshore business.

Barbados has established itself as a politically stable island. It is a member of the United Nations, The Organization of American States, and the Caribbean Community (CARICOM).

It has double taxation treaties with the United States, Canada, the United Kingdom, Finland, Sweden, Norway, and Switzerland.

It is served by major international banks including the Royal Bank of Canada, Bank of Nova Scotia, Canadian Imperial Bank of Commerce, and Barclays Bank; and by major local banks including Barbados National Bank, Caribbean Commercial Bank, and The Mutual Bank of the Caribbean.

Direct air services to North America and Europe are provided by British West Indian Airways (BWIA), American Airlines, Air Canada, and British Airways, among others. The modern harbor serves both passenger and cargo ships.

The population is approximately 252,000, speaks English and is 98% literate. A significant portion of the workforce is trained in the use of computers, data processing and various types of factory machinery.

The legal system is basically English common law together with its own statutes.

Company formation follows the typical British pattern, except that the last word can be Limited, Corporation, or Incorporated (or their abbreviations). Shares may be divided into classes and may have no par value. The company may have unlimited or stated maximum capital. The number of directors is unrestricted, although companies frequently use one or more Barbadian directors to show management and control in Barbados.

There is tax haven legislation giving shipping companies a ten-year tax exemption on profits and gains, and provisions to register ships under the Barbados flag. There is no customs duty on the importation of ships, and their equipment, for this purpose.

One of the major uses of Barbados is for international business companies. They must be resident in Barbados (but not necessarily incorporated there), and have no more than 10% of their assets or capital owned by residents of the Caricom region.

A license to be an international business company is issued by the Minister of Finance. IBCs are usually used as trading companies. However, an IBC, all of whose shares form part of the assets of a foreign trust under the management of an offshore bank is exempt from tax on its profits and gains if its activities are restricted to engaging exclusively in the business of buying, selling, holding or managing securities.

Otherwise, an IBC is subject to income tax rates varying from 2½ on profits and gains up to US$5 million to 1% of profits and gains exceeding US$15 million. Normal business deductions are taken into account in determining the income on which the tax is assessed.

IBCs are not subject to the restrictions of the exchange control act.

The usual forms of trusts are also available in Barbados.

Special provisions also exist for captive insurance companies, offshore banks, and offshore trust companies, all of which are subject to various licensing and supervision requirements.

The primary value in using Barbados over some other country having IBCs is the ability to use the double taxation agreements in many cases.

British Virgin Islands

The British Virgin Islands also has the usual range of international business companies, trusts, and shipping registration. Foreign companies may change their domicile to and from the British Virgin Islands. Most of this legislation came into existence after the double taxation agreements with the United States and the United Kingdom were terminated over a decade ago.

Although a great deal of business has been attracted to the island to take advantage of these newer entities, the really interesting use of this jurisdiction is for forming companies that can use the remaining double taxation agreements with Japan and Switzerland. Most practitioners ignore this possibility and use the BVI as a place to register inexpensive International Business Companies.

The Territory of the British Virgin Islands is constituted by a group of islands in the Caribbean, east of the U.S. Virgin Islands of St. Thomas, St. John and St. Croix. The population is approximately 14,000 with an annual tourist population of about 250,000. The British Virgin Islands are a British Dependency. Their relation to the United Kingdom dates back to the early XVI Century. The Islands have been variously populated, colonized or otherwise influenced by their original indigenous population as well as Spain, Holland, England and Africa.

Her Majesty Queen Elizabeth II is Head of State and is represented by the Governor. The head of government is the Chief Minister. The Territory is endowed with self-government except in matters of defense and foreign affairs. There is a Legislative Council elected by direct vote and a Ministerial Cabinet presided by the Chief Minister.

The legal system is based on English Common Law. The Judiciary is designated by the Territorial Government. Appeals from local courts are in certain instances heard by the English courts.

The Royal Family has visited the territory occasionally. In 1966 Queen Elizabeth II inaugurated Queen Elizabeth Bridge which joins Tortola and Beef Island, where the international airport is located. The Princess Margaret visited the Territory in 1972 and Queen Elizabeth returned in 1977.

The British Virgin Islands enjoy the usual modern system of communications by telephone, telex and telefax. There is shuttle air and sea transport between Tortola and Puerto Rico and the U.S. Virgin Islands, which are in turn serviced by world-wide air transport.

The growth of the corporate and financial services has been primarily the consequence of the policy of the British Virgin Islands to encourage the use of offshore companies organized pursuant to the International Business Companies Ordinance enacted in 1984. Trust services have also developed, primarily because of the background of English trust law and because of the geographical position of the Islands. The U.S. dollar has been legal tender since 1966. As a consequence, all transactions are effected in a universally accepted monetary system and there are no exchange controls.

The government has encouraged the growth of an international banking center in Road Town, Tortola. There are at present four several commercial banks operating within the British Virgin Islands including The Chase Manhattan Bank, The Bank of Nova Scotia, and Barclay's Bank. In addition, there are quite a few banks now licensed to operate solely outside the British Virgin Islands.

There are several law firms, accounting and auditing firms of international standing operating in Road Town, Tortola, assisting clients from overseas. The services are excellent and an efficient clerical staff has developed to manage the work load.

The International Business Companies Ordinance (1984) provides that all dividends, interest, rents, royalties, compensation and other sums payable to persons not resident in the British Virgin Islands, and capital gains realized with respect to any shares, obligations and other securities of a company organized pursuant to the Ordinance are exempt from income tax. In addition, a company organized under the Ordinance is exempt for taxation in the British Virgin Islands. Such companies are subject only to a fixed yearly payment to the authorities.

Company Formation

The organization and operations of international business companies in the British Virgin Islands is governed by the International Business Companies Ordinance No.8 of 1984 enacted by the Legislature of the British Virgin Islands. All information in this section refers only to BVI Companies organized pursuant to that Ordinance. As with the Bahamas, this Ordinance is an add-on to the existing companies law structure, and the old-style companies still exist.

The British Virgin Islands are increasingly becoming an attractive jurisdiction for the establishment of offshore corporations. Among the many advantages are the ease and speed with which a company may be registered, flexible and modern regulations as contained in the Ordinance, and the absence of any taxation on the operations or income of such companies other than a yearly business tax referred to below.

One or more persons, whether natural or legal, subscribe the memorandum and articles of association before a witness, which are then filed with the registrar of companies, who then issues a certificate of incorporation. The company is thereupon registered. This process usually takes two or three days.

It is not necessary that the interested parties be in the British Virgin Islands for the purpose. When the interested parties are not in the British Virgin Islands, any nominee, may act as sole incorporator and executed the memorandum and articles of association.

Once the company has been registered, the subscriber would proceed with the appointment of the first directors and at this point the company is ready to commence operations.

The subscriber to the memorandum and articles of association does not become a shareholder or entitled to subscribe shares by virtue only of having acted as a subscriber. The issuance of the shares is a separate step, and it is possible, although not usual, that no share ever is issued to the subscriber.

The memorandum must include: The name of the company; the address within the British Virgin Islands of the registered office the company, which may be and usually is the address of the registered agent of the company; the name and address within the British Virgin Islands of the registered agent of the company; the objects and purposes of the company; the currency in which shares in the company are to be issued; the authorized capital, which may be designated in terms of shares with par value or in terms of shares without par value; the classes of shares, and the number and par value of each class; the designations, powers, preference, rights, qualifications and restrictions of each class of shares, or a statement to the effect that the directors shall have the power to fix them; the number of shares to be issued in the name of the owner (registered shares) and the number of shares to be issued as bearer shares, and whether registered shares may be exchanged for bearer share, and vice versa; in the case of bearer shares, the manner in which notices are to be given to the holders of bearer shares.

The articles of association contain regulations for the conduct and activities of the company.

The name of the company must contain the word "limited", 'corporation"; or "incorporated", "societe anonyme"; or "sociedad anonima"; or the abbreviations "ltd.", "corp.", "inc." or "s.a."; and must not conflict with the name of any other company already registered. A company may use and may legally be designated either by the full or the abbreviated form of the name.

There are certain restrictions on the choice of name, which for instance may not contain words such as "assurance", "bank", "chartered", "imperial", "royal", etc. It is therefore advisable that the intended name first be cleared with the registrar of companies. A proposed name may be reserved for ninety days on the payment of a nominal fee.

The memorandum and articles of association may be amended at any time by the members (shareholders). They may also be amended by the directors if the directors have been so authorized in the memorandum and articles of association. Such amendments must be registered with the registrar of companies.

The company may perform all lawful acts and exercise all powers provided for in its memorandum and articles of association anywhere in the world. However, according to the ordinance, the company may not:

carry on business with persons resident in the British Virgin Islands; own real property in the British Virgin Islands; carry on banking business (unless licensed) or the business of an insurance or reinsurance company; carry on the business of providing a registered office for companies.

In addition, if the memorandum contains a statement that the object or purpose of the company is to engage in any act or activity that is not prohibited under any law, the effect of such statement is to make all acts or activities that are not illegal part of the object or purposes of the company.

The company is required to adopt a seal, which may be kept outside the British Virgin Islands. The articles of association will designate the person(s) entitled to use the corporate seal.

Seals must be used if the company enters into a contract which, if entered into between individuals, would be required by law to be in writing and under seal. If the corporate seal is not affixed to such document, the contract or other instrument is not thereby rendered invalid. It is not required that powers of attorney or designations of agents be sealed.

A company must have a registered office and a registered agent in the British Virgin Islands.

The business and affairs of the company are managed by a board of directors, which may consist of one person, whether natural or legal. Normally however, a company would have at least two directors and a chairman and a secretary. It is not necessary that directors or officers be residents of the British Virgin Islands.

The names of the directors and officers are not subject of registration with the authorities of the British Virgin Islands.

The first directors are elected by the subscribers to the memorandum and articles of association. Thereafter they are elected by the members (the shareholders).

However, vacancies which arise in the board of directors may be filled by the remaining directors.

Resolutions of directors may be adopted either in meeting assembled within or outside the British Virgin Islands or by written consent. Directors are deemed to be present at a meeting if they participate by telephone or other electronic means and are able to hear each other.

Directors may appoint officers and agents of the company and grant powers of attorney, including general powers of attorney, in favor of third persons to act for the company. The appointment of officers, agents and attorneys-in-fact is not subject of registration in the British Virgin Islands.

It is not required that shares be issued by any particular time, but the company should have members (shareholders) before any business is transacted.

Shares are issued by resolution of the directors and must be fully paid-in when issued. In any event, the name of the shareholder must be entered in the share registry. However, share certificates must be issued in the case of bearer shares.

The identity of the shareholder is not disclosed or subject of registration in the British Virgin Islands.

Resolutions of the shareholders may be adopted in meeting assembled or by written consent or by telex, telegram or other written electronic communication.

Shareholders meetings are called by the directors or by the holders of fifty percent of outstanding shares, and may be held within or outside the British Virgin Islands. Meetings may be held by electronic means if the shareholders are able to hear each other. It is not required that shareholders meetings be held annually or at any other particular interval.

It is not necessary to make any registration or filings in the British Virgin Islands other than the documents for the original incorporation of the company, any amendments to the memorandum and articles of association, any mergers and consolidation, and the eventual dissolution and liquidation of the company.

A company may be merged or consolidated with other companies, including non-BVI companies. Therefore, the effect of such merger or consolidation may be that a new company comes into being as successor to all the assets and liabilities of the consolidated companies, or one of the merged companies continues in existence as successor to the assets and liabilities of the merged companies.

In accordance with the International Business Companies Ordinance of the British Virgin Islands, a BVI company can transfer its place of incorporation to another jurisdiction.

Also, a non-BVI company may continue its existence as a BVI company by complying with certain provisions of the Ordinance. In accordance with such provisions, in order that a non-BVI company continue as a BVI company, articles of continuation must be approved by resolution of the board of directors or other pertinent corporate body under the regulations of its original place of incorporation. The articles of continuation must be signed by such pertinent corporate body but it is not required that they be signed by the registrar or other authority of the original jurisdiction. Such a company will then continue as a BVI company notwithstanding any provisions to the contrary in the laws of the jurisdiction of the place where it was originally incorporated. Upon the registration of the articles of continuation with the Registrar of Companies of the British Virgin Islands, the registrar will issue a certificate of continuation certifying that the company is so incorporated. The International Business Companies Ordinance of the British Virgin Islands also provides for the provisional registration of the continuation to become effective upon the giving of subsequent notice to the Registrar.

The company must have a minutes book and a share register. The records and minutes shall be kept at the registered office of the company in the British Virgin Islands or at such other place as the directors may determine. The share register may be kept anywhere, but a copy must be kept at the registered office in the BVI.

The share registry may be maintained in any form as the directors may approve, including magnetic, electronic or other form of data storage, provided however that the company is able to produce legible evidence of its contents.

Neither the minutes book nor the share register need be issued or authorized or certified by any authority of the British Virgin Islands. Any shareholder may inspect the books and make extracts.

It is not required that the company file accounts with the authorities of the British Virgin Islands. The company should therefore keep its accounts in accordance with the regulations of the place where it conducts business or owns its property.

Taxation and Official Fees

As above mentioned, a company organized pursuant to the International Business Companies Ordinance is not subject to any tax in the British Virgin Islands (other than Registrars Fees) provided it does not carry on business with persons resident in the British Virgin Islands, own real estate in the British Virgin Islands, accept banking deposits or accept contracts of insurance. However, the making of deposits in the British Virgin Islands, making professional contacts, keeping books and records, holding directors or shareholders meetings, holding leases, shares or debt of other such companies in the British Virgin Islands does not generally constitute carrying on business with persons in the British Virgin Islands.

All companies the names of which are on the Registry on 31st December of any year must pay an annual license fee before the 31st July of the following year. Failure to pay the License Fee by 31st July will cause a penalty of 10% of the Fee if the payment is made prior to 31st October and of 50% if payment is made thereafter.

Dissolution & Winding Up

The dissolution and winding up of companies registered under the International Business Companies Ordinance commences with a resolution adopted by the directors on the expiration of the term of existence of the company as expressed in its memorandum and articles of association.

If no shares have been issued the company may be dissolved by resolution of the directors. If shares have been issued, the company may be dissolved by resolution of the members (the shareholders).

Once the winding up and dissolution have been authorized, the directors designate a liquidator. The liquidator can carry on business if he determines that to do so is in the best interests of the creditors of the members.

The time for the liquidation may not exceed two years without permission of a court.

Striking Off From The Register

The registrar shall strike the name of a company from the register if by 31st December of any year the license fee due by the preceding 31st July, and any penalties, have not been paid. Such striking off has no effect on claims, debts, obligations and liabilities of the company.

At any time within three years of such striking off, the company, any creditor, member (shareholder) or liquidator may apply to the registrar to restore the name of the company to the register upon the payment of the appropriate fees and penalties.

During the time when a company is struck from the register, the company may not sue, carry on business, deal with company assets, defend legal proceedings or make any claims except those which arose prior to the time when it was struck off.

Special Provisions For Disposal of Assets

The International Business Companies Ordinance of the British Virgin Islands provides that if a company enters into any contract, deed, arrangement or other instrument relating to the payment of a claim or to the delivery or transfer of property, and the document designates a payee or beneficiary to receive the payment or property (a) upon the death of the person making the designation of, (b) upon the death of another person or (c) upon the occurrence of an event as specified in the document, then such payment, delivery or transfer, the rights of any payee or beneficiary, and ownership of the property, shall not be impaired or defeated by any rule of law governing the transfer of property by will, intestacy or gift. Such rule shall be applicable regardless of any rule to the contrary in the laws of any other jurisdiction, including the law of any jurisdiction where the person making the designation resides or is domiciled.

Such designations may be changed or revoked if the claim is not yet payable or transferable or is subject to withdrawal, collection or assignment by the person making the designation.

DOUBLE-TAXATION-

AGREEMENT HAVENS:

DOUBLE YOUR PLEASURE...

A U.S. taxpayer who pays tax on his investment returns as part of his personal income need not worry about the U.S. withholding tax. This applies only to U.S.-originated incomes — dividends, rent, interest on bonds (but not that on bank deposits), royalties — that are paid to a foreign legal entity. However, once one alienates his investment portfolio to such a foreign entity, either a corporation or a trust, he trades off the usual income tax for the 30 percent withholding tax, paid on the income at its U.S. source before it reaches the haven entity.

The withholding tax is not unqualified. A citizen of a foreign country would hardly be interested in investing in the United States if he had to pay such a tax on top of taxes imposed by his home country. Hence, the U.S. government, interested in encouraging foreigners to invest in America, has double-taxation agreements with many other nations. Such agreements usually include the following provisions: (1) Reduction of the U.S. withholding tax from 30 percent to 15 and sometimes 5 percent (if the foreign corporation involved owns 95 percent of the stock of the U.S. company from which it receives dividends). (2) Acceptance of the U.S. withholding tax as a credit against local tax liabilities. In other words, instead of taxing the 85 percent of the original dividend that remains after deducting U.S. withholding tax as if it were a gross income, the foreign investor's country treats the full amount of the original income as gross income, applies the local income tax, and reduces the tax due by the amount already paid to the United States. (3) A citizen of one of the countries party to the agreement who earns **all** his income in the other can pick which one he wants to pay his taxes to. (4) An agreement to exchange information to facilitate the capture of tax evaders.

Most double-taxation agreements are not of interest to someone seeking a tax haven. They are with highly industrialized, highly taxed countries. Investments in such havens bear a total tax burden equal to the sum of the reduced U.S. withholding tax (usually 5 percent) and the local tax on what remains from the U.S.-source income after deduction of the withholding tax or on the full original income with the U.S. tax accepted as a credit. If this sum is less than 30 percent, a corporation or trust in such a country is preferable to a "pure" haven entity.

With these thoughts firmly in mind, let us now consider the double-taxation havens.

The Netherlands

Holland, originally referring only to the two western provinces of North and South Holland which lay between the Rhine and the Zuider Zee, is now in general use as the popular name for the Kingdom of the Netherlands, and the two are used interchangeably. The people are known as Dutch. This small spit of land, no more than a pinpoint on the globe, lies to the east of England across the North Sea, and is bounded by West Germany to the east and southeast and by Belgium to the south. The land is very low, and at one time in history was in fact known as The Low Countries. Half of the land itself is below sea level. It lies across the mouth of the Rhine and is crisscrossed by two large European rivers, the Meuse and Scheldt, and by its famous canals, giving it the nickname of "Venice of the North." The picture painted indelibly on most everyone's mind of Holland as the land of windmills will soon be just that — an imagined scenery — for although there are still colorful windmills whose arms flash against the sky, most water-pumping work is now done by modern stations using electric power. The hazards of the sea, factualized and fictionalized, have made Holland the land of storied seafarers, barge men, and builders of dikes. Indeed, it is water that made Holland the gateway to Europe, providing the main source of the country's present wealth, and the cause, through directing the warm Gulf Stream along her coasts, of the country's mild climate.

The Kingdom of the Netherlands is a constitutional monarchy with democratic parliamentary government. By this means, the monarch, government, and parliament together rule the country. The kingdom includes the Netherlands Antilles which has its own tax laws and is not included in this discussion.

The Netherlands is a highly industrialized nation with little reliance on agricultural products to bolster its GNP. There is some oil production but of greater importance is the discovery of natural gas.

The Dutch economic system might best be described as a social welfare system similar to that of Great Britain without being beset, at present at least, by the industrial problems afflicting Britain.

The Netherlands, regardless of its own internal tax structure which compares to that of other heavily taxed nations, has nevertheless established itself as a tax haven through legislative action allowing substantial tax benefits to companies formed in the Netherlands for specific business purposes. The Dutch political system is a cumbersome affair and changes within the system are difficult or impossible to achieve. Executives of a tax haven company should be well advised in advance to so design the operation that it falls within the structure outlines of Holland's tax haven legislation and avoids most internal tax liability.

Tax exemptions are provided within the Netherlands on specific qualifying activities, and there are treaties maintained by the government to avoid double taxation.

Generally, the tax treaties will accomplish three reductions:

- Reduce the normal Netherlands withholding rate of 25 percent on dividends paid to recipients in the other country to a lesser rate, i.e., 15 percent (except in the cases of Czechoslovakia, Hungary, Ireland, Israel, Italy, Surinam, and Thailand, where the rates may be either more or less than 15 percent), with an additional provision that if the company receiving the dividend has a minimum capital participation — or in some cases, voting stock — of 25 percent in the dividend-paying company (with the exclusion of Canada and Italy and with an increase to 50 percent in the case of Spain), the withholding rate will be reduced even more. In respect to the United States and United Kingdom, if the recipient company holds 25 percent of the stock in the Netherlands company, the withholding rate is reduced to 5 percent.

- Reduce the withholding tax on interest which a Netherlands-based finance subsidiary of a foreign corporation receives. The withholding rate in the case of the United Kingdom which would normally be 35 percent of the gross, is reduced to 0 percent of the gross, with the net interest income being subject to normal Netherlands corporate tax rate. The United States company, which would normally pay a withholding tax of 30 percent of the gross has the tax reduced to 0 percent of the gross, with the net interest income being subject to the usual Netherlands corporate tax rate.

* Reduce the withholding tax rate on foreign source dividends received by the Netherlands participating company, with an added provision that if the Netherlands company participates in the paying company's **capital** (or in some cases, **voting stock**) to the extent of 25 percent (or 75 percent in the case of a company resident in Italy, and 50 percent in the case of a company resident in Spain), there will be a further withholding tax rate deduction. Dividends received from the United Kingdom are not affected by these provisions, since the United Kingdom does not have a withholding tax on dividends paid. In regards to the United States, the normal 30 percent withholding rate will be reduced to 15 percent through the treaty, with an added provision that if the Netherlands company participates in the dividend-paying company to the extent of 25 percent, the withholding rate will be reduced to 5 percent. All percentage figures apply to gross amounts.

There are three types of foreign companies which can be benefitted by the Netherlands tax haven legislation. These are the finance subsidiary, the holding company, and the participating company.

The Finance Subsidiary

The Netherlands-based finance subsidiary has as its primary activity the financing of the operation of the foreign parent or other closely related companies through the use of Euro-currency loans. The Central Bank of the Netherlands which issues licenses for the formation of companies formed on behalf of or by non-resident legal entities will under certain conditions consider the corporation to be a subsidiary if only 50 percent, or more, of its shares are owned by the foreign parent.

Finance subsidiaries have the following restrictions placed on them by the Central Bank: funds may not be borrowed from residents of the Netherlands; and funds cannot be kept in a bank account in the name of the subsidiary. Such funds include interest and repayments by borrowers.

The finance subsidiary will escape any restrictions on its debt-to-equity ratio as long as the finance subsidiary borrows funds from and relends funds to nonresident affiliate companies. But if funds are borrowed from nonaffiliated lenders to be re-lent to a nonresident affiliate company, a license will be required from the Central Bank, subject to the following conditions:

- Such borrowed funds, including interest and repayments received, must remain outside the Netherlands. In order to open a bank account outside the Netherlands, the finance subsidiary is required to obtain a special license.
- The finance subsidiary must hold an issued and paid-up share capital of at least Dfl 1 million.
- The finance subsidiary may not maintain a debt-to-equity ratio which exceeds 10 to 1.

*   Paid-up capital cannot be used by the finance subsidiary for any purpose, but either must be kept as liquid assets or placed in a deposit account.

It should be noted that the four preceding restrictions are subject to favorable adjustment if the balance total of the parent company amounts to Dfl 1 billion, and if it guarantees unconditionally the loans taken up by the subsidiary.

Interest paid on bonds, notes, and other debt obligations are not subject to any Netherlands withholding tax. When one adds this benefit to the treaty effecting avoidance of double taxation, substantial tax savings can be realized by the Netherlands finance subsidiary.

Also, deductible as an expense against the profits of the company is interest paid by the finance subsidiary, otherwise liable to the normal corporate tax rate after allowable deductions.

The withholding tax rate on dividends paid by the Netherlands-based finance subsidiary to a foreign entity is 25 percent, unless subject to a tax treaty.

Holding Companies

To qualify as a holding company for Netherlands tax purposes, the company must be a corporation with virtually no assets other than a majority of shares in other companies. It must also fulfill an essential function within the operating structure of the organization to which it belongs.

The Netherlands holding company's chief tax benefit is an exemption from corporate tax on dividends received by the company. Moreover, if the source of dividends paid to the Netherlands company is a country involved in a tax treaty with the Netherlands, there will be a decrease of the withholding tax at its source.

The major consideration, as regards corporate income tax, is not the qualification as holding company, but the qualification as "minimum minority-participation" company. This is the Netherlands participating company whose tax benefits are outlined as follows:

The Participating Company

To qualify for this category, the Netherlands corporation must own at least 5 percent of the outstanding shares of the capital stock of another corporation. For Netherlands tax purposes, the other corporation is called the **subordinate company**. To be exempt from corporate income tax on dividends and profits received, the participating company must, in addition to its minimum participation qualifications, meet the following conditions:

*   The subordinated company must be taxed on its profits in the country where it was established.
*   Neither the Netherlands participating company nor the subordinated company may meet the Netherlands definition of investment company.
*   The participating company may not participate in the capital stock of the subordinated company for the purpose of dividend stripping.
*   The participating company may be required to accept a nominal management fee from the foreign parent, which would be subject to the normal Netherlands corporate tax.
*   If the participating company's scope of ordinary business is to own shares of capital stock of other companies, or if acquisition of such stock is for public interest, not all of the above requirements need be met for the Netherlands

company to qualify as a "minimum minority-participation" company.

A participating company has two acceptable ways to finance participation in the capital stock of other companies. These are (1) through use of equity capital, and (2) through use of borrowed funds. Interest and other expenses attendant upon borrowed funds used for capital participation in other companies are not considered a deductible expense for Netherlands corporate income tax purposes. On the other hand, the interest on borrowed funds that are re-lent is a deductible expense.

If, through the alienation of capital stock of a subordinated company, the participating company realizes capital gains, such gains will be exempted from taxation. However, if capital losses are incurred in such transactions, such losses are not considered deductible expenses for corporate income tax purposes unless the losses are in connection with the dissolution and liquidation of the subordinated company.

There are two types of Netherlands companies under which a corporation can be organized. One is a **Naamloze Vennootschap** (N.V.), which is like the United States corporation or the public limited liability company in the United Kingdom. The other type is the **Besloten Vennootschap Met Beperkte Aansprakelijkheid** (B.V.), which can be compared to the private company in the United Kingdom.

Before a Netherlands corporation can be established by a nonresident individual or legal entity, a special license must be obtained from the Central Bank of the Netherlands, and until the license is issued no transactions whatsoever can take place. Regarding exchange control, the bank has a liberal policy of allowing current payments in both directions, as well as stock exchange transactions, free of any fee. There are banks and brokers officially authorized by the Central Bank through which payments or transactions must be channeled.

Generally, the bank will issue a license in almost every case. However, there are instances wherein the license is issued subject to certain conditions, which are a corollary of the objects of the corporation.

Legal Forms of Business Enterprises

There are three principal forms of business enterprise in the Netherlands: (1) public limited liability company (N.V.); (2) private limited liability company (B.V.); (3) the partnership.

The **public limited liability company (N.V.)** is a legal entity with its capital divided into shares. Shareholders are not personally liable for corporate debts or obligations which exceed the amount of their shareholding. A N.V. is established by legal deed containing the articles of association ("Statuten"), which must be in the Dutch language. These Statuten are subject to the approval of the Minister of Justice, and an announcement of the formation must be made in the Official Gazette (Nederlandse Staatscourant).

A public limited liability company can be established by one or more individuals or corporate entities. After establishment, one person or corporate entity may own all of the issued shares. There are no discriminatory rules about the nationality of shareholders or officers of the N.V. The financial statements of all N.V.'s are subject to an annual audit requirement, and the annual publication of balance sheet, profit and loss account, explanatory notes and the auditor's certificate is obligatory. Minimum capital to be issued and paid up initially is Dfl. 100.000,-.

The same rules generally apply to a **private limited liability company (B.V.)**. The minimum paid-up capital for a B.V., however, is Dfl. 40.000,-. In addition, there are two other important differences:

- The transferability of shares of a B.V. is restricted by law, and can be further restricted in the articles of association. The B.V. is not allowed to issue bearer shares; rather all shares must be registered.
- Only medium and large B.V.'s are subject to an obligatory audit and must publish their financial statements in full.
- In order to set up a private limited liability company in the Netherlands ("Besloten Vennootschap"), the following information is required:
- Name of company to be formed.
- Statement of the amount of capital to be issued and paid up initially. The company may have an authorized capital of five times this amount, which means that the capital may be increased to the amount of the authorized capital without amendment of the articles of association.
- The company's founder may choose between using managing directors only or have both managing directors and supervisory directors.
- Full names, private addresses, date and place of birth and nationality of the future directors.
- Recent financial statements of the shareholders and preferably a corroborating statement of their bankers.
- — A short description of the object of the company, which can be rather broad (e.g. engineering of and trading in waste-heat recovery devices for industrial applications and all activities related to such object).
- — The financial year to be observed by the new company (e.g. July 1st to June 30th).

Apart from legal fees, which are dependent on the amount of work involved, the incorporation costs for a B.V. company with a minimum capital of Dfl. 40.000,- are as follows:

capital duty (1% of paid-up capital)	Dfl. 400
name clearance by Trade Register	Dfl. 250
statement of no-objection from Ministry of Justice	Dfl. 150
notary fee (minimum)	Dfl. 2.500
Trade Register fee for first year	Dfl. 175

The third type of business enterprise in the Netherlands is the partnership, of which there are two kinds: general and limited.

A **general partnership**, "Vennootschap Onder Firma" (usually called V.O.F. or Firma), may be formed by individuals or corporate entities. The necessary regulations — comparable to the articles of association of a N.V. or B.V. — are summed up in an (informal) agreement concluded by the partners ("vennoten"). Each general partner is personally liable for the obligations of the partnership. Like corporations, partnerships must reveal a certain amount of information for the Trade Register.

The same rules apply to a **limited partnership** or "Commanditaire Vennootschap" (C.V.). A C.V. is a partnership of one or more general and one or more limited partners. Limited partners are only liable for the amount of their respective capital contributions, provided they do not take part in the management of the partnership.

Corporate Tax Rate

Corporate tax is levied upon both resident and non-resident taxpayers. Companies are considered as resident if they are effectively managed and controlled in the Netherlands. Corporate taxpayers are deemed to be resident when incorporated under Dutch civil law, even if actual management is abroad. Dual residence of a company is normally avoided by tax treaty provisions in favor of the country where the company is effectively managed and controlled. Resident corporate taxpayers are subject to Dutch tax on their worldwide income. Such companies may also be subject to foreign corporate tax on their profits earned outside the Netherlands. To avoid double taxation, Dutch tax law contains various rules that exempt income which has already been taxed or is subject to taxation in another country. This avoidance of double taxation is provided for in the participation exemption, bilateral tax treaties, or the Unilateral Decree.

Non-resident corporate taxpayers are those entities not established in the Netherlands, whose capital is wholly or partly derived from shares. Non-resident corporate taxpayers are only subject to tax on their Dutch-source earned income: (1) business income from a permanent establishment, and (2) income from immovable property located in the Netherlands. The profits of a Dutch permanent establishment are determined following Dutch rules, as if it were an independent enterprise. Interest or similar charges (e.g. royalties) from the head office are non-deductible, unless it can be proved that these charges are based upon transactions made by the head office specifically on behalf of the permanent establishment. A deduction from taxable profit is allowed for head office expenses which can be attributed to the activities of the permanent establishment.

Dutch corporate tax law, in general, does not distinguish between capital or other gains. All gains are in principle part of the taxable income for the year during which they are generated. Annual taxable income should be calculated in accordance with sound business practice and in a consistent manner. A change in accounting method is allowed if and insofar it conforms with generally accepted accounting principles.

These rather general tax law provisions allow Dutch tax authorities to apply a pragmatic attitude toward taxable profit calculations. It is common practice to negotiate advance agreements regarding elements of the method used to calculate taxable profit, such as the moment of profit recognition, intercompany transfer pricing and intercompany cost-sharing arrangements. Thus, considerable freedom exists in adopting a suitable system as long as it is in accordance with standard methods of accounting.

Dutch corporations, including holding companies, enjoy **participation exemption**, which means they are exempt from Dutch corporate tax on "benefits" connected with certain qualifying shareholdings. "Benefits" include cash dividends, dividends in kind, bonus shares, "hidden" profit distributions and capital gains realized on disposal of the shareholding. A capital loss resulting from disposal of a shareholding is similarly non-deductible (although a loss upon liquidation of a subsidiary is deductible). The fact that capital gains are exempted by the participation exemption facilitates reorganization of a group structure and thus increases the flexibility of the group as a whole.

To qualify for the participation exemption, the following conditions for a shareholding must be met:

- The participation must represent at least 5 percent of the nominal paid-up capital of the subsidiary.
- The shares must have been held since the beginning of the accounting year.
- The subsidiary company should not be a Dutch qualified investment company; this company itself is exempt from corporate tax.

If the subsidiary is foreign, some additional conditions apply:

- The subsidiary must be subject to a foreign profits tax. The relative tax percentage levied is unimportant. Also, the existence of a tax holiday does not affect availability of the exemption.

- The shareholding of foreign subsidiaries cannot be a mere "portfolio investment." Advance rulings can be obtained from the Dutch tax authorities which establish this fact.

Before October 1, 1988, taxable profit was subject to a flat corporate rate of 42 percent. A reduced corporate tax rate became effective on October 1, 1988. For taxable profit up to Dfl 250.000,- a 40 percent rate is applied. Taxable profit in excess of Dfl. 250.000,- is subject to a reduced rate of 35 percent.

Dutch tax law also has provision for loss carry over, allowing an eight year carry forward and three year carry back of losses. However, losses incurred during the first six years of a company's existence can be carried forward indefinitely. Losses are offset in the sequence in which they occur, with the provision that normal (i.e. non-start up) losses are compensated first. Losses are first offset against the oldest profits.

The avoidance of double taxation by treaty or Unilateral Decree normally does not take the form of a foreign tax credit against Dutch tax on worldwide income. Instead, an exemption is granted for Dutch tax on the foreign source income, even if the foreign tax is very low or nonexistent. Contrary to most treaties, however, the basic principle applied in the Unilateral Decree is that income is exempt for Dutch tax purposes only if such income is subject to a tax on income by the foreign State, regardless of the tax rate applicable in such a State, or that no foreign tax has actually been paid.

Corporate Tax: Subsidiary Versus Branch

In considering the establishment of a company in the Netherlands, one is well advised to weigh the advantages and disadvantages of proceeding either with a subsidiary or a branch. While in general, the subsidiary is more expensive, complicated and time-consuming, the liability of shareholders is limited to the extent of their capital contribution, and, unless otherwise agreed to by contract, the foreign parent company is not responsible for the debts, obligations and liabilities of the Dutch subsidiary. Moreover, Dutch nationals often prefer dealing with a Dutch subsidiary instead of a foreign branch office. Major advantages of the branch are that it is relatively easy to start and its costs are usually lower than a subsidiary. However, the foreign company is fully responsible for any debts, obligations and liabilities incurred by the branch.

In determining whether to establish a subsidiary or branch, potential tax implications should also be examined. Bilateral tax treaties concluded by the Netherlands generally provide that withholding tax on dividends from a Dutch subsidiary to its foreign parent is in many cases 5 percent (see Table 1). Assuming that the 5 percent rate applies, total effective Dutch income tax on remitted earnings would approximate 38.5 percent. In the absence of a treaty the dividend withholding tax rate is 25 percent.

A Dutch branch of a foreign company is also subject to tax at 35 percent. However, no withholding tax on remitted earnings is due. Therefore, the initial advantage of a branch is that the total Dutch effective income tax rate on remitted earnings can be limited to 35 percent rather than 38.5 percent. If initial losses are anticipated, the Dutch branch of a foreign company has another advantage. For Dutch tax purposes these losses can be compensated with future Dutch profits. For foreign tax purposes, the losses can often be utilized by the head office in its current year tax return.

Use of a Dutch branch may not be advantageous in situations where it is anticipated that the operation will initially break even, or both the Dutch branch and the foreign head office are profitable as the branch income is subject to current taxation in the foreign country. However, in many cases, the Dutch source income will be tax exempt in the other country. Alternatively, use of a Dutch subsidiary may avoid or defer foreign taxation simply by not paying dividends to the foreign parent company and reinvesting the Dutch subsidiary's earnings.

Still another advantage of a Dutch subsidiary is the amortization of intangible assets (e.g. technology) over its economic life, generally in 5-10 years. If intangible assets are transferred (and contributed as equity) by the parent company to its Dutch subsidiary, such assets can be amortized for Dutch tax purposes. Note that a 1 percent Netherlands capital tax is due on the value of the capital contribution. If intangibles are transferred in exchange for shares in the Dutch subsidiary, the parent company is often not subject to taxation in its home country upon receipt of such shares. Thus, depending on dividend policy, a tax deferral of up to 35 percent of the intangible asset value can be achieved. Issues concerning the amortization of intangible assets require justification of the amounts involved, and should be discussed with the tax inspector.

The Netherlands currently enjoys more than 40 bilateral income tax treaties with the industrial and developing nations throughout the world. A list of treaties and the applicable withholding tax rates or dividends can be found on the next two pages.

Corporate Taxation of Regional Headquarters, Service Companies and Branches

Regional headquarters are generally established to supervise the operations of European and/or Middle East subsidiaries. Typical activities of regional headquarters include: sales coordination, administration and accounting, advertising, and public relations as well as holding shares in subsidiaries, group financing and licensing.

As the activities of such entities are usually only of an administrative and supporting nature (as opposed to profit-generating activities like actual sales), the Dutch tax authorities are generally willing to issue advance rulings pursuant to which the taxable profit of such a company or branch is fixed on a cost plus basis (between 0 percent and 25 percent of the Dutch operational cost such as salaries, leasing of office space and general office expenses). These rulings may be granted for a period of three to five years, and may be extended for additional periods unless the circumstances have changed materially.

Ordinarily, a subsidiary or branch established in the Netherlands, which carries on supporting, preparatory and auxiliary activities for one or more foreign affiliated enterprises, would be liable to taxation at typical rates and conditions. Examples of such auxiliary activities include: administrative functions at the executive level, the keeping of an area to store or display goods, purchasing, advertising, the collecting and supplying of information, and the carrying out of scientific research. However, the Ministry of Finance has issued a regulation concerning the tax treatment of intercompany services performed in the Netherlands by or on behalf of multinational groups. Based upon this regulation, it may sound attractive for (from a corporate tax standpoint) a nonresident company to incorporate a Dutch subsidiary or open a Dutch branch to perform such services.

The regulation indicates that where a business, liable to taxation in the Netherlands, carries out transactions with affiliated businesses, the conditions agreed upon with the affiliated business should be in agreement with the arm's length principle. However, the primary yardstick for applying the arm's length principle, comparative market price, is lacking in many cases. Where it is inapplicable or where it cannot be unconditionally applied, the preferred methods for determining the profit of activities as described above is the so-called "cost-plus" method. An advance ruling can be negotiated with the Dutch tax inspector establishing the terms for application of the cost-plus method.

As an example of arrangements for which a comparative market price is unavailable, the regulation specifically mentions cash management. In this case, cash management might vary from centralized bookkeeping and administrative activities to the actual management and application of all liquid resources of a group and the preparation and determination of the relevant policy management of currency exchange risks, centralization of insurance and reinsurance activities (not including underwriting activities).

For the activities discussed above, the costs which form the basis for a ruling are generally all costs directly connected to the activity performed by the Dutch business, including cost of accommodation, office costs, salaries and reimbursement of employment expenses, an arm's length return on equity as well as interest expense on borrowed funds. The Ministry of Finance has stated that activities of a supporting, preparatory or auxiliary nature are to be taxed at a 5 percent cost-plus basis. Should more than insignificant business risks be attached to activities performed in the Netherlands, a profit mark-up of more than 5 percent may be required by the tax inspector. According to these rulings, any profit actually attributed to the Netherlands' activity which exceeds the cost-plus profit will normally be taxable as well.

This means, for instance, that interest income received by the Dutch entity will be taxable at the normal rate, and that an actual profit mark- up exceeding 5 percent will not be tax exempt.

It should be noted that a Dutch permanent establishment has no treaty protection with regard to income received from sources in third countries (not being the country where the head office is situated). However, most tax treaties concluded by the Netherlands provide that a branch for tax purposes shall not be deemed to exist (and thus no liability for Dutch income tax even on a cost-plus basis), if:

- Facilities are used **for the sole purpose** of warehousing, display or delivery of goods or merchandise.

- A stock of goods or merchandise is maintained **for the sole purpose** of warehousing, display or shipment, processing or conversion.

- A fixed place of business is maintained **for the sole purpose** of purchasing goods, collecting information, advertising, providing information, or similar activities for the benefit of the foreign head office, which are of a preparatory or supporting nature.

The Use of Dutch Intermediate Companies for Holding, Financing and Licensing Activities

The Netherlands is frequently used as a location for intermediate holding companies, principally because of the participation exemption (see above), but also because it can be advantageous to route finance and royalty activities through a Dutch company. These activities can also be combined in one company.

The Netherlands has a more extensive tax treaty network than most EU countries. A regional headquarters can benefit from these treaties in collecting dividends, interest and royalties from subsidiaries. The treaties provide for an exemption from or a reduction of foreign withholding taxes on dividends, interest and royalties. Moreover, the Netherlands do not levy a withholding tax on interest and royalties. The favorable tax treatment of these activities is described below. A note of caution is in order here, however, as the new treaty with the United States has a number of clauses designed to limit treaty-shopping by residents of other countries using The Netherlands as a conduit. Such arrangements are still possible, but you should get advice from a Dutch tax professional who is familiar with the requirements that have to be met.

Holding of Shares in Subsidiaries. Holding companies do not have a separate tax status under Dutch law. Tax benefits which are available can be enjoyed by any type of company which holds shares in foreign subsidiaries. Dividends received by a Dutch company from both resident and nonresident subsidiaries are fully exempt from Netherlands' income tax under the participation exemption. The exemption also includes capital gains made upon disposal of the subsidiary's shares. Capital losses, on the other hand, are not tax deductible (except for capital losses sustained upon dissolution and subsequent liquidation of the foreign subsidiary).

Tax treaties concluded by the Netherlands generally provide that withholding tax on dividends distributed to a Dutch company holding at least 25 percent of the shares in the distributing company is reduced or even eliminated. The treaties also provide that Dutch dividend withholding tax on dividends distributed by the Dutch company to its foreign parent (normally 25 percent) is generally reduced to 5 percent or zero.

The conditions which a company must meet to qualify for the participation exemption have been described above. A specific problem in this area is determining whether the participation constitutes a portfolio investment. To avoid disputes of a factual nature, under certain conditions a ruling can be obtained from the tax authorities establishing that the participation is not such an investment. In return, the holding company is obliged to pay corporate tax at the normal rate on an agreed minimum taxable profit normally equal to 25 percent of the costs related to the holdings activities.

Group Financing. The Netherlands is particularly attractive for group financing activities because its tax treaty network typically reduces or even eliminates the foreign withholding tax on interest paid to a Dutch company. Moreover, the Netherlands do not impose any withholding tax at source on interest paid to non-Dutch creditors, nor any duty on the issuance of bonds.

Tax rulings available to a Dutch finance company generally provide for income tax on a minimum nominal spread of generally 1/8 percent or 1/4 percent between incoming and outgoing interest. For very substantial loans, the spread can be reduced to 1/16 percent or even 1/32 percent.

Furthermore, no debt/equity ratios need to be observed for legal, exchange control or tax purposes. Agreement may also be reached with the tax authorities on a favorable treatment of central invoicing, leasing and foreign exchange clearing within the group.

Licensing. In order to benefit from the tax treaties, an intermediate royalty company is often set up between payer and recipient. The Dutch tax treaties often provide for a reduction or elimination of withholding tax on royalties received by a Dutch resident. In addition, the Netherlands does not levy a withholding tax on outgoing royalties. As a result, royalties can flow through a Dutch company at nominal cost. For tangible and intangible licensing purposes, the Dutch authorities are usually willing to issue rulings according to which Dutch subsidiaries of foreign companies engaged in licensing will be subject to tax on a spread between 2 percent and 7 percent of incoming and outgoing royalties. The percentage is determined according to a sliding scale as follows:

Foreign Withholding Tax. The next two pages summarize withholding tax rates applicable to incoming dividends, interest, and royalties under tax treaties concluded by the Netherlands.

Property Tax (Rates)

Property tax is a local tax, levied yearly by the municipality. The primary basis for taxation is the ownership and/or use of buildings and land. Property is assessed at its real value on the market in an unoccupied condition or at an approximate cost of rebuilding if market value is not obtainable due to the special character of specific real estate.

A levy of Dfl. 15,- for each Dfl. 3.00,- of this calculated value is payable for combined ownership and use. This latter amount varies per municipality but does not usually exceed Dfl. 20,-. If the premises are leased, this levy is partly paid by the owner and partly by the user. Property tax in the Netherlands is therefore of minor importance and very low in comparison with surrounding countries.

Depreciation

Generally, all assets owned or used by a corporation for purposes of its trade are depreciable if the values of these assets necessarily diminish with time. Depreciation is calculated on cost less residual value.

The basis for depreciable costs is the purchase price or production cost. This basis may not be regularly adjusted for depreciation of the currency. Depreciable basis must be decreased, however, by amounts received as capital grants (cash grants) from the government as an encouragement for capital investment (e.g. the Investment Premium Regulation).

Depreciation allowances may be taken during years in which an asset is used in the business. The time at which the asset is ordered or the purchase price is paid is not, therefore, decisive. However, any reduction in commercial value between the time at which an asset is ordered and the time it is put into use may be deducted immediately. Permissible depreciation methods include the straight line and declining balance methods and methods based on the intensity of use. Depreciation is compulsory; no deferral is permitted.

Depreciation rates are usually based on the expected economical life of an asset. Rates can be negotiated with the local tax authorities. Typical rates allowable for the more common business assets are detailed below:

Office buildings	2 - 3%
Industrial buildings	2 - 5%
Office furniture	10 - 20%
Office machines	up to 100% small machines, others, 20 - 50%
Motor vehicles	25 - 33-1/3%
Machinery	10 - 20 - 33-1/3%
Small tools	100%
Intangibles	100%, 20 - 10%

Taxation of Foreign Employees

Employees transferred to the Netherlands (who are not Dutch nationals) can apply for a special tax concession known as the 35 percent ruling. When granted, the foreign employees are treated by the Netherlands' tax authorities as nonresident taxpayers, both as regards to wealth tax and income tax (including wage tax, which is an advance levy on income tax). The rules have changed a number of times, and it is important to check on the current status at the time the application is made.

The inspector of Direct Taxation handles applications for the 35 percent concession. The address is: Inspectie der Directe Belastingen (Buitenlanders), Akerstraat Noord 69, Postbus 300, 6440 LA Brunssum, tel.: 045-217333.

Value Added Tax

Value added tax (V.A.T.) is levied in the Netherlands on entrepreneurs on the delivery of all goods (both movable and immovable) and services rendered in the Netherlands and, generally, on the importation of goods. The term "delivery" includes the transfer of title goods, lease/purchase agreements and the disposal of goods for non-business purposes.

V.A.T. is levied at each stage of production and distribution on the basis of amounts invoiced to the purchaser, including shipping, handling and insurance charges but excluding the V.A.T. tax itself and cash discounts for prompt payment or deposits on returnable containers. For imported goods, the taxable basis is the import value as determined for customs duty purposes, together with all import duties and inland freight. The delivery of goods is deemed to be a taxable event if the place where transportation begins or where the goods are located at the time of delivery is within the Netherlands. Services are normally considered to be supplied where the supplier of the services is established or has a fixed establishment. However, numerous exceptions exist for specific services.

The following tax rates are currently in force:

* A standard rate of 17.5 percent applicable to all goods and services not exempt or subject to the reduced rate or zero rate.

* A reduced rate of 6 percent for those goods and services considered essential (i.e. necessaries of life).

* A zero rate for goods and services related to export and import (e.g. any activities within bonded warehouses or their equivalent).

V.A.T. is charged to the customer and must be stated on the invoice for all goods and services supplied. V.A.T. is paid to the tax authorities through a tax return that must be filed on a monthly or quarterly basis as decided by the local tax inspector. The return and related payment are sent to the tax collector within one month after the end of the applicable period.

V.A.T. is paid to suppliers on purchased goods and services (input tax), and is deductible from the V.A.T. charged to customers (output tax). Both amounts must be stated on the tax return. If the V.A.T. paid exceeds the V.A.T. charge, the excess is refunded by the tax authorities. The right to deduct V.A.T. paid from V.A.T. charged arises when the invoice is received and not when it is paid. Conversely, V.A.T. charged is payable to the tax collector at the time the invoice is rendered to the customer and not at the time when payment is received.

Although the Netherlands should not be considered as a tax haven country in any general sense, it does offer considerable advantages to holding and finance companies. In appropriate circumstances, formation of a Dutch company might be the correct choice as a vehicle to finance other companies in a group, while it may at the same time function as a holding company.

Austria

Austria has holding company legislation that is in many ways similar to that of the Netherlands for receipt of dividends from subsidiaries. Austria is a neutral country with strong trade ties to Eastern Europe, which may be useful for a holding company making investments in that area. It is now a member of the European Union, but this is unlikely to have any effect on the holding company situation.

Austria has an extensive system of double taxation agreements, covering nearly 40 countries. In the 1989 tax reform in Austria normal corporate taxation was reduced to 30 percent.

A corporation is subject to Austrian tax on its earnings worldwide if the head office or registered office of the company is in Austria. The head office is assumed to be where the center of senior management is situated. The registered office is the place defined by law where an Austrian corporation is headquartered. Corporations that have neither their head office nor their registered office in Austria are subject to tax in Austria on their domestic earnings.

If a corporation (parent company) has a holding in another Austrian company (affiliated company) all of the parent company's profit-sharing is tax exempt. This tax exemption applies both to disclosed dividend payouts and to disguised profit distribution.

Apart from the general exemption for holding earnings in Austria, there is also what is known as the "international intercompany tax concession." An Austrian corporation is exempted from paying Austrian corporation tax on any form of profit-sharing from a holding in a foreign corporation provided the following conditions are met: the foreign corporation must be a corporation (not a partnership or other form of enterprise); and the Austrian corporation can show evidence to have directly possessed a holding interest of at least 25 percent in the shares of the foreign corporation continuously for at least one year before the balance sheet date applicable to the income assessment.

An Austrian holding company may thus collect dividends from its foreign subsidiaries tax free. The "international intercompany tax concession" covers both disclosed dividend payouts and disguised profit distribution.

The "international intercompany tax concession" does not contain an "activity clause." It is thus of no consequence whether or not the Austrian holding company or its subsidiary have active earnings — in other words, whether or not they are actively engaged in business transactions.

Once the requirements for the "international intercompany tax concession" have been met, not only the regular dividends but the capital gains generated in Austria which arise from the sale of such qualified affiliated holdings are tax exempt. Tax exemption for capital gains applies only to holdings in foreign companies, however. The capital gains arising from holdings in Austrian corporations are entirely subject to taxation.

There are no provisions stipulating that mere holding companies are excluded from the privileges provided for in Austria's double taxation agreements. On the other hand, Luxembourg's double taxation agreements contain such provisions.

If an Austrian corporation pays dividends to a foreign corporation, a withholding tax of 25 percent is withheld (some double taxation agreements provide for lower rates of withholding tax). This raises obvious problems in paying the money from Austria to a pure tax haven. Of course the problem only arises if and when there is a need to pay out a dividend, rather than reinvest the money.

The conversion of interest into dividends and vice versa often makes sense for taxation purposes. For example, if a Swiss company purchases bonds, any interest therefrom is fully liable to taxation in Switzerland. If the Swiss company instead establishes a subsidiary in the Netherlands Antilles and the subsidiary purchases the bonds, the subsidiary earns interest thereon which is taxable in the Netherlands Antilles at a maximum level of 3 percent. The subsidiary subsequently pays the Swiss parent company dividends, which are not subject to withholding tax in the Netherlands Antilles. In Switzerland the dividends received are tax exempt. In this case the interest was converted into dividends in the Netherlands Antilles.

Converting interest into dividends and vice versa is generally possible in Austria (provided no fake transaction or breach of the law is involved) and may well pay off.

For example, a Saudi Arabian company wishes to invest in a Dutch company. As Saudi Arabia has not concluded any double taxation agreements, dividend payments from the Netherlands to Saudi Arabia are subject to a withholding tax of 25 percent. On the other hand, the Saudi Arabian company may establish an intermediate holding company in Austria which in its turn acquires a holding in the Dutch company. By the terms of the Austrian-Dutch double taxation agreement, dividends can be transferred tax-exempt from the Netherlands to Austria. In Austria neither these dividends nor any capital gains arising out of the sale of the holding are subject to tax.

However, the tax-exempt transfer of the dividends to Saudi Arabia is not possible, since Austria has not concluded a double taxation agreement with that country. But it is possible to convert dividends into interest. The Saudi Arabian company first establishes a second subsidiary (sister company of the Austrian holding company) in a country which levies either no tax or only low levels of tax on interest and no withholding tax on dividends (e.g. an offshore company in the Channel Islands or the Netherlands Antilles).

The Saudi Arabian company provides this offshore company with the appropriate equity capital. The offshore company passes on this equity capital as a loan to the Austrian holding company. The latter acquires the Dutch company with the loan from the offshore company.

Dividends and capital gains from the holding in the Netherlands are temporarily invested in Austria tax-exempt. The profits temporarily invested in Austria are transferred out of Austria in the form of interest payments on the loan from the offshore company. This flow of profits is exempt from tax, because such interest payments are not subject to tax in Austria. The offshore company, too, receives the interest tax-exempt. The interest is again converted into dividends and is transferred exempt of withholding tax to Saudi Arabia.

In the above example the withholding tax is lowered from 25 percent to 0 percent. It should be noted, however, that arrangements like this need to be examined very closely to ensure that they are not classified unilaterally as fake transactions or abusive practices.

By contrast with most countries' tax law systems, Austria's commercial and tax law do not prescribe minimum debt equity ratios.

LUXEMBOURG: A TRADITIONAL HAVEN FOR HOLDING & FINANCE COMPANIES

Luxembourg is a full member of the European Union. Most Luxembourg taxes are the same as in its neighboring countries, Belgium, France, and Germany. However, Luxembourg is especially well-suited as a tax haven for specific purposes.

The Holding Company Act of 1929 makes Luxembourg an attractive tax haven for the holding company, provided it meets prescribed qualifications: It must be a "pure" holding company; it cannot conduct "actual business"; and it cannot be a "commercial establishment open to the public." The "no actual business" clause is interpreted to mean no industrial activity. In effect, this means that there are many business activities in which the pure holding company can participate. Several thousand holding companies are presently located in Luxembourg, with the number constantly increasing.

For the purpose of tax havenry, it is important to make the distinction between the **mixed** holding company and the **pure** holding company.

Mixed Holding Company

The mixed holding company is defined in Luxembourg as one that administers an investment portfolio, takes participating interests, develops patents, and also engages in direct industrial and/or commercial activity. The Holding Company Act of 1929, and the tax advantages that it provides, **does not apply to the mixed holding company**.

Pure Holding Company

In Luxembourg, the pure holding company is defined as one whose "...sole object is the taking of participating interests, in whatever form, in other Luxembourg or foreign undertakings, and the administrating and development of such participating interest, so however that company shall carry on no industrial activity, nor maintain a commercial establishment open to the public." The Holding Company Act of 1929 applies specifically to this type of holding company.

The pure holding company may only hold negotiable securities as assets. This is not as restrictive as it may first appear. It does not mean that the company must be an inactive body with a fixed portfolio; it can, for example, sell a portion of its securities to dispose of some participations, and can, in turn, reinvest the proceeds of the sale by taking participating interests in another enterprise. Again, the distinction is that the company has not engaged in any industrial activity, nor attempted to do business with the public. Further, the pure holding company is permitted to develop its interests by supervising the financial administrations of its affiliates, even to the extent of exercising technical and commercial control.

Moreover, it is expected that the pure holding company will take an active interest, either as a shareholder, or as a lender, in its affiliate firms. Thus, the legal interpretation of the clause "administration and development of such participating interests" is that the holding company can grant long-term and short-term loans to the various enterprises in which it takes a participating interest, as well as guarantee increases in their capital. However, such loans must be terminated if and when the holding company withdraws participation in the enterprise. Also construed as loans for the purpose of this provision are any advances that a holding company might make to an enterprise, the securities of which do not make up a sufficient percentage of the holding company's portfolio. (This is not applicable, however, to finance holding companies that were formed in accordance with regulations that the Minister of Treasury issued on September 9, 1965).

Although the holding company may hold participating interests in other undertakings, "in whatsoever form," Luxembourg legislation does not permit holding company association with a partnership firm, or permit a holding company to be a partner in a firm. The one exception to this is a holding company acting as a "sleeping partner" in a partnership limited by shares.

The intent of the 1929 legislation is that the holding company cannot own real estate, with the rare exception in which real estate is necessary to accommodate the company's administrative departments. However, its portfolio may contain shares of a real estate company.

Capitalizing the Holding Company. The holding company is capitalized in much the same manner as the stock company, by issuing either shares or bonds. This may or may not be by public issue, and the bonds may be securities for either long- or short-term loans. The notable restrictions placed on the capitalization of the holding company is that it cannot operate a "commercial office open to the public," and is therefore not allowed to operate as a banking institution that solicits deposits from the public.

Liabilities. The holding company is expected to have liabilities just as any other company. The creditors of such commitments are the company's shareholders, or banking institutions. So long as the liabilities are considered normal, and are a result of activities consistent with the articles of association, the creditors are liable for no taxation under Luxembourg legislation. The intent here is that the revenue authorities want to prevent a disproportional difference between the capital of the company and the amount owed to creditors. A disproportional difference, for example, would be liabilities that are two to three times greater than the normal amount of capital. However, finance holding companies are exempt from this law.

Holding Company Act of 1929

The wording of the 1929 law refers only to "holding companies." However, the intent of the legislation was not to restrict the effects of the legislation to standard holding companies, but extend it to "financial participating companies," of various functional capacities. Among these are controlling companies, investment trusts, and finance companies. Luxembourg law follows the standard practice of other countries in using the generic term, **holding company**, to encompass institutions of various kinds, even though such institutions may not have a common character.

The Finance Holding Company

Tax advantages to the Luxembourg finance holding company become obvious when we consider that several countries (Germany and the U.S., for example) levy a withholding tax on interest accruing to foreign bondholders. This would be an inhibiting factor for the purchase of bonds on the international market from companies domiciled in such countries. By contrast, the Luxembourg finance holding company, which need not withhold tax on interest paid out, is in an excellent position for an international bond issue. The parent company would, of course, guarantee the bonds issued by the Luxembourg holding company. To qualify as a holding company, however, the finance company launching the bond issue is required to hold an adequate percentage of shares of affiliated companies that are multinational company subsidiaries.

Under a new system introduced in 1965, the concept of the financial or industrial group controlling several related companies that are linked by economic, financial, and legal interests, was created. This concept came about through the influence of multinational firms that formed holding companies with large amounts of capital, which ultimately resulted in the formation of international industrial and financing groups. Under this system, a holding company is permitted to extend loans to nonsubsidiary companies, providing the following conditions are met:

- The constitution of the finance holding company must be as a public company.
- So that Luxembourg authorities can ensure that sufficient and permanent economic links are in force between the holding company and the founding companies, the parent company (or companies) forming the financial or industrial group must be stated as the founders on the deed of constitution. Also, articles of the constitution must provide for the registration of the shares issued by the finance holding company.
- Persons outside the group cannot profit from the sale of shares in the finance holding company until the company has repaid all its borrowings; however, shares may be assigned.

- The finance holding company's portfolio must consist of the stock of companies in the same financial or industrial group.
- If a company is to be the recipient of a loan from the finance holding company, it must meet the conditions for membership in the group.
- If debenture loans are to be issued, the articles of the constitution must include a clause stating that the yield from the loans can only accrue to the benefit of companies in the financial or industrial group in which the holding company is participating.
- Authorities must be consulted before any company that intends to use these facilities is formed.

The September 9, 1965 ruling by the Minister of the Treasury allows Luxembourg holding companies to finance companies belonging to the same group, without the necessity of holding an adequate percentage of the shares of such companies. This ruling had the effect of enabling the holding company to participate in the capital market. However, to derive benefit from this ruling, the following conditions must be met:

- The Luxembourg holding company must be established as a public limited company.
- The parent company or affiliates of the groups must appear as founders of the Luxembourg holding company.
- The Luxembourg holding company's shares must be in registered form.
- If bond issues are outstanding, the shareholders must not sell their equities to third parties.
- The Luxembourg holding company's portfolio must contain shares that are issued by enterprises belonging to the same group. This condition is met when the parent

company's equity investment in the Luxembourg holding company is paid for by contributing shares of the parent company. This is called **cross-shareholding** between the parent company and the holding company.

• Proceeds from a loan must be used only for enterprises of the group in which the holding company has participating interests. This restriction must be explicitly stated in the articles of association.

Still another way that the finance holding company differs from the ordinary Luxembourg holding company is that it may issue bonds in the ratio of 10:1 to the share capital, as well as have liabilities of 3 times its share capital.

Management Holding Company

The management holding company is another of the various entities classed under the general term holding company. Since there is no specific legislation in Luxembourg that applies to open-end investment funds, the management company functions as the trustee and administrator of the assets invested in these funds. In the absence of such legislation, the open-end investment trust has no legal status; therefore, when third party transactions are called for, the management company acts on the trust's behalf.

Adhering to the principle of the distinction of competencies, the open-end investment holding company consists of three separate organs: the management company, the joint trust, and the trustee bank.

The management holding company is a capital share company, usually assuming the form of a public holding company. The Minister of Treasury, together with certain Luxembourg legislation, has imposed the following rules on such companies:

- Their only purpose must be to form and administer the joint investment trusts for which they were constituted.
- At the time of constitution, they must be capitalized in the amount of at least 5,000,000 francs, subscribed and paid in full.
- Their shares must be registered.
- Their assets must be managed so as to provide a guarantee for the bearers of the investment trust's certificates. In effect, this means that they must employ their own funds.
- The shareholders, or persons for whom the investment funds are originated, must provide a joint guarantee to comply with the administrative regulations in any undertakings that are initiated.

At the outset of its formation, the management holding company is subject to the standard tax system. However, there is a reduction of the annual subscription duty, to six-tenths percent of the inventory value of the portfolio of the funds administered, payable in four quarterly installments. The fiscal privileges provided to holding companies by Luxembourg legislation are equally applicable to both the management company and the open-end investment company it administers.

Joint Investment Trust

The joint investment trust is an organic joint possession that has a specific legal status. Persons or entities with holdings in the trust are considered co-owners of its underlying assets, with ownership rights, represented by either bearer or registered stock instead of being considered as owners of corporate shares. This would be equivalent to units of beneficial interest in a British or American trust. A holder in the trust has the privilege of demanding redemption of his stock anytime.

The Minister of Treasury must approve the administrative regulations when the company is formed. Holdings in the trust are contingent upon adherence to these administrative regulations. The regulations outline the rights and obligations of the holders, as well as the conditions under which the management company is mandated. It is essential that the regulations define (1) the issuing and redemptions conditions for the co-ownership stock, (2) the method and frequency for assessing the value of the shares, (3) the method and costs of administering the trust's assets, and (4) the rules that apply to the spreading of assets.

Concerning the spreading of assets, however, there are certain restrictions that must be complied with in any case, as regards the amount of the trust's assets that are invested in stock issued by one company, or in unquoted stock. Still another restriction imposed by Luxembourg legislation is that the open-end joint investment trust cannot borrow from or hold shares in other investment trusts.

To make public issue, or to be quoted on the stock exchange, an investment must have assets of at least 100,000,000 francs. The trustee bank holds the assets of the investment trust, and jointly guarantees adherence to administrative regulations. An investment trust may utilize more than one trustee bank. Luxembourg authorities must approve the bank or banks that are chosen.

Closed-End Investment Holding Company

The constitution of the closed-end investment holding company calls for the form of a public holding company, in which shareholders own shares of the corporation rather than shares of the underlying assets. This form of the Luxembourg holding company would not be unique, except for its popularity, and the resultant issuance by Luxembourg authorities of the following recommendations concerning its form:

- At the outset, the concept of authorized capital is acceptable, and, at a general meeting of the investment company's shareholders, authorization may be given to the board to increase the registered capital up to a given amount. The method of generating this increase must be by the most suitable methods, and be consistent with capital requirements. However, this resolution must be submitted within five years to the extraordinary general meeting for ratification regarding the portion of authorized capital that may not have been subscribed.

- On the date of the company's constitution, the subscription price for issued shares may not include a premium that is overly large in comparison to the nominal value of the stock. Previously, nominal value of the stock has always represented at least ten percent of the initial subscription price.

- At the time of a capital increase, the subscription price for the offered shares must be equal to the net value of the shares that were issued previously (including any expenses).

- If certain persons are granted special financial advantages—preference shares, bonus shares, or options—in return for their assistance in the formation or development of the company, such advantages will be allowed only on the condition that a detailed and accurate description of them is given in the prospectus. Further, the results of granting special financial advantages must be specified individually in the financial statements, and explained in the periodic reports to shareholders.

- A distinction must be made between actual funds, on the one hand, and registered capital and legal reserves on the other, if the company elects to buy back its own shares, subject to the following provisions: (a) Actual funds must be used for the purchase; (b) The company's articles of constitution must allow for such transactions; and (c) Equal treatment must be afforded shareholders in applying for and repurchasing the shares.
- In the event that the company repurchases shares, it must then provide accounts and reports to the public that clearly outline the terms of the repurchase.

The methods for implementing repurchases of shares varies. Some investment companies do their own repurchasing, while others prefer to form subsidiaries for that purpose. The subsidiary, whose only purpose is to repurchase the parent company's shares, is also classed in the holding company system. The repurchased shares no longer confer a voting right, or distribution right in the event of liquidation.

Unlike joint investment trusts, closed-end investment companies face no restrictions in the choice or spreading of the investment. For example, they may hold stocks and shares in investment trusts or other investment companies in their portfolios. Further, if the general provisions applying to holding companies are adhered to, the closed-end investment company may employ capital other than that received from the sale of ordinary shares. The closed-end company is subject to the same taxation as are holding companies.

Therefore, we can say that the closed-end investment company is a sort of hybrid of the open-end investment company and pure holding company. Because it is subject to fewer restrictions than the open-end investment company, it is becoming a preferred form for an increasing number of international promoters. As a typical comparison, the open-end company is not permitted to borrow money, either on a short- or long-term basis, and is therefore not able to use the "leverage" technique in the management of the fund's assets.

From a legal viewpoint, the closed-end investment company's capital structure and general form are (briefly) as follows:

Based upon a decision taken by the general meeting of shareholders, the board of directors is given the authority to increase capital up to the specified amount of authorized capital. This increase is effected over a period of time determined by the subscriptions that are received by the company. Such subscriptions may be made to the board of directors at specific intervals. The essence of this procedure is that new shares may be issued continuously. The successive increases of the issued capital are recorded periodically, by deed established by a Luxembourg notary public, and are required to be published in the **Official Gazette**. The duration of the effect of the shareholders' original decision is five years; at the expiration of this period, if the authorized capital has not been issued in its entirety, the decision has to be renewed.

In order that the closed-end investment company operate to fulfill its corporate objective, certain standards regarding share values have to be set. Since the net worth of the company's assets is established (in most cases) daily or weekly, it is essential that the subscription price, as paid by the investors, correspond exactly to the net worth of the share. To effect this, the issue price is made up of two factors: the par value of the share, which is constant; and the par value plus the added premium, which varies according to the issue price.

The premium serves the following function: The closed-end investment company must be able to redeem its shares at net asset value anytime shareholders present such shares for redemption, just as does the open-end investment company. To do this in accordance with Luxembourg law, the redemption can only be financed by a specific reserve account provided by the premiums collected from subscribers, but not through the firm's capital or legal reserve accounts.

The relation between the par value of the capital and the premiums of the investment company varies from 1:10, to somewhat less. According to Luxembourg law, premiums should not be overly disproportionate to the par value of the capital, with a ratio of 1:5 being considered in the tolerable range for the purpose of the repurchase company's pursuing redemption.

We have already touched upon the functions of the repurchase holding company, which is also subject to the Luxembourg laws applicable to holding companies. While the decision to utilize the purchase holding company is optional, its use is recommended by both Luxembourg authorities and the promoters of closed-end investment companies. As a practicality, the repurchase company can be a holding company, owned in its entirety by the closed-end investment company.

The repurchased shares cannot be resold to the public, and do not have a voting or liquidations dividend right. They can be managed separately from those owned by shareholders of the closed-end investment company. The net value of the repurchased shares must be deducted from the total net assets value of the shares of the closed-end investment company.

Luxembourg law is fairly stringent regarding the information that must be published by the closed-end investment company. This information must be complete and detailed. The ruling applies specifically to yearly and periodic reports, which should clearly state the amounts of the issued and authorized capital, the par value and premium of the investment company's issued shares, the number of shares redeemed by the repurchase company, the balance sheet of both the parent company and the repurchase company, and a detailed statement of the assets and securities that the company holds in its portfolio.

Patent Holding Company

Patent holding is an important function of the investment holding company, with patents being considered as much a security in the portfolio as are shares and bonds. Patents must be exploited by ordinary commercial and industrial enterprises. When this is done, the holding company is the ideal form for the patent business. This has resulted in the formation of many holding companies whose primary purpose is to hold patents; moreover, with the advent of the common market, the number of patent holding companies will surely increase. The portion of Luxembourg legislation that applies to patents is specific in declaring that patents are commercial securities with a special character, and appropriate as a means of financial participation in commercial enterprises. Soon after the legislation was passed, the Luxembourg revenue authorities responded to a questionnaire concerning the new laws. The following points are a result of that questionnaire.

- One of the most effective operations that a holding company can participate in, from the viewpoint of increasing the value of its securities, is the purchase of patents for the specific purpose of granting licenses to affiliates or other companies. The granting of patents may be implemented by exchanging them for shares, or cash payments in any form (such as annual payments), or for a percentage of the profits, a percentage of the runover, or by whatever means is viable for the principals concerned.

- A holding company can acquire patents, either by outright purchases, or by taking them on a royalty arrangement. The acquisition of patents is looked upon as much the same as increasing securities by acquiring cash, whether such cash is acquired through loans, granted credits, or by an increase in capital. In the case of patents, they may be acquired either through third parties, or through affiliated companies.

- The holding company can only transfer patents to third parties (whether individuals or companies) in which the holding company does not have substantial holdings if certain requirements are met — the transfer must be a method of raising funds that will be used within a year to purchase securities. When this is done, no taxation is applicable during the year, allowing the company sufficient time to convert patent sales revenues into company securities.

- The foregoing requirement is flexible to the extent that a holding company may make one of several isolated patent transactions to third parties without reinvesting the proceeds of the transactions into securities, and without losing its holding company status so long as it continues to conform to the Holding Company Act of 1929. Thus, the law recognizes the possibility that a reinvestment of funds in securities may, under certain circumstances, be too costly to be practical, or may be impossible. (This concept of flexibility in the Luxembourg law is much the same as that of other countries where holding company patents are considered special cases, to be dealt with by special rules.)

- Luxembourg law also permits the holding company to assume the role of an agent in the sale of patents that belong to affiliated companies.
- If, in transactions involving the purchase and sale of patents, holding company actions imply that it is operating a patent agency, such action can be construed as commercial activity. The company would no longer benefit from holding company legislation. Therefore, the holding company must attempt to reinvest the proceeds of patent sales into securities within a reasonable time, or show sufficient cause why this cannot be done.
- If either foreign or home patents are transferred, the transfer must be registered at a flat registration fee.

New Holding Companies

A 1990 law permits a second type of international holding company that can benefit from tax treaties. Companies under this law are subject to full corporate taxation at a rate of nearly 40%. However, they take advantage of Luxembourg's *participation exemption* so as to avoid tax on dividends and capital gains derived from its foreign affiliates. The exemption for dividends requires a shareholding of at least 10% and it must be held during the entire year in which the dividend is paid. The affiliate paying the dividend must be subject to a corporate income tax in its home country of at least 15%. The exemption for capital gains requires a holding of at least 25% and the required holding period is longer. Luxembourg's participation exemption works like the Netherlands substantial-holding privilege. Dividends received by a resident company are exempt from Luxembourg corporate tax if a shareholding of at least 10% has been held since the beginning of the year. The exemption has been extended to cover capital gains if a shareholding of at least 25% has been held for at least 12 months.

English Equivalent to the Luxembourg Holding Company

In its legal structure, the Luxembourg holding company may assume one of the following English equivalencies:
- General partnership.
- Limited partnership.
- Partnership limited by shares.
- Public limited company (joint stock company).
- Private limited company (limited liability company).
- Cooperative society.

Public Limited, Joint Stock Company

The most commonly encountered type of holding company is the public limited, joint stock company, which may be organized as either a closed-end or open-end company. It may utilize a management company, a repurchase company, and a trustee bank. The assets of the investment trust are kept in the trustee bank. A relatively small operation may forego the management company and trustee bank; however, in any case, a repurchase holding company may be used as a vehicle for acquiring patents. It may be as diversified as any stock company; however, to use the stock exchange for a public share issue, it must have assets of at least 100,000,000 francs.

Signing the Deed. If a holding company is to be a joint stock company, it must be formed under a notarial deed. Founders who live in another country may give powers of attorney to third parties for the signing of the notarial deed, thereby relieving themselves of the necessity of being present at the signing. These third parties who attend the signing of the deed (before a notary) may be entered on the deed as nominees. It is noted, however, that such nominees have no specific mandate, and that the subscribed shares will be transferred to the principals.

Residence Requirements. Luxembourg legislation recognizes that the founders, directors, auditors, managers, managing directors, etc., may be of any nationality, and moreover, may be residents of another country.

Books of Account. Company books, which may first be initialed, and subsequently signed by competent authorities, must be kept at the registered office.

Shares. Shares of the company are registered shares, and must remain registered shares until they are paid, or until bearer shares are issued. There is no legal necessity to provide printed shares. The capital of the company and the nominal value of each share may either be expressed in Luxembourg francs, or in any other currency.

Term. The duration of the company's term is 30 years. This term may be renewed repeatedly, so long as it is done with adherence to legal requirements (renewals are also for 30-year periods).

Meetings. The joint stock holding company must hold ordinary, annual meetings at its registered Luxembourg office, and must submit the company's accounts to the shareholders. In the case of absentee shareholders, proxy attendance is permitted, with no expense incurred to the shareholder who does this. The presence of a notary public is not required at the ordinary meetings. However, in the event of an extraordinary meeting, convened to amend the articles of constitution, a notary public must be present.

Publication. The joint stock holding company must publish its annual balance sheet, and an abstract of its profit and loss accounts in the Luxembourg **Official Gazette**. This publication must also state the composition of the board of directors and auditor or auditors. Luxembourg law does not require that a list of the company securities be published in the **Gazette**.

Luxembourg Services

Both foreign and domestic banks are on the increase in Luxembourg. Much of this increase is because the Luxembourg stock exchange is extensively used for the issuance of Eurodollar bonds. Because of the highly developed business atmosphere of this tiny country, a complete range of legal and accounting services is available.

There are no exchange controls.

Taxation

Luxembourg has double taxation treaties with Holland, France, Austria, the United States, and the United Kingdom. Generally, since Luxembourg holding companies are not really being doubly taxed, they are not qualified for a reduced withholding tax.

Summary

Luxembourg legislation is designed to attract holding companies. The establishment of a holding company can result in a considerably reduced expense budget for a corporation. As evidence of this, consider the following:

- Regardless of a company's profits, there is only a single, small annual tax.
- The judicial system of Luxembourg, which is liberal, is geared toward the needs of the holding company.

- All the principals of a company, such as the promoters, directors, auditors, managers, etc. may be of any foreign nationality, and may reside in other countries.
- There is no communal taxation.
- There is no Luxembourg tax levied against dividends distributed by the company, either against the company itself, or against foreign shareholders.
- There is no Luxembourg tax levied against coupons of foreign securities — such as shares and bonds — that are held by the company.
- There is no taxation on the proceeds of liquidations.
- The law does not require the publication of the list of company securities.
- Luxembourg revenue authorities do not examine or supervise the books of holding companies.

NEVIS: A SUPERIOR ASSET PROTECTION HAVEN

The "sovereign democratic federal state" of St. Christopher-Nevis (as its 1983 constitution ceremoniously describes it), has a governmental form and name almost bigger than its population (45,000), and total land area (267 sq. km.).

But this tiny West Indies island nation, known to the natives as "St. Kitts-Nevis," has become very big in certain exclusive international financial circles. That's because Nevis has no taxes, extremely user-friendly incorporation and trust laws, and an official attitude of hearty welcome to foreign offshore corporations and asset protection trusts.

In his second voyage to the New World in 1493, the year after Columbus discovered what was to become known as "America," (actually landing first at what is now the Dominican Republic), his explorations included two of the Leeward Islands. One of these he named (perhaps for a bit of ego gratification), St. Christopher, much later shortened to the current "St. Kitts."

It is reliably reported that when Columbus saw the smaller of the two islands, two miles south of St. Kitts, he was instantly impressed by the majestic volcanic mountain in its center, an almost perfect cone rising 3,232 feet, smothered in thick clouds. His diary indicates the intrepid Columbus was reminded of the snow-capped peaks of the Pyrenees, and so he named the island **Nieves**, the Spanish word for "snows."

Though Columbus claimed the islands for Spain, the first colonization was by the British in 1623 and 1628 respectively. In fact these islands became the mother British colony in the Caribbean, the launching pad for other settlements in Antiqua, Barbuda, Tortola, and Monserrat. The French arrived a few years later, inexplicably bringing a bunch of monkeys with them, and they (the French, not the monkeys) also used the islands as a starting point for their West Indian colonial designs in Martinique, Guadeloupe, St. Martin, St. Barts, La Desirade, and Les Saintes.

Located 225 miles east of Puerto Rico and about 1,200 miles south of Miami, until the islands September 19, 1983 declaration of independence, both were British colonies.

The islands are now a member of the Commonwealth of Nations and recognize as nominal head of state, Queen Elizabeth II, who appoints a local Governor General. The elected unicameral Parliament sits in the capital of Basseterre on St. Kitts (population 35,000), but Nevis (10,000) has its own Island Assembly as well, and retains the constitutional right of secession from St. Kitts. Now and again newspapers in Nevis (pronounced **NEE-vis**) issue heated editorial demands for separation, but if it happens, it will be without shots being fired, other than a few verbal salvos.

The tiny 2-island nation is a member of the United Nations, the Organization of American States (OAS) and is an associated Commonwealth participating state of the European Union (EU). It is also a member of the Caribbean Community (CARICOM) economic and trading group, along with fourteen other area nations including the Bahamas, Bermuda and Belize.

Although it was formerly a member of the British sterling bloc, the country's currency is now the Eastern Caribbean dollar used by several CARICOM nations, pegged to the United States dollar at a rate hovering around EC$ 2.60 to 2.70, to US$ 1.00. U.S. currency is freely accepted, but your change will be in EC dollars.

Most St. Kitts-Nevis islanders are descendants of African slaves imported by the British and French, the original American West Indian natives being long since extinct. The population is 94 percent black, 40 percent urban. English is the official and spoken language, but with a lilting West Indian accent, "mon."

The legal and judicial system, originally based on English common law, has now incorporated many of the basic elements of United States commercial law, especially that of New York and Delaware, for good reasons that will be clear in a moment.

The islands have a pleasant, healthy climate, warm with cool breezes throughout the year, low humidity and no real demarcated rainy season. Average annual rainfall is about 55 inches, most of it in the fall, which is also the hurricane season. The official tourist "season" is from December 15 to April 14, only because that's when weather is nastiest in the northern hemisphere and Caribbean islands most fashionable. Temperatures year-round average 78 to 85 degrees Fahrenheit, and from November through January the islands experience increased "Christmas winds," as they are called locally.

A low-key economic promotional program authorized by the 1984 "Citizenship Act" offers nationality and a passport in return for a $200,000 investment, usually the purchase price of a seaside condominium and certain "fees." Citizenship for the investor and spouse are included in the deal. (A less expensive route to citizenship is marriage, since St. Kitts & Nevis is one of the few countries that gives instant citizenship upon marriage to a spouse of either sex.)

Nevis is attractive for financial reasons, as we shall see, but it is also known for its natural beauty — long, curving beaches of white and black sand, lush foliage and flowers, mineral spa baths and restored sugar plantations now used as charming country inns, many nestled high in the mountains surrounded by lavish tropical gardens. For the energetic resident there is mountain climbing, swimming, tennis, horseback riding, snorkeling. But the going is easy here with hammocks for naps, lobster bakes on palm-shaded beaches, candlelight dinners in stately dining rooms and relaxation on romantic verandas.

Nevis is located two miles south of St. Kitts, a leisurely 45-minute ferry ride away, except Thursday, which is ship maintenance day, and the Sabbath. There is also inter-island air service.

The "Premier Off-Shore Corporate Jurisdiction"

That's the way local boosters describe the smaller of the two islands, Nevis, where its capital, Charlestown, has become a miniature international corporate business center.

About 1,200 of the island's 9,300 inhabitants live in the town, founded in 1660, a place full of ancient buildings with fanciful galleries, elaborate gingerbread woodwork, shutters, colorful hanging plants — and a small but effective cadre of international corporate and asset protection experts, both lawyers and bankers.

Based on the Island Assembly's adoption of the "Business Corporation Act of 1984," Nevis has an established, decade-long record of catering to foreign off shore corporations, with the welcome mat always out. Patterned after the extremely liberal (towards business) corporation laws of the American State of Delaware, English commercial law is also blended into the statute, so UK solicitors should have little fear about navigating its provisions.

The corporation statute allows complete confidentiality for company officials and shareholders, and there is no requirement for public disclosure of ownership, management, or financial status of a business.

Although they must pay an annual fee of US$450, "international business corporations," or "IBCs" as the law calls them, are otherwise exempt from taxes — no withholding, stamps, fees or taxes on income or foreign assets. Individually negotiated government-guaranteed tax holidays are available in writing for IBCs, provided they carry on no business locally. Official corporate start-up costs can be under US$1,000 including a minimum capitalization tax of US$200, and company formation fees of US$600. These low government levies compare very favorably with those imposed by other corporate-friendly havens, like the high-profile, high-cost Cayman Islands.

On Nevis there are no exchange controls, no tax treaties with other nations (including the U.S.), and the government will not exchange tax or other information with any other foreign revenue service or government. Principal corporate offices and records may be maintained by Nevis companies anywhere in the world the owners wish.

The Nevis corporation law is almost unique in that it contains a very modern legal provision allowing the international portability or transfer of an existing foreign company from its country of origin to the island. Known as the "redomiciling provision," this allows the smooth and instantaneous transfer of an existing American, British, Panamanian or any other nation's corporation, retention of its original name and date of incorporation — all without interruption of business activity or corporate existence. The only requirement is the amendment of existing articles of incorporation to conform with local laws.

New company creation and registration is fast in Nevis — accomplished by the simple payment of the capitalization tax and fees mentioned earlier to the Register of Corporations. Within ten days thereafter formal incorporation documents must be filed, but there are corporate service firms waiting to assist the foreign incorporator with ready-made paperwork.

Small wonder that in ten years since the law's original adoption, thousands of foreign corporate owners have established their companies in Charlestown, Nevis.

Asset Protection Trusts — A New Offshore Service

Building on their record for statutory corporate cordiality, on April 28, 1994 the Island Assembly adopted the "Nevis International Trust Ordinance," a comprehensive, clear and flexible asset protection trust (APT) law comparable to, and in many ways, better than that of the Cook Islands in the South Pacific, already well-known as an APT world center.

The new Nevis law incorporates the best features of the Cook Islands law, but in many ways is more flexible. The basic aim of the law is to permit foreign citizens to obtain protection against threats to their property and assets by transferring title to an APT established in Charlestown, Nevis.

Nevis simply is taking advantage of the fact that in many parts of the world, especially the U.S., medical, legal and professional malpractice law suits, as well as legislative and judicial imposition of no-fault personal liability on corporate officers and directors have become a nasty fact of business life. A Nevis trust places personal assets beyond the reach of potential foreign governments, litigious plaintiffs, creditors and contingent fee lawyers.

Under the new law, the Nevis judiciary will not recognize any non-domestic court orders regarding its domestic APTs. This forces a foreign judgment creditor to start all over again, retrying in Nevisian courts, with Nevisian lawyers, the original claim giving rise to the foreign judgment. A plaintiff who sues an APT must first post a US$25,000 bond with the government to cover court and others costs, before a suit will be accepted for filing. And the statute of limitations for filing legal challenges to a Nevisian APT runs out one year from the date of the trust creation. In cases where fraudulent intent on the part of the trust or its officers or beneficiaries is alleged, the law places the burden of proof on the foreign claimant.

Nevis has an established international bar and local trust experts who understand and can assist in furthering APT objectives. The APT act has proven very popular and a considerable number of trusts have been registered in Nevis.

Under the statute, basic trust documents are not required to be filed with the Nevis government, and are not a matter of public record. The only public information needed to establish an APT is a standard form or letter naming the trustee, the date of trust creation, the date of the filing, and the name of the local trust company representing the APT. The only governmental fee charged is US$200 upon filing, and an equal annual fee to maintain the filing.

Once established, the Nevis asset protection trust can consist of as little as a trust account in a local bank offering international services. Nevis has many of them, including Barclays International, Royal Bank of Canada, the Bank of Nova Scotia, the Bank of Commerce, the Nevis Co-operative Bank, the St.Kitts-Nevis-Anguilla Bank and the Nevis Bank in Charlestown. Banking hours vary but generally are 8-2 Monday through Thursday, Friday 8-5 and Saturday 8:30-11:00 a.m.

These established banks have full international departments. Most international banks offer U.S. dollar-denominated accounts that often pay better interest rates than U.S. institutions. With modern fax machines, telex, telephones, instant communications and international banking facilities, it is just as convenient to hold assets and accounts in Nevis as it is in any major financial center — and a lot safer in many personal and financial respects.

Under the provisions of the Nevis International Trust Ordinance, the same person can serve in the triple role of creator (settlor), beneficiary and protector of the APT, allowing far greater control over assets and income than U.S. domestic law permits. Generally,

Anglo-American common law forbids a settlor to create a trust for his or her own benefit.

The basic structure of a foreign asset protection trust differs little from an Anglo-American trust.

The settlor creates the trust by executing a formal declaration describing the purposes, to which he transfers assets to be administered according to the declaration by the named trustees. Usually there are three trustees named, two in the settlor's country and one in Nevis, the latter known as a "protector." Named trust beneficiaries can vary according to the settlor's estate planning objectives, and under Nevis law the settlor may be the primary beneficiary.

Nevis requires the appointment of a trust "protector" who, as the title indicates, oversees its operation to insure trust objectives are met and the law is followed. A protector does not manage the trust, but possibly can veto some actions — and Nevis allows a beneficiary to serve in the dual role as protector.

Tax and Legal Advantages for American Readers

Under U.S. tax law, foreign asset protection trusts are "tax-neutral." They are considered as domestic trusts, meaning income from the trust is treated by the Internal Revenue Service as the settlor's personal income and taxed accordingly. Because the settlor retains some control over the transfer of his assets to any foreign trust, including those established in Nevis, U.S. gift taxes can usually be avoided. Although Nevis has no estate taxes, U.S. estate taxes are imposed on the value of trust assets for the settlor's estate, but all existing exemptions for combined martial assets can be used. Foreign asset protection trusts are not subject to the 35 percent U.S. excise tax otherwise imposed on transfers of property to a "foreign person."

One device a settlor may employ to retain optimal control of assets is to form a limited partnership, making the Nevisian trust a limited partner. This allows a general managing partner/settlor to retain active control over all assets he transfers to the Nevis trust/ limited partner, while trust assets are protected from creditors or other legal assaults.

It goes without saying that assets located in the United States, title to which are held by a foreign APT, are certainly not immune from American court powers. U.S. judges have shown an increasing tendency to justify such jurisdiction, but in appropriate cases cash and certain types of portable personal property easily can be transferred physically to a foreign situs such as Nevis.

Nevis — An Obvious Choice

Aside from the undoubted protection offered by the new Nevis International Trust Ordinance, this is a small nation with great economic and political stability, a highly reputable judicial system, favorable local tax laws, no language barrier and excellent international communication and financial facilities.

These combined virtues of St. Kitts-Nevis explain why it is already taking its rightful place as a leader among other offshore financial centers with legal systems hospitable to foreign-owned asset protection trusts, among them the other Caribbean nations of the Cayman Islands, the Bahamas, Belize, the Turks and Caicos islands, the Cook Islands in the south Pacific near New Zealand, as well as Cyprus and Gibraltar in the Mediterranean.

LIECHTENSTEIN: A BIT OF UTOPIA IN OLD EUROPE

The reader may wonder what else there is to discuss, what other categories of tax havens can exist apart from those already covered. Liechtenstein logically falls in the category of foreign-source-income havens, but it has certain features that merit special attention. In addition to "standard" corporate entities, it offers certain other possibilities. These can provide many of the benefits of corporations and trusts in flexible combination, almost "to order," without many of the disadvantages of both usual forms.

There is one important caveat to keep in mind however: tax officials have a very deeply entrenched conditioned reflex of vast suspicion toward any business related to Liechtenstein. They "know" tax evasion is involved. Thus, it is better to use a Liechtensteinian entity indirectly, through at least one intermediary entity.

Another preliminary point about Liechtenstein that must be mentioned is that it is a civil law country, not a common law one. Its legal tradition has considerable Swiss-German ancestry. Thus, one would not expect trust-like entities to be possible. But, surprisingly, they are.

Unlike most other tax havens, Liechtenstein is not geographically isolated. It is a tiny principality on the banks of the Rhine, sandwiched between Austria and Switzerland. It is 16 miles long and, on the average, 3.7 miles wide. It is indirectly accessible by air. One can fly to Zurich and drive from there, or fly to any other European capital and go from there by train. The telecommunication and airmail services are excellent. Satellite direct-dialing makes telephone communication extremely easy.

Politically, Liechtenstein is a constitutional monarchy. Legal sovereignty is exercised cooperatively and wisely by a hereditary prince and a democratically elected parliament. The tiny nation is very stable and prosperous, economically and socially.

Liechtenstein is now heavily industrialized, though not long ago it was mainly agricultural. It is economically united with Switzerland. There are no customs barriers separating the two countries, and their joint currency is the rock-solid Swiss franc.

The legal code has an interesting history. It originated in Austro-Hungarian law. In 1914, local legislation amending this basic law began to be enacted, influenced by both the German legal tradition and Swiss property law. In 1926 a unique, locally originated code dealing with property of both "physical" and "juridical" persons was drawn up. This code is the third chapter of a more general locally developed code of civil law. It defines various forms of available legal personalities—the "establishment," the "foundation," the company limited by shares, and the trust—and relates the defined entities to tax law.

The most important feature of this law from a tax haven point of view is that a holding company, a company whose main purpose is the management of property and participation in other business organizations or the permanent management of holdings in other business organizations, is exempt from capital and earnings (income) taxes. Such a company pays a minimal annual tax on its total paid-up capital and reserve.

A similar tax immunity is granted to "domiciled" companies, companies defined not by reference to the specific nature of their business activities but by reference to their noninvolvement in local business. Again, a minimal tax on total paid-up capital plus reserves is payable by such companies.

Even better tax treatment is granted to "foundations," which, as against companies limited by shares (essentially standard corporations), are unique local creations. Foundations enjoy special sliding tax rates on capital. They are also exempt from the requirement of registration in the commercial register, thereby combining the advantages of privacy with that of virtually no taxes. There are two basic kinds of foundations. Family foundations are granted the tax benefits of the sliding rate scale on all capital over 10 million Swiss francs. Ordinary foundations enjoy these benefits on everything above 2 million francs.

Another advantage of Liechtenstein is its bank secrecy. In fact, Liechtenstein preserves the Swiss tradition better than Switzerland. It enforces bank secrecy laws with great severity and is in no way committed internationally to relax these laws. This, combined with its lack of exchange controls, the world's strongest currency, unique corporate and tax laws, and excellent professional services, make Liechtenstein very attractive indeed.

What merits it a special place in our considerations are the unique legal entities, the foundation and the establishment. The best way to understand the former is as a variation of the trust. It can be set up to allocate future property, generated by the investment of an original endowment, to family members or other beneficiaries. Instead of a trustee, there is a board (usually provided by a local trust company) that manages the principal fund (the endowment) and makes grants to the intended beneficiaries out of the returns on the investment, out of the principal invested, or both.

A foundation need not be limited to such trustlike functions. It can, in principle, simply manage one's estate with the distinct advantage of untaxable returns derived by a separate legal person. A foundation is not locally taxable if it is mainly involved in investment in other companies or if it has no local business involvements apart from its own management.

To return to the nature of foundations, the most prominent type of the straight family foundation, designed to support family members, provide for their education, etc. A mixed family foundation is similar, only it serves to provide for members of other families as well. The establishment of a foundation requires the separation of the endowment, constituting the foundation's property, from the estate of the settler and giving it a special name, purpose, and internal organization. It is these legal acts that give the foundation its "legal personality." Because this legal personality is not constituted by state registration, a foundation can be validly constituted in a private manner.

Apart from the foundation's property (its endowment), a basic document signed by the settler, called the memorandum of settlement, is required. It is here that privacy may be compromised because the settler must sign and the signature must be officially certified. This can be taken care of by establishing a foundation through another legal person (such as a tax haven corporation) or through a lawyer with power of attorney, thus maintaining privacy.

The memorandum of foundation must specify: (1) name of the foundation, (2) domicile of the foundation, (3) objects and purposes of the foundation, which can be quite vague and general, (4) specification of the nature and amount of the endowment, (5) organization of the foundation, and (6) how the property of the foundation is to be finally distributed, to what beneficiaries, in what manner, under what conditions, and when the foundation is to be dissolved.

Clearly, this is quite similar to a trust deed. But there is a special local flexibility: the document, apart from meeting these requirements, can contain anything one wishes. Moreover, the discussion of the constitution of the foundation can be set forth in a separate document that also specifies the articles of settlement. Such a separate document would require another certified signature of the settler.

Still another legal possibility is to have a letter of settlement, specifying the terms of the settlement and empowering the foundation board or any third party to specify details about benefits, modes of distribution, and so on. This approach is advisable only for a testamentary foundation, applying after the settler's death, for it means foregoing the power to make decisions and changes on such issues.

One can specify the beneficiaries in extreme detail, or be quite general. It is also possible to have separate by-laws supplementary to the memorandum and the articles of settlement added at any time after the foundation is set up, specifying beneficiaries and benefits. Moreover — and this is the major advantage of a foundation — the founder can at any later time change his mind about any specific provision. Unlike a trust, under which one can only send a "memorandum of wishes" to the trustees which they can follow or ignore as they choose, a foundation allows one continued control without liability for foundation debts or taxes.

The various items that must be included in the basic document defining a foundation are as follows:

Name. The name of the foundation can be virtually whatever one chooses, provided it includes no national designations and does include either **Stiftung** ("foundation") or **Familienstiftung** ("family foundation") as its last word. Moreover, the name must involve nothing illegal or immoral and should not conflict with the name of any other existing foundation. Similarly, if one wants to set up a business foundation, it is impermissible to call it a family foundation, and vice versa. It is possible to establish a family foundation with business involvements as a subsidiary function if one so chooses, but the original and principal purpose of a foundation whose name includes "family foundation" must be the support of one's family. Still, if unforeseen circumstances make the primary purpose obsolete, no change of name is required.

The Purpose of the Foundation. This is generally similar for all: the administration of property and the distribution of income derived from that property. It can involve accumulation of property by self-insurance. The statement of purpose cannot include profit making as an independent objective. This does not mean that a foundation is barred from making, accumulating, and reinvesting profits for a given time — but this is the means, not the end. The end of a foundation, its proper and legitimate purpose, is to support beneficiaries. The point is that the foundation is trustlike in having a limited perpetuity period, at the end of which money must be distributed. It cannot go on making money indefinitely.

Apart from this general consideration, the statement of purpose can be as vague and general or as specific as desired. The details can be left to the foundation board, and when it comes to investment policies, the wisest course is to leave this to the managers. To formulate a business policy for decisions that may take place twenty-five years after the settler's death would be extremely unwise. What is important is to have some basic guidelines and competent managers.

The distribution of the foundation proceeds should be as specific as possible. If one wants to take care of his great-grandchildren yet unborn, a general description of this category of individuals is needed. One simple possibility is having a maintenance foundation paying a specified portion of its income to specified individuals without any extra set conditions or purposes. If, however, conditions or purposes are spelled out, they must be both legal and moral.

The Capital Requirement. This is the strictest requirement of all. Capital must be irreversibly transferred to the foundation. If the assets do not consist of cash, one must provide proof by competent and independent assessment that their total value does not fall below the minimum paid-in capital limit. Moreover, if the assets include IOUs, these IOUs can later be legally enforced on the settler by the beneficiaries.

There is a bright side to the irreversible alienation. The foundation's capital is not any longer the settler's, and his creditors cannot make claims against it. Nor can the creditors of the foundation make claims against the settler. This may be important if one is the sole beneficiary of his foundation and he goes bankrupt. He can still enjoy the fruits of the foundation without any creditor access to the property; at most, they could make claims against benefits from the foundation, but not the foundation's assets.

The Organization of the Foundation. This constitutes the specification of foundation governing bodies. The settlor can appoint them directly or appoint someone, such as the executor of his will, to appoint them. The first element is the "supreme authority." This is the settlor. He determines the use and ultimate allocation of the foundation property. He appoints the original board members and can retain the right of dismissing them at will and appointing replacements. He establishes the beneficiaries, decides the distribution of benefits, etc. He can even maintain the right to revoke the foundation, amend its memorandum, add or delete new by-laws, or finally liquidate, dissolve, or merge the foundation with remaining property reverting to himself, to the beneficiaries, or to whomever he chooses. These extreme powers of "legislation" allow him to maintain day-to-day control over both the use of the money and its ultimate enjoyment, spared from the liabilities inherent in the normal management of personal property. He can make all investment decisions himself, make himself sole beneficiary, and still not be personally liable for taxes on the income the foundation earns or for whatever debts it may incur. Thus, one can have the advantages of a corporation coupled with those of a trust, and with complete privacy.

The second element of foundation organization is the board. The terms of settlement of the foundation must specify how the board is appointed, how its members are dismissed, how a vacated position of a resigned board member is refilled. These decisions can be transferred to the board itself, reserved to the settler, or vested in whatever third party the settler chooses, including the beneficiaries. In the latter case, one must be specific about whether or not one of the beneficiaries can be appointed or elected a member of the board by other beneficiaries, if this is permitted, the method of doing so must be spelled out.

There is a legal presumption in foundation law that if authority to nominate board members and the authority to dismiss them are not explicitly separated, these two powers are united in one person or body, but the settler can leave to himself the right of dismissal and allow the board (including the dismissed member in his last act of involvement with the foundation) to elect the replacement member.

Obviously, board members cannot be nominated without their consent, and they can resign at any time. However, their initial consent to serve implies that they have to continue on the board until replaced. Alternatively, one can allow the board to act in the absence of a resigned member.

The functions of the board are similar to those of a trustee of a trust or, more accurately, to that of a corporate board of directors. They decide on the administration of investments and the distribution of benefits. The settler can, however, restrict the board's range of powers as he thinks best.

Board decisions are put into effect by majority vote, binding the minority, but even this "normal" feature can be altered in the terms of settlement. Any way one does it, though, the board's functions are administration and management. Any employee empowered to manage any part of the foundation's activities is considered to be acting on powers delegated to him by the board, which can be revoked at any time by dismissing and, possibly, replacing him.

Members of the board are bound by "proper business practice," and they are liable for any default on this practice or any breach of responsibility. They must act to the best of their knowledge and ability in their efforts to implement the settler's instructions concerning distribution of benefits. It is normally presumed that the board does not nominate beneficiaries. But one can give them this right, or, as is more common, designate beneficiaries on a group basis (e.g., "all my grandsons"), with the board specifying the individual beneficiaries. This power of designation becomes larger if the original specification is vague. Does one's "family" include an illegitimate son? The illegitimate daughter of the cousin of one's mother-in-law? If a settler were to be so unfortunately inexplicit as to what he meant by "family," and he is no longer around to ask, the board will have to decide to the best of its knowledge.

The board's primary responsibility is to the settler. But he can transfer to it his power of supreme authority, transfer it to someone else, or simply die. In the latter case, it is the public supervisory authorities of Liechtenstein and the foundation's beneficiaries to whom the board becomes responsible. If one so wishes, the terms of settlement may allow the beneficiaries to sue the board collectively, or its individual members, for not respecting the rights and benefits granted them by the terms of settlement. Similarly, anyone who can prove a legitimate interest in the foundation's property can lodge a complaint with the authorities against the board for failing to act on the settlement terms or for violating the purposes of the foundation.

A third foundation official that may but need not be appointed by the settler is a custodian. He can be given the power, say, of supervising payments of benefits as to amount, type, and recipients.

Or he can be appointed to take care of the money due untraceable beneficiaries, in which case it is his duty to manage the money properly.

A fourth body, optimal for board supervision, is a body of auditors. They, too, are not legally required. One can decide if such a body should exist, how its members are to be selected, what its range of responsibility should be, and so on.

Another optional body is that of collators. They can handle the function of nominating beneficiaries within the limited range the settler prescribes. They can also be empowered to implement the settler's general instructions concerning mode, time, and conditions of benefit payments. In this case, the board is left only with the duty of management and administration.

Of course, the more optional bodies employed, the greater the defense provided for the beneficiaries—and the larger the operating costs of the foundation. Thus, one's choice in these matters should balance up the risks to beneficiaries against the costs of maintenance.

There are some fixed statutory requirements a foundation board must satisfy: keeping normal accounts and issuing statements of liabilities and assets and of profits and losses on fixed specific dates. This duty can be transferred to an accountancy firm the board nominates. If one so decides, he can retain the power to inspect the accounts and to make decisions based on them. Alternatively, some independent party may supervise the board to guarantee due performance. Thus, the beneficiaries or any subgroup of them could be granted the right to audit the accounts and act on the basis of the audit.

A foundation can be revoked before registration (if such is necessary) or before documentation is completed, and if it is testamentary, any time before the settler's death. If the terms of settlement so specify, one can leave the right of revocation to himself, in the same way he can explicitly empower himself to modify the terms of settlement. The right of revocation can also be left to one or more heirs.

There is a legal distinction between the two basic types of revocation. A foundation revoked before full documentation or registration has taken place is revoked "on the grounds of insufficiency of intention" as a special case of "insufficiency of contract." This is known as revocation **ex tunc,** or retroactive revocation. It legally cancels the existence of the foundation before its inception. In this case, no claims can be made against the foundation; all liabilities incurred by it become the settler's personal liabilities.

The second type of revocation is that of a fully constituted foundation. This is known as **ex nunc** ("from now") revocation. All rights and liabilities incurred by the foundation are then valid, and it cannot properly be liquidated without full discharge, to the extent of its existing assets, of all liabilities. The only exception here is that in the terms of settlement one can provide for an automatic and immediate and even retroactive expiry of the benefits granted to beneficiaries.

Thus, a foundation can cease to exist because it is revoked by whoever has the right under its terms to revoke it. Of course, it can be liquidated once it has accumulated money for its perpetuity period, distributed all of it, and discharged all its debts. It can also be annulled by the government if the object of the foundation becomes unattainable or unworthy of pursuit (e.g., the beneficiaries have all died); if the foundation cannot act any more to achieve these aims due to insolvency; or if the terms of settlement are legally defective beyond cure. The state supervisory authorities impose and execute annulment, but have no further right to supervise or inspect in any way the day-to-day activities of the foundation unless the settler specifically grants them this right.

The concept of "beneficiary" is further refinable. One can separate **beneficiaries** in law — those granted the right to legally enforce on the board the benefits they are due — from the **beneficiaries in fact**, those not granted enforcement rights. Similarly, one can nominate **conditional beneficiaries**, those entitled to benefits only if certain conditions obtained as spelled out in the terms of settlement (e.g., other beneficiaries are dropped, a certain age is reached). Conditional beneficiaries have to agree in writing to accept the status of beneficiaries and, when the time comes, provide proper proof that whatever conditions were stipulated for benefits have been fulfilled. Unconditional beneficiaries are assumed to have agreed to receive benefits.

One can empower the board to revoke beneficiary status if certain conditions are fulfilled. But the board has to exercise this power within five years of the event that constitutes satisfaction of the condition. Alternatively, one can set as a condition that, say, a beneficiary must have no criminal record of a certain kind, in which case the time limitation does not apply.

As for oneself being a beneficiary, there can be circumstances under which a court may order a foundation to support the settler when it is proved that due to the establishment of the foundation he became incapable of paying his own debts. This implies, in effect, that one cannot abuse the foundation's status as a legal person and his power as supreme authority to establish a foundation from borrowed money, name himself sole beneficiary, and then declare bankruptcy.

If the mode of paying benefits is not specified, then they are assumed to be in cash. If they are supposed to amount to a specified fixed sum per year without specifying that this sum actually will be given each year, it is possible to discharge them in one lump payment that can be proved to be equal to the purchase of an annuity that would yield the specified annual sum.

Beneficiaries can go into court to defend their rights, as in a case where the board treats differently beneficiaries that are not differently treated in the terms of settlement. There is a legal presumption that equal benefits are to be given to all beneficiaries unless the settler has explicitly indicated otherwise. Also, the board cannot nominate beneficiaries if not explicitly given the right to do so, or if they have a closed list of beneficiaries, or if a body of collators exists for the purpose.

If no specification of either beneficiaries or of a way to nominate them exists, the settler and his legal heirs after him are legally assumed to be sole beneficiaries according to the following rules: If one's children are appointed beneficiaries, the law considers them all to be his issue otherwise entitled to be his heirs. If his spouse is nominated as beneficiary, his surviving wife is deemed legally to be beneficiary if she has not remarried. (Remember, this happens when one does not stipulate to the contrary.) When no beneficiaries have been nominated and the settler is dead, the Liechtensteinian inheritance law applying to heirs when there is no will would specify beneficiaries.

It is important to understand the way Liechtensteinian foundation law works as exemplified by the second rule. It is primarily a system of presumptions, not rigid restrictions. These presumptions apply when one does not specify something explicitly and do not apply when one's specific formulation excludes them. Where no presumptions exist, one must make a specification; otherwise, the foundation will be inoperative. For instance, one must spell out for each beneficiary (or for all of them as a group) whether or not benefit claims are to be made against the foundation investment returns or the original endowment. Otherwise, the board makes the decision, however arbitrarily.

To avoid the abuse of foundations there exist some statutory requirements that are inflexible. Among them is the rule that creditors take precedence over beneficiaries. A foundation cannot legally pay benefits and avoid paying debts. Creditors, naturally, have the right to sue the board for failing to comply with this requirement. Also, there exists a legal requirement that whoever is granted by the terms of settlement the power to dissolve the foundation also has the power to make a partial distribution to the beneficiaries and, thereby, reduce their rights.

It is easy to see that this system of presumptions and rules, combined with a settler's very wide powers and the fact that board powers are, essentially, residual, make the foundation much more flexible than corporations and trusts. One can reserve all powers and not be bound by the inflexible powers of a trustee or board of directors. Moreover, one can enjoy the "alter ego" of a legal entity without any public scrutiny such as that resulting from incorporation. A corporation must be registered; a foundation, like a trust, can be constituted with complete privacy and can operate with truly confidential, impenetrable numbered bank accounts.

As good as it is, the foundation is not the optimal Liechtensteinian profit-making entity. The prize in this category goes to the establishment.

Unlike the foundation, the establishment exists for economic purposes and not family or other "supporting" ends. It is a corporate body, with its own assets serving as sole backing for its own liabilities. It has its own internal organization and its own basic initial capital, allowing it to pursue lasting economic aims with no perpetuity period.

An establishment has a founder, similar to a foundation settler. The founder is a legal personality, not necessarily a physical one. He can be one's agent or attorney. He can also be the owner of a certificate on which there is no name, like a bearer share. The founder must sign the articles of incorporation, and his signature must be authenticated by a notary.

The articles of incorporation must specify:

Name of the Establishment. This can be any fancy designation that includes no national names or references to Liechtenstein or any sort of subtitle. It must include the word **Anstalt** ("establishment"), and it must not be misleading as to the nature of the foundation or immoral or illegal.

The name may include two parts, one of general application, which can be used by many establishments simultaneously (such as "establishment for timber processing"), the other specific, original, or descriptive. This second part can be used only by the originating establishment, which thereby gains exclusive right to it.

The limitations on names implies, of course, that establishments, as against foundations and trusts, and like corporations, must be registered. It is up to the registrar to guarantee that the name satisfies all legal requirements and does not violate any prior right of use. Failure to register may incur serious penalties under the law.

Purpose of the Establishment. This can be, but need not be, private profit, as well as public utility. It can be stated narrowly or broadly. Any later change in purpose requires an amendment of the articles. Of course, the purpose must be both legal and moral; failing that, it is assumed that the establishment never existed as a legal person. If it becomes legally established, it has all the legal rights of a person to property, name, and honor (i.e., it can sue for libel and slander). Dissolution on the grounds of immoral or illegal purpose, however, is a **retroactive** annihilation of this status of legal personality. It requires the decision of an administrative tribunal following an administrative complaint or a trial. When such an unhappy event occurs, the court is empowered to suspend all the activities of the establishment, to confiscate all its property, and to use it to pay the establishment's creditors. Any remaining assets can be confiscated by the government.

Dissolution can also take place when the original goals of an establishment were not illegal or immoral but the establishment operates outside its allowed zone of activity as delimited by its articles. In this case, the state can take over the management of the establishment to pursue the original goals, and it can also, in the case of serious trouble, confiscate whatever remains of the establishment's property after debts have been paid.

Capitalization. There is a minimum paid-in capital requirement of 30,000 Swiss francs if there are no participation shares or associates' rights. Otherwise, the minimum is 50,000 Swiss francs. The appropriate minimum can, if cash, be proved by bank certificate. If the minimum is not met by a cash deposit in a bank but is in other forms, evidence of its assessed value by recognized competent assessors must be provided.

If participation shares are included, these can have a par value or represent a proportion of ownership. In the latter case, a specific, explicit statement to that effect must be included in the articles. Also, all shares must be fully paid-in, registered in a special ledger, and a specific body, as indicated in the articles, must be authorized to allow or disallow their transfer. All these complications can be avoided if the establishment has a single owner, the founder. Then he has the right to allocate profits as he likes, as well as the rights to change the articles when he sees fit, appoint and dismiss directors, etc. His legal heir inherits his founder's rights.

When ownership is divided among shareholders, founder's rights are conferred upon the general meeting of shareholders. Alternatively, the articles may specify that the board of directors inherits from the general meeting part or all of its powers. Again, it is assumed, unless specifically excluded by the articles, that only beneficiaries of the establishment are members of the general meeting and that they all have equal voting rights. But the articles may explicitly allow for nonbeneficiary founders with voting rights, or for unequal voting rights.

Organization. The articles must specify the operating organs of the establishment. The founder, as supreme authority, or alternatively, in the case of several founders and divided ownership, the general assembly, has already been discussed. Another indispensable organ is the board of directors. This can include any number of legal persons having the right to represent the establishment to third parties and sign contracts and commitments in its name, either individually, collectively, or in any combination provided by the articles. The assumption is that the term of appointment is three years, but the articles can specify any period and can allow for the firing and replacement of any director at any time by the supreme authority. There is a presumption that when the number of directors has been reduced by firing, resignation, or mortality, the board can continue business as usual with a reduced number.

There is one inflexible requirement: There must be at least one Liechtensteinian citizen resident director. He can, however, be a proxy supplied by a local representative. The names and addresses of all directors, managers, and those proxies allowed to sign for the company, must be entered in the government company register.

The board may act within the limits determined by the founder in the establishment articles and usually is assumed to have the right to hire employees for the establishment. The board is presumed, unless otherwise stated in the articles, to act collectively, and if individual directors are allowed to act individually under certain circumstances, the validity of such action is lost if objected to by another director. On the other hand, once the board signs a contract with the intention of binding the establishment, such legal binding exists, even if the establishment is not explicitly mentioned. The board is bound by standard business practice and responsible to the supreme authority. Its normal responsibilities include appointment and dismissal of staff, implementation of the founder's instructions, organization and expansion of the activities of the establishment within the limits set by the articles and by law, keeping complete accounts and records, and submission of annual reports to the supreme authority to permit it to reach independent conclusions.

Being a member of the board imposes certain duties on an individual. He cannot start a business competing with the establishment or be involved with one unless already so involved when he took his office, this fact being known to the establishment founder at the time. In this case, it is presumed that he is free of the normal obligation not to work for the competition by virtue of special permission from the founder. In case of violation of this conflict-of-interest principle, both immediate dismissal by the founder, without compensation, as well as a legal case for damages against the offending director is possible. It is possible, for instance, to demand that he transfer the advantages of a deal he made for himself to the establishment or give it whatever benefits he received from such a deal. But such action can be taken only within a year of discovery of the improper behavior of the offending board member.

The right to represent the company is transferable from the board to specific managers, each within the domain allocated to him as his responsibility by the board. The board's method of operation, meeting, reaching decisions, and signing in the name of the establishment has to be specified in the articles.

Methods of Accounting, Handling Balance Sheets, and Giving Notices to Relevant Parties. A body of auditors can be included in the organization, authorized to ascertain that the balance sheets, inventories, and profit and loss accounts agree with the books, that the books are properly kept, and that the information in them is accurate. It is their duty to report to the supreme authority (founder) any discrepancy or irregularity. Bookkeeping, annual balance sheets, annual statements of assets and liabilities, and copies of correspondence are required by law for all corporations and corporate-like business organizations, including establishments. The auditors may, additionally, represent the establishment to third parties unless they are explicitly denied this right in the articles. They can be appointed, for only one year at a time, and reappointed only twice, a maximum of three years altogether.

The articles must also comply with statutory requirements for giving notices. If the establishment deals locally, all communications must be published in the official gazette. If not, a legal representative (a Liechtensteinian citizen and resident) has to post them on a court notice board.

Provisions for Liquidation and Dissolution of the Establishment. These are restricted by law and must involve giving notice to creditors through a public notice in the publication organ specified in the articles. Within six months, if all liabilities have been duly discharged, the name of the establishment is struck off the books. If the liquidator finds out that liabilities exceed assets, all activities must be suspended and the courts informed about the bankruptcy. In the period of liquidation, the establishment is still a legal person, but the words "in liquidation" must be included in its name. Its liquidators gain the rights of directors and are bound with respect to the founder, his heirs, and creditors in the same way normal board members are, though they are exempted from the prohibition against working for competing firms or competing with the establishment that is imposed on board members.

Liquidation also involves its accounting counterpart. Liquidation balance sheets, indicating all liabilities discharged, debts paid, assets sold, and cancellation of registration effected must be submitted to the founder. During the period of liquidation, no dividends to shareholders are payable. The books of the liquidated establishment must be preserved for ten years, and anybody with valid claims after liquidation is completed will be granted permission to inspect them. Such claims become valid against the legal successors of the establishment, those who collected what was left of the assets after all preceding debts have been repaid.

An establishment must be registered by the state. Costs for this are information duty, registration fees, and variable stamp duties.

If an establishment trades locally, it must pay a capital tax plus a profits tax. The profits tax ranges from 5 percent to 12 percent, and within these limits the rate is one-half the ratio of the net profit to the total capital. For example, if the profits are 10 percent of capital, a 5 percent profits tax is due. If an establishment trades only outside Liechtenstein, its sole liability is an annual capital tax. If ownership is divided into shares, 3 percent of dividends paid is taken as a coupon tax — another good reason to set up an establishment without shares.

The possibility of taxes because of either local involvement or divided ownership implies the general necessity of annual tax returns of profit and loss to show whether or not an establishment has any tax liabilities apart from the basic standard capital taxes. All these monies are official payments.

It is hard to establish general figures for annual maintenance and management because there are so many variables. Individual circumstances will dictate whether or not a Liechtensteinian establishment is worth setting up.

Apart from the foundation and the establishment, simple incorporation in Liechtenstein may offer benefits similar to those that can be obtained in other no-tax-on-foreign-income havens. These advantages should be considered carefully, since Liechtenstein offers Swiss-type bank facilities, monetary freedom, and privacy. On the other hand, one should bear in mind that a Liechtensteinian corporation is much more suspect in the eyes of tax authorities than, say, a Hong Kong corporation.

In Liechtenstein, ownership of a corporation can be divided not only into shares but into fractions, or quotas, and the relevant documents must specify the total sum of capital and reserves.

Division into fractions or quotas simply means that each certificate represents a percentage of the corporation instead of a fixed number of shares. For example, it may be for 10 percent of the capital, and would simply state on the certificate that it represents 10 percent ownership of the corporation. Shares can be without par value, and bearer shares are also allowed. The articles of incorporation can allow conversion of one kind of share to another, as well as for variable capital, within certain limits. The latter possibility requires the use of shares rather than certificates of ownership of fractions or quotas. Further, Liechtenstein allows the articles of incorporation to specify the proportion of bearer shares to be paid-in, subject to a legal minimum of 50 percent.

The articles of incorporation have to specify the usual things: corporate name and registered office address, capitalization (amount of initial capital, division into shares, nature of shares, nature and amount of paid-up capital, and the amount to be paid-up for each share), method of calling the general meeting of shareholders, governing bodies of the corporation and the manner in which members are appointed and dismissed to and from positions on them, and the form of communication of notices to shareholders and third parties.

Apart from these standard clauses, one could add extra provisions that may relate to the value of non-cash contributions, special privileges of founding shareholders as against those who buy in later, and provisions relating to special amendments needed to general corporate law in its application to the particular corporation (e.g., how articles can be amended, how changes of authorized capital are to be executed, how mergers are to be performed). Additional restrictions, such as a built-in limitation on the life of the corporation, limits on the transfer of registered shares, differentiation in the voting power of certain kinds of shares, etc., can also be included.

An extra flexibility is offered by the fact that local law allows two forms of incorporation, so as to permit appeal to public finance in the process of formation itself. The first mode, "simultaneous" incorporation, involves the standard procedures. The founders sign a memorandum declaring incorporation of the company, sanction the articles, confirm their acceptance of all shares, and pay for them.

The second mode is "successive" incorporation. Here the founders need not subscribe to all shares, but merely to some of them. They lay down and sign the articles, subscribe to their part of the share issue, and offer the remaining shares to the public. After all shares have been subscribed to, a general meeting of all shareholders is convened to decide on the appointment of officers and the confirmation of the articles. Successive incorporation requires a prospectus specifying all relevant details concerning the articles, times for subscription and payment, subscription offices, the issue price of shares, and how much has to be paid-in before the first general meeting of shareholders.

Under either method, incorporation requires a minimum paid-in capital of 50,000 Swiss francs. Registered shares can be subscribed to by a mere 20 percent premium, as against the already mentioned 50 percent premium on bearer shares. As usual, the difference between the issue price of a share and the premium is a liability of the shareholder to the corporation.

In an instance in which the paid-in capital includes noncash assets, or in which some shareholders are granted certain special privileges by the articles, the founders must publish a written report setting forth the cash value of the noncash contributions and/or why privileges have been granted. These reports must be open to public inspection in any subscription office, because when an individual subscribes he is entitled to know why other shareholders will have privileges he will not have, what they are, and how noncash payments are valued. Moreover, any group of shareholders controlling 10 percent of the shares is entitled to enforce expert evaluation of the noncash assets as well as independent evaluation of any special privileges. If this right is invoked, both reports would be discussed in the next general shareholders' meeting, and if they are rejected by majority vote, the shareholders are entitled to a refund. Any such peculiarities as noncash contributions and special privileges to special shareholders require the approval of three-fourths of the shareholders.

Only when this sequential process is completed, all shares subscribed, all special features are approved, and officers appointed, is registration in the commercial register effected. Registration cannot be accomplished unless the minimum paid-in capital of 50,000 Swiss francs is fully certified by bank documents or assessment of noncash contributions or both.

Sequential incorporation allows one to solicit strangers to participate in a corporation. Another possibility for financing comes from the right Liechtensteinian companies have to float bonds to shareholders and the general public. Bonds may entitle their owner to the right to buy future shares when issued, but they do not carry voting rights.

While Liechtensteinian corporations are flexible, the flexibility has its own built-in restrictions. Variable capital is allowed, but it is only allowed with registered shares. Increasing capital requires selling more shares. Decreasing capital requires buying up shares and canceling them. The maximum capital cannot be more than ten times the minimum, as specified in the articles, and must be specified as well. Any act of purchasing and canceling shares requires a liquidation balance sheet showing that after repayment the liabilities of the corporation are still covered by its remaining assets, reserves, and capital. The specific mode of buying shares back must be set forth in the articles.

Another possibility for handling repurchased shares is to "freeze" them for awhile and resell them later. Since such "frozen" shares have neither voting nor dividend rights, this is equivalent to canceling and reissuing the same shares — within the limits of variability of capital allowed by the articles. Another restriction is that if the minimum authorized capital of the corporation is higher than the legal minimum of paid-in capital (more than 50,000 francs), there is a statutory requirement of a yearly accumulation of 10 percent of net profits in a reserve fund until the minimum is reached. This 10 percent is, therefore, not distributable as dividends.

Liechtensteinian corporations can be liquidated in a number of ways: by court action due to illegal or immoral operations or bankruptcy; in accordance with specifications in the articles; and by a majority vote to liquidate in a general shareholders' meeting.

A corporation must keep books, and its board must submit annual balance sheets to the general meeting within six months of the end of the accounting year. For a corporation with more than one million Swiss francs' capitalization and for any corporation with bonds outstanding, balance sheets and profit and loss accounts must be publicly published.

Apart from the minimum capitalization requirement, the cost of incorporation depends on the capital involved. On top of this, there are small stamp duties and certification costs.

As for maintenance, there is an annual capital tax on the total capital (with a minimum tax of 1,000 Swiss francs). If a company is either a holding company or a domiciliary company—that is, if it specializes in holding investment portfolios or if it operates only outside Liechtenstein—no further taxes apply. Local operations, however, involve some additional taxes. There is an earnings tax and a higher capital tax. All companies, including domiciliary and holding companies, pay a 3 percent coupon tax on dividends and a 3 percent tax on interest paid to bondholders. And every company must annually file with the government a balance sheet, a profit and loss account, and details concerning the coupon tax. Of course, to these taxes must be added the expenses associated with paying board members, company officers, and so on.

Liechtenstein is outstanding among civil law countries when it comes to trusts. It is an exception to the rule that civil law nations either do not allow trusts or, if they do, the trusts they allow are less than desirable.

In Liechtenstein, trust law considers a trust to be a contract between the trustor and the trustee. It is a private contract that does not require registration with a public registrar and is thus a very private affair. The trust property is whatever estate, funds, or other property one allocates to the trust, and it can be described in the trust instruments in as great or as little detail as one might like. It contains, of course, the principal plus accumulated revenue of investment returns and/or compensation for damages incurred to property. The trust, in view of its private nature, is **not** a separate legal entity, and does not have limited liability. The trustee is personally or corporately liable for debts (not including taxes) incurred by the trust property he manages, and he has the right of legal recourse against both the trustor and the beneficiaries, unless the trust instrument explicitly excludes this right.

The trust property is managed, legally, under the title of the trustee, in accordance with his appointment by the trustor. The trustee is entitled to a salary for his services and reimbursement of all expenses incurred by him in managing the trust and for damages that might be incurred by his property by the trust property.

An advantage of Liechtensteinian trusts is that they can operate under the laws of, say, the Cayman Islands or Hong Kong, to be applied locally by Liechtensteinian courts. The major drawback is the fact that the trust is not a legal person, and thus its income is taxed to the trustor. To avert this, another special Liechtensteinian entity exists: the trust enterprise.

The trust enterprise is a legal person, managed by a trustee. It must be registered in the commercial registry as a "registered trust." This is in line with the fact that legal entities can **usually** be formed only through the state. Private agreements usually cannot create legal entities (Liechtensteinian foundations excluded).

The corporate document of the trust enterprise, the trust statement, must specify all that is usual for corporations: the name of the trust, the registered office address, the perpetuity period (not limited by law), the purposes and objects of the trust enterprise, and a statement of limited liability. Apart from the trust statement, trust articles are needed, specifying the amount and nature of funds (with a separate list of items), the number of trustees and the method of appointing and replacing them.

The minimum capital required of a trust enterprise must be fully paid-in. As against common law trusts, the purpose of a trust enterprise can be business, family support, or philanthropy. The trustees are legally free to make investment decisions in accordance with whatever provisions are specified in the trust articles. Their expenses and salaries are paid out of the trust enterprise's revenues unless the articles otherwise specify. The trust enterprise, being a legal personality, covers its liabilities through its assets alone. The trustor, trustee(s), and beneficiaries become legally liable only due to some violation of the trust articles or through illegal exploitation of the trust.

Trust entities are taxed like other corporate entities in Liechtenstein. If all income comes from abroad, a minimal annual capital tax is due. Local activities are penalized by the local taxes mentioned above. Finally, trust enterprises, like private trusts, can be made subject to any other country's laws, with local courts applying them.

The great flexibility of Liechtensteinian corporate and trust laws, the various tax advantages, the absolute privacy available, the monetary freedom, and the soundness of the Swiss franc together explain why 20,000 companies are registered in Liechtenstein. Since each of them pays the government a minimum of 1,000 Swiss francs a year, this adds up to very important revenues for a country with but 20,000 citizens. It is unlikely, to say the least, that this paradise for wise investors will disappear any time soon.

SWITZERLAND: MONEY HAVEN BUT NOT A TAX HAVEN

The reader may have wondered why Switzerland and Liechtenstein are not considered together in a chapter on European havens. The reason is simple: Switzerland is **not** a tax haven.

This may come as a shock. Many people think "tax haven" means a numbered account with a Swiss bank. This is a fallacy. Such a conclusion is liable to be greeted with considerable skepticism. So let us detail why Switzerland is not a tax haven and why those seeking a tax haven should stay out of the Swiss Alps, and the one major use that Switzerland has for the individual investor.

Why is Switzerland so widely considered a tax haven? To begin with, there is its remarkable internal and international political stability. It has been a most successfully neutral country in many European wars and both world wars, so in modern times, its economy has never been devastated by war's destruction. Also, it is a basically free enterprise country with little government regulation and economic control and relatively low taxes. Its banks have had a tradition of inviolate secrecy, stability, and reliability. Its currency, the Swiss franc, has a very good reputation and is very strong and stable.

The country is geographically in the center of Europe, where major continental roads from east, west, north, and south intersect. Its internal roads and railways are excellent, and all its transportation services are punctual. It is also accessible by river barge directly from the sea. Airline service is tops, and telecommunications are the very best available. Needless to say, professional services are of the very highest quality and reliability.

As we have noted, Switzerland is politically stable, as is well attested to by its history, legal structure, and present socioeconomic situation. Its basic constitution, enacted in 1848 and slightly revised in 1974, gives the country a confederation system. It has 123 articles, specifying rights and duties of both citizens and the government. The twenty-five cantons (states) have inalienable constitutional rights that cannot be usurped by the federal government. There is a seven-man national cabinet, nationally elected. The foreign policy has for centuries been peaceful neutrality concerning all international conflicts. The legal system is grounded in the civil law tradition.

Switzerland is multilingual; German, French, Italian, and Romansch are official languages. German is the most widespread tongue, having a variety of local dialects. The business community is widely conversant with English.

Both the federal government and the cantons as well as the municipalities tax separately, with cantonal taxes the heaviest. Companies are taxed both on their profits and on their capital by the federal government and the cantons, as well as the "community."

Company taxes are not flat but progressive. The brackets depend not on the total volume of a company's profits, but as in Liechtenstein, on the "profit intensity," the ratio of profits to capital. All taxes on worldwide income add up to usually 25-35 percent. Switzerland is clearly no tax haven. The individual income tax is also progressive and is levied on the total of one's worldwide income.

There is special tax treatment for holding companies. This special treatment applies also to ordinary companies to the extent that they operate as holding companies and derive income from merely "Passive" sources (dividends, interest, etc.). Such tax exemptions are highly limited, however; for instance, they do not apply to interest from loans and royalties from leases paid by companies in which one has stock ownership. Still, a pure holding company pays no federal income tax, only a federal capital tax on the value of share capital and a similar canton capital tax.

Domiciliary companies, those based in Switzerland but doing business only outside the country, have been granted exemptions from local income taxes by some cantons. The applicable taxes are reduced cantonal capital tax, federal income tax, and federal capital tax.

Apart from these taxes, one has to consider a turnover tax of 4-5 percent against payment on the internal delivery of goods by a wholesaler. This can be avoided if the goods are immediately exported or if they are merely in transit. There is a similar tax on imported goods, on top of the import duty.

Even with a purely investment-holding company, there is one huge liability: a 35 percent withholding tax imposed on dividends paid to foreign stockholders. It applies indiscriminately to dividends, interest on bonds, and interest on bank deposits; only royalties are exempted.

Might not the double-taxation agreement between the United States and Switzerland allow one to consider Switzerland as a base for a holding company? On the surface, this seems to be so. The agreement reduces the U.S. withholding tax on dividends to 15 percent. However, the Swiss government has taken special measures to restrict the usability of the agreement for tax minimization purposes. If, say, more than 50 percent of the profits of a Swiss company derived from U.S. sources are paid to aliens, no withholding tax benefits can be claimed. One may think that the way out is not to distribute to himself dividends from his Swiss company and instead reinvest all profits. However, another law requires a company to pay as dividends at least

25 percent of the gross income derived from tax-relief benefits. Thus, there are narrow limits to using the agreement.

On top of these disadvantages, Swiss incorporation is expensive. There is a stamp duty of 2 percent on authorized capital.

If all this is not enough, neither the joint stock company nor the private limited liability company, the two business entities most readily available in Switzerland, offers any particular tax advantages.

There are some excellent Swiss banking services, investment management services, and insurance products and this is the area in which you can put Switzerland to use.

The Swiss Franc — Pillar of Financial Stability

The Swiss franc is more than a paper currency — it is backed by gold. Swiss law requires a minimum 40% gold reserve for every franc in circulation. Actual gold reserves amount to 56% and are valued at the old Central Bank price of US$42.22 per ounce. At today's market price the actual gold reserves would amount to many times the amount of Swiss francs in circulation. There is no other currency in this position.

On April 18, 1999, Swiss voters gave their qualified approval to a new constitution which contains a provision effectively ending the statutory gold backing of the Swiss franc. Some 57% of voters approved the overhaul of the 125 year old constitution, or 12 of Switzerland's 26 cantons. (A majority of both votes and cantons is needed to pass.) Among other proposals enshrined into law by the referendum's results were the right to strike and equal rights for the handicapped.

Under the old constitution, every Swiss franc in circulation had to be backed by 40% in gold reserves. Using the artificial price of Sfr. 4,596 per kilogram as mandated by that Constitution, Switzerland's gold reserves of some Sfr. 12 billion were just more than enough to cover the statutory level at 43%. Applying current market prices, however, gold reserves of Sfr. 43 bn significantly exceed currency in circulation at about 130%.

In the new constitution, specifically Article 99, paragraph 3, it merely states that the Swiss National Bank accumulates reserves, a portion of which shall be in gold. With the independence of the SNB now also newly guaranteed in the constitution (paragraph 2 of Art. 99), the SNB can choose what portion of reserves to hold in gold. A specific level of gold relative to the currency is no longer mandated.

Switzerland's political and economic stability has contributed to the Swiss franc's superior level of performance. The Swiss franc has steadily increased in value against all other currencies. Long term, the Swiss franc has been the world's best investment currency.

There is no question that the Swiss franc has been the best managed currency in the world. Others have been rising stars — the German mark and the Japanese yen for example — but they rose as part of a speculation on the rapid growth of their underlying economies, not because the currency was well managed. And they didn't remain rising stars. The yen has been affected by severe Japanese economic problems, and the mark by the high cost of reunification of Germany — a cost that may go on for decades yet.

Historically, the Japanese yen has been a heavy loser of monetary value against the Swiss franc. The Japanese paper and debt crisis may turn out to be worse than the American one.

The German cost of reunification has already been vastly more than the politicians estimated. Taxes and deficit spending are sharply on the rise. The reasons are understandable, but understanding doesn't change the economic result and the effect on the strength of the mark, which may become a far weaker currency than many economists expect.

For many, Swiss interest rates seem low, yet viewed historically, the total long term return has run higher than 10% when measured in U.S. dollars. So many investors make the mistake of comparing yields expressed only in the currency of the investment, and fail to calculate the relative yields including the currency fluctuations.

The Swiss Insurance Industry

Insurance companies belong to one of the most important sectors of the economy in Switzerland. It is also extremely conservative and safe. In 130 years none have failed, a record that even Swiss banks cannot match. Unique tax advantages combined with conservative money management cause Swiss insurance products to perform much better than one might expect. Conservative does not have to mean low returns. (If the insurance company doesn't have to deduct losses on a lot of bad investments, it is much easier to maintain a conservative, safe, high return.)

Swiss government insurance company regulation keeps investment portfolios at a nearly no risk level. Liquidity and valuation of investments are ultra-conservative. Only a maximum of 30% of investible funds may be put in real estate. Swiss real estate has always held the highest values, but this is ultra-conservatism at work. If it should go down, it might not be liquid enough to cover claims — so let's be ultra-conservative and severely limit the exposure. A philosophy that a lot of American banks and insurance companies are probably now wishing they had followed — or at least their policyholders are wishing they had.

Then just in case this isn't enough, Swiss insurance companies often carry their real estate holdings at less than half their present market value, allowing a very wide margin of price changes before safety can possibly be affected.

Swiss accounting in general seems to be on the conservative side. Companies tend to have hidden reserves of millions, rather than the North American style of overvaluing assets to achieve a high stock market price for takeover bids. This conservatism applies all the more to the insurance industry.

The Swiss insurance companies offer a great range of services. In fact, the range is broader than that offered by most Swiss banks. There are only about 20 insurance companies in Switzerland. This concentration makes the industry strong, and easy to supervise. There are no weak insurance companies in Switzerland, unlike the United States were insurance laws in many states permit an insurance company to be formed with capital as low as $100,000, and licensed, empty insurance company shells are frequently sold in classified ads in The Wall Street Journal and other newspapers.

The industry is regulated by the Swiss Federal Bureau of Private Insurance — a very strict regulator. There is no rate competition — the emphasis is on maintaining the strength of the insurer, and prohibiting risky investments (although it is unlikely that a Swiss insurance manager would even **think** of making a risky investment).

Regulation of private insurance companies has been established by a clause in the Swiss federal constitution since 1885. Contrast this to the United States where insurance companies are often regulated only by rules promulgated by a politically appointed insurance commissioner, who expects to be employed by an insurance company when the governor who appointed him is retired in a few years.

Swiss Annuities

Swiss annuities are heavily regulated, to avoid any potential funding problem. They denominate accounts in the strong Swiss franc. And the annuity payout is guaranteed.

Swiss annuities are **exempt** from the famous 35% withholding tax imposed by Switzerland on bank account interest received by foreigners. Annuities do not have to be reported to Swiss or U.S. tax authorities, nor to those in most countries. (Australia has become an exception, and now taxes profits in foreign annuities, even though they have not been paid out.)

A U.S. purchaser of an annuity is required to pay a 1% U.S. federal excise tax on the purchase of any policy from a foreign company. This is much like the sales tax rule that says that if a person shops in a different state, with a lower sales tax than their home state, when they get home they are required to mail a check to their home state's sales tax department for the difference in sales tax rates. Readers in other countries will not generally have even this type of tax to deal with. The U.S. federal excise tax form (IRS Form 720) does not ask for details of the policy bought or who it was bought from — it merely asks for a calculation of 1% tax of any foreign policies purchased. This is a one time tax at the time of purchase; it is not an ongoing tax. It is the responsibility of the U.S. taxpayer, to report the Swiss annuity or other foreign insurance policy.

Swiss insurance companies do not report anything to any government agency, Swiss or foreign — not the initial purchase of the policy, nor the payments into it, nor interest and dividends earned.

For readers who are U.S. citizens or residents, a swiss franc annuity is not a "foreign bank account," subject to the reporting requirements on the IRS Form 1040 or the special U.S. Treasury form for reporting foreign accounts. Transfers of funds by check or wire are not reportable under U.S. law by individuals — the reporting requirements apply **only** to cash and "cash equivalents" — such as money orders, cashier's checks, and travellers' checks.

If any government which currently has free transfer of funds were to eventually institute exchange controls, the government might require that most overseas investments be repatriated. This has been a common requirement by most governments that have imposed exchange controls. Insurance policies, however, would likely escape any forced repatriation under future exchange controls, because they are a pending contract between the investor and the insurance company. Swiss bank accounts would probably not escape such controls. (To the bureaucrats writing such regulations, an insurance policy is a commodity already bought, rather than an investment.)

No creditor may attach a Swiss annuity, if the purchaser's wife or children are named as beneficiaries. Liens cannot be attached to these assets. This way, the purchaser knows that at least a portion of his wealth is beyond reach and will, indeed, go to his designated heirs.

With most Swiss annuities an investor can liquidate up to 100% of the account without penalty (except for a SFr500 charge during the first year.)

In the U.S., and in most countries, insurance proceeds are not taxed. And, in most countries, earnings on annuities during the deferral period are not taxable until income is paid, or when they are liquidated (except in Australia).

For our American readers, we should mention that Swiss annuities can be placed in a U.S. tax-sheltered pension plans, such as IRA, Keogh, or corporate plans, or such a plan can be rolled over into a Swiss-annuity. (To put a Swiss annuity in a U.S. pension plan, all that is required is a U.S. trustee, such as a bank or other institution, and that the annuity contract be held in the U.S. by that trustee. Many banks offer "self-directed" pension plans for a very small annual administration fee, and these plans can easily be used for this purpose.)

Investment in Swiss annuities is on a "no load" basis, front-end or back-end. The investments can be canceled at any time, without a loss of principal, and with all principal, interest and dividends payable if canceled after one year. (If canceled in the first year, there is a small penalty of about 500 Swiss francs, plus loss of interest.)

Swiss Annuity Products

Swiss annuity products bring offer the benefits of Swiss bank accounts without the drawbacks — presenting the best Swiss investment advantages for investors.

Although they are annuities, they act more like a savings account than a deferred annuity. But it is operated under an insurance company's umbrella, so that it conforms to the definition of an annuity in most country's tax laws (including the United States), and as such, compounds tax-free until it is liquidated or converted into an income annuity later on.

Swiss annuity accounts earn approximately the same return as long-term government bonds in the same currency the account is denominated in (European Union bonds in the case of the ECU), less a half-percent management fee. That may not seem like much, but when combined with the depreciation of other currencies against the Swiss franc, the return rates are far better than appear at first glance.

Upon maturity of the account, the investor can choose between a lump sum payout (paying capital gains tax on accumulated earnings only), rolling the funds into an income annuity (paying capital gains taxes only as future income payments are received, and then only on the portion representing accumulated earnings), or extend the scheduled term by giving notice in advance of the originally scheduled date (and continue to defer tax on accumulated earnings).

Protection Of Assets In Swiss Annuities From Lawsuits

Growing the wealth is important, but so is protecting it, and Switzerland excels at this. Almost anybody with wealth is at risk — from lawsuits, tax collectors, confiscating governments. With everything that can happen to savings, it is nice to know that there is something, somewhere, nobody can touch.

According to Swiss law, insurance policies — including annuity contracts — cannot be seized by creditors. They also cannot be included in a Swiss bankruptcy procedure. Even if a foreign court expressly orders the seizure of a Swiss annuity account or its inclusion in a bankruptcy estate, the account will not be seized by Swiss authorities, provided that it has been structured the right way.

There are two requirements: A person who buys a life insurance policy from a Swiss insurance company must designate his or her spouse or descendants, or a third party (if done so irrevocably) as beneficiaries. Also, to avoid suspicion of making a fraudulent conveyance to avoid a specific judgment, under Swiss law, the person must have purchased the policy or designated the beneficiaries not less than six months before any bankruptcy decree or collection process.

The policyholder can also protect the policy by converting a designation of spouse or children into an irrevocable designation when he becomes aware of the fact that his creditors will seize his assets and that a court might compel him to repatriate the funds in the insurance policy. If he is subsequently ordered to revoke the designation of the beneficiary and to liquidate the policy he will not be able to do so as the insurance company will not accept his instructions because of the irrevocable designation of the beneficiaries.

Article 81 of the Swiss insurance law provides that if a policyholder has made a revocable designation of spouse or children as beneficiaries, they automatically become policyholders and acquire all rights if the policyholder is declared bankrupt. In such a case the original policyholder therefore automatically loses control over the policy and also his right to demand the liquidation of the policy and the repatriation of funds. A court therefore cannot compel the policyholder to liquidate the policy or otherwise repatriate his funds. If the spouse or children notify the insurance company of the bankruptcy, the insurance company will note that in its records. Even if the original policyholder sends instructions because a court has ordered him to do so, the insurance company will ignore those instructions. It is important that the company be notified promptly of the bankruptcy, so that they do not inadvertently follow the original policyholder's instructions because they weren't told of the bankruptcy.

If the policyholder has designated his spouse or his children as beneficiaries of the insurance policy, the insurance policy is protected from his creditors regardless of whether the designation is revocable or irrevocable. The policyholder may therefore designate his spouse or children as beneficiaries on a revocable basis and revoke this designation before the policy expires if at such time there is no threat from any creditors.

These laws are part of fundamental Swiss law. They were not created to make Switzerland an asset protection haven. There is a current fad of various offshore islands passing special legislation allowing the creation of asset protection trusts for foreigners. Since they are not part of the fundamental legal structure of the country concerned, local legislators really don't care if they work or not. And since most of these trusts are simply used as a convenient legal title to assets that are left in the investor's home country, such as brokerage accounts, houses, or office buildings, it is very easy for a court to simply call the trust a sham to defraud creditors and ignore its legal title — seizing the assets that are within the physical jurisdiction of the court.

Such flimsy structures, providing only a thin legal screen to the title to foreign property, are quite different from real assets being solely under the control of a rock-solid insurance company in a major industrialized country. A defendant trying to convince a court that his local brokerage account is really owned by a trust represented by a brass-plate under a palm tree on a faraway island is not likely to be successful — more likely the court will simply seize the asset.

But with the Swiss annuity, the insurance policy is not being protected by the Swiss courts and government because of any especial concern for the foreign investor, but because the principle of protection of insurance policies is a fundamental part of Swiss law — for the protection of the Swiss themselves. Insurance is for the family, not something to be taken by creditors or other claimants. No Swiss lawyer would even waste his time bringing such a case.

One firm specializes in dealing with foreign investors in Swiss insurance products, and everybody in the firm speaks excellent English. Contact:

> JML Swiss Investment Counsellors
> Germaniastrasse 55, Dept. 212
> Ch-8033, Zurich, Switzerland
> Tele: (41-1) 368-8233
> Fax: (41-1) 368-8299 Mark fax Attn: Dept. 212

The firm is able to correspond in English, French, and German.

Lattman's success can in part be measured by the thousands of satisfied clients around the world who have been counselled by his firm. His very first client, dating from 1973, is still active, prosperous, and happy.

Swiss Bank Services

Switzerland's banking system has a centuries-old heritage of secrecy, but that heritage was not put into law until 1934. In effect, the Swiss opted to hold on to their secrecy while other banking systems around the world were beginning to compromise on secrecy. In the 1930s, many other nations, including the United States, were creating a distinction between deposit banks and investment banks, and the Swiss legislature refused to follow that trend. The Swiss opted to retain "universal" banking, or full-service type banking, which means that your Swiss bank can be a deposit bank, a checking account bank, a stock broker, a commercial lender, an investment bank — everything you need.

In addition to the formal requirements imposed by the Banking Act of 1934, and strict supervision by the Banking Commission, the Swiss banks are also subjected to regular audits. The first audit is to comply with the Swiss corporation law, which every Swiss corporation must have. The second audit is the banking audit, which must be conducted by one of a total of 17 audit firms that have been specially approved by the Banking Commission to conduct bank audits. Over the years, these bank audits have become very complex and exacting. The audit firms have a whole set of detailed rules by which they go over the bank's books.

The audit has become the primary guarantee for the legal protection of Swiss bank depositors. The Swiss banks and the 17 audit firms actually supervise and regulate banking in Switzerland to a far greater extent than governments regulate banking in other nations.

The banking law also requires stiff liquidity and capital requirements for the operation of a Swiss bank. These are among the most rigid in the world. The liquidity formula is rather complicated, but the end product is that most private Swiss banks have liquidity at or around 100%, which is unprecedented in other national banking systems. The formula for capital requirements in Swiss banks means that around 7 to 9 percent of total liabilities must be equity. this is a high percentage in relation to other countries. Swiss banks who own securities must write them down to market, or cost (whichever is lower), every month, so no Swiss bank will have unrealized paper losses on its securities, as often happens to banks in other countries.

Swiss banks, as a whole, are very safe, and they take the necessary measures to regulate the entirety of their industry so that Swiss banking does not lose any of its reputation for sound money management.

The Swiss commercial banks adhere closely to policies established by banks throughout the world. From the purely local viewpoint, Swiss credit policies apply to virtually all types of loans; however, credit extended to foreign customers is limited to top-ranking companies, and to the financing of exports from Switzerland. Loan terms vary with such factors as the value of collateral, but are generally more favorable in Switzerland than in many other countries.

To a large extent, the amount of bank credit that a company can get depends upon how much confidence the company can generate in the banker's mind; therefore, each individual case is subject to different treatment. To this end, a typical, business-oriented Swiss bank goes to considerable trouble to analyze its clients' needs, and provide solutions that are fitting to the capital requirements of each case. To customers domiciled in Switzerland, the following services are typically offered:

1)   Short-term credit of all kinds is extended, whether secured or unsecured. This may be in current account form, or as a fixed advance in either Swiss francs or foreign currency.

2)   Mortgage loans.

3)   Leasing and factoring.

4)   Refinancing of leasing operations.

5) The discounting of acceptances, including the financing of medium term receivables, that result from the export business.

6) The opening of letters of credit.

7) Guarantees, sureties, and bonds for public authorities and/or private persons.

To further broaden their scope in the world money market, Swiss banks place the following facilities at the service of Swissdomiciled clients:

1) Direct, short- to medium-term loans, which may be in Swiss francs or other convertible currencies, on fixed interest or a roll-over basis.

2) Financing of Swiss merchandise (together with an export risk guarantee by the Swiss government).

3) "Bridging" loans as a means of preliminary financing, prior to capital market transactions in Switzerland and on the Euromarket.

The banks of Switzerland not only assist corporations, but business and private clients as well, in specialized ways. Advice or other services through some banks include:

1) Transfer of payments in the national and international sectors.

2) Buying and selling bank notes and paying instruments in foreign currencies.

3) Negotiation of stock market transactions internally and abroad.

4) Securities management and custody.

5) Establishment of trusts, and counseling in investments.

Extremely sensitive to and knowledgeable of business and commerce conditions in Switzerland, Swiss banks help to establish contacts necessary to launch a Swiss enterprise. Some publish brochures and booklets containing detailed information on economic and business conditions. Such publications also provide information on special features; of specific regional industries. Some major banks have branches throughout Switzerland, as well as in London, Tokyo, New York, Luxembourg, and Panama. The typical major Swiss bank has representation in most major financial centers, and can be in continuous communications with thousands of correspondent banks world-wide.

Switzerland has been a most successfully neutral country in many European weirs and both world wars, so in modern times, its economy has never been devastated by war's destruction.

Also, it is a basically free enterprise country with little government regulation and economic control and relatively low taxes.

The country is geographically in the center of Europe, where major continental roads from east, west, north and south intersect. Its internal roads and railways are excellent, and all Swiss transportation services are punctual. It is also accessible by river barge directly from the sea. Airline service is tops, and telecommunications are the very best available. Needless to say, professional services are of the very highest quality and reliability.

Portfolio Management From A Swiss Base

The fine art of Swiss money management has a long and successful tradition for which Switzerland is often justifiably envied world-wide.

Using an independent portfolio manager rather than a bank offers better service, and better control over the account. It also eliminates the conflict of interest that naturally arises between the banks commissionable role as stockbroker and its role as investment manager (a conflict that has long plagued U.S. securities firms as well).

An excellent choice is Weber Hartmann Vrijhof & Partners, an independent Swiss portfolio management firm that can manage your investment account, whether it be an individual portfolio or a portfolio for your offshore trust or corporation.

Their office will assist you in opening an account with one of Switzerland's first-class banks in Zurich, which will be the custodian of your assets.

It is not feasible to manage an account of less than U.S. $100,000 (or the equivalent in other currencies), because of the transaction costs and inability to properly diversify.

Highly-experienced financial consultants of excellent repute make up the team at the disposal of their customers.

The banking career of Senior Partner Robert Vrijhof began in 1978 with the Union Bank of Switzerland, working his way through the international securities trading department. Later, with Credit Suisse, he held the senior position as manager of the Foreign Stock Exchange trading section. In 1987, he accepted an offer by Foreign Commerce Bank as portfolio manager. His profound knowledge in this area soon led to the position of Vice-President and head of the portfolio management group at Focobank.

René Schatt, Executive Director, started his banking career in 1977 with the Thurgauer Cantonalbank, where he finished his basic training. In 1984, he joined the Foreign Commerce Bank and worked his way through the securities administration and trading department. At the same time, he continued studying and in 1987, he achieved the "Federal Diploma of Banking Expert." In 1990, he was promoted to Vice-President and head of the securities department. In 1992, he joined the first Korean Bank in Switzerland, KDB Bank (Switzerland) Ltd., working as Senior Vice-President and being the Swiss Member of the General Management.

For more information contact:

> Weber Hartmann Vrijhof & Partners Ltd.
> Zurichstrasse 110b
> CH-8134 Adliswil
> Switzerland
> Telephone +41 1 709 1115
> Fax +41 1 709 1113

Purchasing Swiss Mutual Funds

One of the very best ways to purchase offshore mutual funds is through private Swiss banks.

Jurg Lattmann, founder of JML Swiss Investment Counsellors (Dept. 212, Baarerstrasse 53, CH-6304 Zug, Switzerland) has special arrangements with some of the best of these banks to handle portfolios for the firm's clients.

JML's Personal Portfolio Management Program allows clients to customize and control their investments, while still receiving constant expert management advice.

Readers of this book may obtain a free one-year subscription to the JML monthly newsletter, Swiss Perspective, which gives in depth coverage of international investment topics, by writing to the address above.

Swiss Gold Certificates Provide Portable Privacy

A gold certificate provides you with an attractive alternative to investing in physical metal, and offers a way to transfer assets out of the country.

The Mocatta Delivery Order (MDO) is a title document representing ownership of a specific, numbered unit of gold, silver or platinum. With origins dating back to 1671, Mocatta is the oldest bullion trading firm in the world. As one of the world's most experienced precious metals organizations, Mocatta created the MDO to satisfy the highest criteria of privacy, safety, liquidity and flexibility.

You can choose storage in either Wilmington, Delaware or Zurich, Switzerland. During the storage the metal is fully insured under a Lloyds of London insurance policy.

The certificate is issued in your name (or the name of a corporation or trust, if you prefer) and identifies the physical gold, silver, or platinum owned. MDOs offer transfer of ownership features that enable the owner to sell, assign or collateralize the metal easily, yet provide the protection of non-negotiability, since a lost document can be replaced, unlike a bearer security. American readers will be interested to know that since the order is non-negotiable, it does not have to be reported if it is taken in or out of the United States. There is no reporting of the purchase to the IRS. An MDO can be issued in the name of a family limited partnership or offshore trust, or assigned to one of them as a means of transferring ownership of the metal when the asset protection entity is created.

For more information on the MDO contact:

> Asset Strategies International Inc.
> Suite 400A
> 1700 Rockville Pike
> Rockville, Maryland 20852 U.S.A.
> telephone (301) 881-8600; fax: (301) 881-1936.

Asset Strategies International was founded in 1982 by two of the former senior officers of Deak-Perera, at the time the nation's oldest and largest precious metals and foreign exchange firm. The principals, Michael Checkan and Glen Kirsch have been in the precious metals/foreign exchange business for a combined total of 50 years. They are well known in the financial newsletter industry and at one time or another have been recognized as a "recommended vendor" by many of the writers in the newsletter industry.

Asset Strategies International helped the Government of Western Australia create the Perth Mint Certificate Program, a program with some similarities to the MDO, but with a wide range of choices of metals and quantities.

IRELAND: SPECIAL HAVEN FOR ENTREPRENEURS

For the rest of the world, the arrival of the single European market in 1992 was both a promise and a threat. The promise is the lure of a market of 340 million well-heeled consumers. The threat is that the high taxes, sky-high wages, innumerable languages, and entrenched levels of bureaucracy associated with the European Union (EU) will effectively deny access to firms outside it.

Using Ireland as a base is one way to lock in low labor costs and a 20-year tax holiday in the process. In some cases, you can even get free government money to fund your start-up costs.

Only one EU country offers foreign entrepreneurs the benefits of an English-speaking work force, labor costs that are only 60% to 70% of U.S. levels, a 10% ceiling on taxes, and cash grants to help them get started. That country is Ireland.

Since the 1970s, the Irish government has pursued an aggressive foreign investment program. To encourage foreign entrepreneurs to set up businesses in Ireland, the government created the Irish Development Authority (IDA).

The IDA has broad powers to approve applications and make grants to prospective employers. It also operates branch offices in the United States, Australia, Japan, South Korea, Taiwan, Britain, Germany, and the Netherlands.

To start up a business and win special grants for creating jobs, entrepreneurs need only contact the nearest IDA office. Local Irish IDA officials will be available to provide back up assistance.

One-stop shopping spares prospective investors the long-winded dealings with local authorities or agencies that can make foreign investment difficult elsewhere. A considerable number of large multinational companies have already taken advantage of the benefits of setting up Irish subsidiaries. But don't get the idea that Irish incentives are only for big companies. The average foreign company in Ireland employs only 40 to 50 workers.

To qualify for IDA incentives, a company must be engaged either in manufacturing or in international services. The latter category includes computer or software services, back offices for insurance companies, and financial and other primary services.

Financial companies are required to set up in the new International Financial Services Center in Dublin, a brand-new, high-tech development near the refurbished Dublin docks. To qualify for IDA tax breaks and capital grants, a financial company must employ a minimum of 10 people. There is no minimum size, however, for manufacturing companies or other service operations.

The Irish parliament passed a law extending through the year 2010 the maximum corporate tax rate of 10% on foreign investments. Thus, companies investing now can look forward to at least two decades of tax relief. The government will also make cash grants to deserving prospective employers. These can take the form either of picking up the entire first year's payroll for a labor intensive business, such as software development, or of capital grants for factories or other more capital-intensive operations.

Grants are made according to the quality and number of jobs to be created. The IDA looks with particular favor on those projects that will employ some of Ireland's many university graduates. A project will also be more attractive if it will obtain supplies locally or will otherwise contribute to the local economy. Companies receiving IDA grants are free to lay off employees. But they must carry the grant on their books for ten years as a self-amortizing liability, secured by equipment or some other guarantee. Thus, if a company eliminates jobs during the first ten years, it will probably have to give back part of the grant. After ten years, however, the liability is gone. So far, however, firms have tended to expand Irish operations rather than cut them back — thanks to the favorable tax conditions. Many smaller companies that set up shop in the past have grown into medium to large companies.

In addition to the IDA program, Ireland offers other programs. One of them is the Shannon Free Zone program. Incentives are similar to those of the IDA, with taxes held to 10% and capital grants available. Companies are required to locate near Shannon Airport. The Shannon Free Zone operation is administered separately from the IDA.

In just a few years, Dublin's International Financial Services Center (IFSC) has emerged from a derelict docklands site to be a new European hub for the management of the financial assets of some of the biggest corporations in the world.

Since the first, new office building on the 27-acre site opened in 1990, familiar names associated with diverse manufacturing activities, such as IBM, Alcan, Volkswagen, Volvo, Grand Metropolitan and Outokumpu, have all chosen Dublin as a location from which to manage their world-wide corporate treasury operations.

Others, such as Asea Brown Boverie, BMW, Ericsson and Coca-Cola, have chosen the IFSC as the hub from which to manage their world-wide insurance needs. Large corporations such as these, with manufacturing assets and properties scattered in scores of locations around the world, set up their own insurance companies through which their subsidiaries then place their property insurance.

Captive insurance, as it is known, has developed well and quite unexpectedly. On the back of this business, re-insurance operations have also grown rapidly.

Far from being a glass and chrome shell, housing dubious "brass-plate" operations often associated with offshore centers, the IFSC now has 140 financial services companies, giving direct employment to 986 people.

One hundred and ninety five projects have been approved, which have made commitments to employ eventually almost 3,000 people.

The IFSC was conceived as a means of transforming the derelict docklands area of Dublin into a new European financial center, which would complement the growth in new manufacturing industries that have sprung up across Ireland under the stimulus of the IDA.

Ireland offers many advantages compared with rival centers such as Luxembourg and the Channel Islands, through lower wage and housing costs, a skilled and abundant labor force and good communications with other European business centers.

The IFSC is just a 10-minute walk from Dublin's city center and a 20 minutes' drive from the airport. The development site has plenty of room for expansion and is planned to have complementary developments of a 300-bedroom hotel, a marina, shopping and restaurant facilities and residential properties.

If a planned development of a light rail transport system gets European Union approval and funding, much of Dublin's traffic congestion problems can also be overcome, which is one of the city's few drawbacks for developers of services-related industries.

One of the IFSC's attractions has been the possibility for cash-rich firms to place their surplus cash in investment funds which are then managed in Dublin by specialist companies. Profits are taxed at the 10 per cent rate and can be repatriated without further tax liabilities due to Ireland's double taxation treaties with its EU partners.

Many leading foreign banks, such as Dresdner Bank, Citibank, Chase Manhattan and Deutsche Bank, have established fund management operations in Dublin.

Dublin's tax advantages disappear in 2005 but this is sufficient time for many institutions to be interested. With 550,000 square feet of office space completed at the IFSC, the government, through its Customs House Docks Authority, is now negotiating the center's second stage of development, which includes a museum, an hotel, retail facilities, housing and further office buildings.

A special source of help in Ireland

There is an Irish firm that I am particularly pleased to recommend. Fitzgerald & Associates, one of Ireland's leading accounting, financial and tax consulting firms, is a dynamic, growing firm of registered auditors, business advisers and accountants with offices in Cork and Dublin. The head of the firm, John Fitzgerald, is a law graduate and barrister as well as an accountant.

Apart from the usual accounting and auditing services, they are involved in comprehensive tax planning for both individuals and corporations, in corporate finance services such as advice on funding, financial planning, management buyouts, and the negotiation of Irish government grant assistance. They give advice on mergers and acquisitions and preparation of documents for public securities issues by Irish companies.

They form Irish companies, and can provide the company secretary and other statutorily-required company services.

To discuss specific services with them, please contact:

John Fitzgerald
Fitzgerald & Associates
6 Sullivan's Quay
Cork, Ireland
Telephone: +353 21 963877
Fax   +353 21 310273

THE UNITED STATES AS A
TAX HAVEN

The United States is considered a tax haven by many foreign investors. While U.S. citizens are struggling with federal, state, and local tax burdens of 40% or more of their total income, foreign investors often can invest in the United States tax-free or almost tax-free.

The country is not a straightforward no-tax haven like the Cayman Islands or the Bahamas. Instead, it has some complicated tax laws and tax treaties that, when taken together and fully understood, provide opportunities for the foreign investor to make low-tax gains in U.S. investments. Unknown to the average American is an elite group of U.S. tax lawyers and accountants who refer to themselves as "inbound specialists." This means they specialize in structuring transactions for foreigners who seek to invest capital in the U.S.

The United States encourages tax-free foreign investment because it needs foreign capital to finance the economy and the government budget deficit. For example, the U.S. generally imposes a 30% withholding tax on all interest payments to foreign residents and corporations. Foreign investors let it be known quickly that they would take their money elsewhere if the withholding tax remained, however, and exceptions to the tax now exist.

The great benefit of the U.S. tax haven for many foreigners occurs when the U.S. tax rules are combined with those of other countries. The United States taxes its citizens and residents on their worldwide income. But noncitizens and nonresidents are not taxed on income from certain sources within this country. As a result, there are a number of foreign businesses who invest in the United States to take advantage of these non-taxable situations.

The key to tax-free or almost tax-free investing is to ensure that the offshore corporation is considered a foreign corporation not engaged in a U.S. trade or business under U.S. tax law. There are detailed regulations that give numerous rules and examples. The important points are that generally there cannot be a U.S. office or agent in the United States, books and records must be maintained outside the U.S., and management and control must not be located there. Directors' and shareholders' meetings should be held outside the country, and the corporation cannot have a business there. It is vital that a U.S tax adviser structure the arrangement to comply with the law and furnish a complete list of dos and don'ts.

The foreign investor benefits from no U.S. taxes on bank-deposit interest and no U.S. tax on capital gains earned on U.S. stocks and bonds. There will, however, be some tax on dividends from U.S. stocks.

In cases in which a tax might be incurred, such as on dividends, this often can be reduced or avoided by locating the offshore corporation in a country that has a favorable tax treaty with the United States. The Treasury Department has renegotiated a number of the tax treaties, but there still are some under which the U.S. withholding tax rate on dividends is significantly reduced.

The advantages foreign investors have over U.S. ones were most apparent in the junk bond crisis and the problems it created for some insurance companies and savings and loan associations. Only foreign corporations or partnerships were submitting the best bids for the portfolios of junk bonds that these institutions were trying to sell. The primary reason for that is the tax advantages the foreign investors would enjoy. Any U.S. buyer of the bonds would have to pay taxes on any interest and capital gains they earned. The foreign investors face no U.S. taxes and, if they are based in a tax haven like Hong Kong, no domestic taxes either. This allows them to make bids 10% or more above those of U.S. competitors.

Investing in U.S. real estate used to be an easy way to tax-free income and gains for nonresident aliens. But the rules were changed in 1980, and the profits no longer will be tax-free. Still, investment in U.S. real estate through an offshore corporation can result in lower tax on profits if the transaction is structured properly. This is a complicated and rapidly changing area, but the general approach is to set up an offshore company in a country that has a favorable tax treaty with the United States. (The Netherlands is the historical favorite.) The offshore company then creates a U.S. corporation, which buys the real estate. Sometimes, it makes sense to have one U.S. company own the real estate while another is set up to manage the property and collect management fees.

The U.S. periodically issues revenue rulings to attack schemes that it has heard are being used. To get any of these results, up-to-date advice from an experienced U.S. tax adviser is essential.

REGIONAL BRANCH

HAVENS: AND HOW YOU

CAN USE THEM

A number of countries have passed special legislation to attract branch offices of foreign companies that will use the country only as a regional base and not do local business. The package of incentives is generally very extensive, including complete tax exemption for the company and its employees, customs duty exemptions for both company and personal goods, and sometimes a duty-free car.

Although intended for multi-national corporations, in fact these special laws are available to any company. They can provide a very useful loophole for establishing your personal base in a convenient country. For example, Greece, a full member of the EU, was the pioneer of this type of legislation. With a Greek residence permit in hand, and a small working base somewhere on Greek soil, you would then be free to travel and conduct business anywhere in the EU.

Greece

Greece consists of the mainland, a few large islands, and many smaller islands. The mainland is bordered on the north by countries of southeastern Europe, and on the south by the Mediterranean Sea. A major portion of its external boundaries comprise the shorelines of the Ionian, Aegean, and Mediterranean Seas. The largest of the islands is Crete, lying southeast of the mainland in the Mediterranean Sea. The capital city of Greece is Athens.

Greece's tax haven laws, especially as they affect foreign firms with shipping interests, have been responsible for the sound economic growth of the nation. Apart from the tax haven industry, there has been a gradual but decided transition from an agriculturally-based economy to one that is divided between industry and services. And, as has been the case for many centuries, shipping plays an extremely important role in Greece's economic development. The gross national output is making steady annual increases.

A majority of the general populace speaks the Greek language; however, many persons in the business community have a working familiarity with English.

Except for the specially designed tax haven laws, which exempt qualified regional headquarters of multinational companies from tax, taxation in Greece is a reality of life (the corporate tax rate is in the neighborhood of 40%, and inheritance tax rates are on a progressive scale that reaches 75%. Tax evasion in Greece is a risky venture.)

In addition to extremely well-developed facilities for shipping, Greece has a well-developed banking system, including a central bank, several commercial banks, investment banks, credit institutions, and branch offices of foreign banks. Many major airlines serve Greece. The country has a good communications system, as well as an efficiently operated postal service. The national currency is the drachma.

Any foreign commercial or industrial company that establishes a regional office in Greece, under Law 89, will receive 100% exemption from income tax, as well as other significant tax benefits. The title of this Greek tax law in its entirety is "Establishment in Greece of Foreign Commercial and Industrial Companies."

The establishment of a Greek regional office is subject to the approval of the Minister of Coordination. The Minister of Coordination approves or disapproves the application within several days. Approval is contingent upon granting power of attorney to a permanent Greek resident who will act as the foreign company's legal representative. The law requires that a Greek consular officer in the home country of the foreign company authenticate the power of attorney. It must be translated into the Greek language.

To effect the power of attorney, a statement must be written in the home country, stating that the party giving the power of attorney is a duly constituted corporation. This statement must be notarized by a local notary public. The foreign parent company may also be asked by the Minister of Coordination to file a copy of the annual balance sheet and profit and loss statement (your local attorney may also suggest sending a copy of the parent company's articles of incorporation.)

Thousands of foreign companies that operate shipping fleets have established Greek regional offices to take advantage of the tax benefits on non-Greek source income from around the world.

Provided that the regional office is legally structured in accordance with Law 89, and provided that it derives no income from Greece, it receives the following benefits:

1). Exemption from all Greek taxes.

2). Exemption from income tax on earnings of foreign personnel who work for the regional office.

3). Exemption from all customs duties, stamp duties, import taxes, and luxury taxes on items imported to equip the regional office.

4).   Exemption from duties on the importation of household items by the firm's foreign personnel.

5).   Exemption from any requirement to keep books in the Greek language.

6).   Exemption from requesting the approval of the Post Office to post registered letters abroad.

7).   Exemption from any export-import duties relating to samples of advertising material by the regional firm.

8).   Exemption from tax on interest received from deposits in Greek banks or from government bonds.

9).   Exemption, for certain, specified enterprises, from a tax on the profits from sale of securities.

10).   Exemption from any tax on interest from loans granted by foreign banks or firms to certain Greek entities, regardless of whether or not Greece has a double taxation treaty with the home country of the foreign firm granting the loan.

11).   Exemption from duties on the conversion of bond or preference shares of corporations, and on the replacement of share or bond certificates.

12).   Two-year work permits for foreign personnel, with extensions obtainable.

Under Greek Law 89, and other laws that supplement it, a shipping company established in Greece will enjoy the twelve benefits previously listed. Approval for the establishment of the regional shipping firm must come from both the Minister of Coordination and the Minister of Mercantile Marine.

Jordan

Jordan, a small Arab nation strategically located near the Red Sea, Mediterranean Sea, and the Arab markets of the Middle East, is making a bid, through special tax haven legislation, to induce international business firms to locate regional headquarters there. Now that Beirut is no longer available as a regional headquarters for international trading companies, Jordan may well achieve the status of a major tax haven and regional headquarters location, for trade in the Middle East.

The Jordanian law is called the Foreign Companies Registration Law. Under the law, a foreign company can establish a Jordan-based branch for engaging in business outside Jordan. The fact that the law does not permit the foreign company to conduct business in Jordan should present no obstacle to the enterprising firm that can use such a strategic location to reach Arabian Gulf markets.

As a part of the oil-producing Arabian region, Jordan's physical location provides access to the Persian Gulf, the Mediterranean trade routes used by oil-producing companies, as well as to the Red Sea and the Indian Ocean routes that serve Asia, Africa, and Australia. It also has excellent highways and air service to link it to Europe and neighboring countries. Its location gives access to a consumer population comparable to that of the U.S., with a combined national product of approximately $150 billion.

Jordan's business community seems to have a stronger base in the principles of free enterprise than other countries in the region. Combined with a history of economic stability, high educational standards, a high literacy rate, and excellent living conditions, the Jordanian penchant for free enterprise should provide the elements for important economic growth.

Because of its importance in the industrial and commercial world, Jordanian officials have made English a mandatory subject in government schools. Eight years of English language instruction is required for all secondary and vocational school graduates. Moreover, the Jordanian business and professional community (including government offices) is staffed with English-speaking Jordanians, many of whom are graduates of American or British colleges and universities.

Banking facilities are good, with a large network of commercial banks -- including several foreign banks -- and many specialized credit institutions to provide short- and long-term money for qualified business firms.

Although not much can be said for the efficiency of Jordan's seaports, which seem to be continually clogged with ships, the excellent network of highways in the area provides a viable transportation system. Also, Jordan's air service from many major airlines places it within a few hours of European and Arab capitals. The only executive jet service in the Middle East is located in Jordan.

Jordan maintains a dependable mail service, with air mail from the United States arriving in four or five days. A direct-dial telex system is connected with the major international carriers. The direct-dial system for telephone calls to the United States and Europe is constantly being improved -- new satellite telephone equipment has been installed. Jordan gives priority to any foreign company that requests telex services.

Amman, the capital, has international schools for elementary and post-elementary students. Hospitals and other medical facilities are modern. Churches are of many denominations because Jordan has a large Christian population. Local shops and supermarkets are stocked with familiar American and European household items and products. Shopping or dining out is easy, with storekeepers and other businessmen speaking English. There are French, Chinese, Polynesian, and Turkish restaurants in addition to the more familiar American and Arabian ones.

Amman also offers cultural events found in any major city -- concerts, art exhibits, lectures, and films. The entire country is somewhat like an open museum because Greeks, Romans, Nabateans, Canaanites, Persians, Crusaders, Arabs, and Ottoman Turks have, at various times throughout history, held or dominated some or all of Jordan. Jordan differs from most Arab countries in that it engages in and provides equipment for a variety of sports activities, including tennis, basketball, soccer, horseback riding, hunting, horse racing, squash, cricket, fishing, sailing, water skiing and scuba diving.

Amman provides deluxe housing at rates below the average for the area. Housing consists of single dwellings with attractive gardens. A variety of modern apartments are also available. Foreigners may be pleasantly surprised to find that household servants work at modest wages.

A company registering under Jordan's Foreign Companies Registration Law will find itself in line for many tax benefits, including: total exemption from income and social security taxes; exemption from registrations with the Chamber of Commerce, and from the payment of business registration taxes; exemption from customs duties on the furnishings and equipment for the Jordan branch office; and exemption from duties on the importation of commercial samples. Jordan also grants nonresident exchange control status to the regional office so that it may maintain bank accounts in foreign currency.

Not only does the Jordan-based regional office receive direct tax benefits, its employees also receive substantial privileges from the Jordan government. These include exemption from social security and income taxes for non-Jordanian employees; an exemption on customs duties on household furniture imported by the non-Jordanian employees; duty-free importation of a car every two years, granted to each employee; and the availability of residential and work permits for the non-Jordanian employees.

It seems likely that Jordan's bid to attract international business will be successful. Some years ago Greece offered a similar package of tax benefits and experienced an influx of regional headquarters of multinational companies. Jordan's tax exemption law for foreign companies, together with the many other concessions and incentives that are offered, should create a healthy international business scene in the Arab kingdom.

Tunisia

In 1989, Tunisia passed legislation authorizing a package of tax exemptions for international service companies, following the same basic pattern as the Greek and Jordanian legislation. The one major difference is that approval can be obtained to do some local business, which is taxed at the normal local rates. It is too early to tell how well Tunisia will develop has a regional headquarters site. The climate is lovely, and it is an attractive tourist destination, but it does not have the advantages of Jordan as to being in the center of a booming market. However, as development programs continue in the western North African countries, Tunisia may become an interesting base.

Philippines

In an effort to bolster the local economy, the Philippines has enacted legislation that incorporates certain restrictions and provisions which may ultimately make the Philippines of little value as a tax haven. The body of the legislation is Decree 218, "Prescribing Incentives for the Establishment of Regional or Area Headquarters of Multinational Companies in the Philippines." Companies that qualify for tax benefits under this decree usually establish regional offices in the Manila area.

The essence of Decree 218 is that any regional headquarters organized in the Philippines that is managed and controlled from outside the country, and that does not derive local income, may be entitled to a 100% tax exemption. The intent of the law is to make the regional office act only in a supervisory, communications or coordinating capacity for other affiliates or branches in the Asia-Pacific area. This means that the parent company must be extremely careful to segregate and limit the functions of the regional office. Some provisions of the decree are:

1. Either a Philippine commercial attache or a Philippine consul in the home country of the multinational firm must present certification to the Philippines government that the foreign firm is a legal entity engaged in international trade with affiliates, subsidiaries, or regional offices in the Asia-Pacific area.

2. A principal officer of the multinational firm must present a certification to the Philippines government stating that the multinational firm has been authorized by its board of directors to establish regional offices in the Philippines. This certification must state that the regional office will act only in a supervisory, coordinating, or communications capacity for its affiliates, subsidiaries, and branches in the Asia-Pacific area; and further, that no income will be derived in the Philippines.

3. The multinational firm must agree to spend at least $50,000 U.S. (or equivalent) annually, to cover the expenses of its operation in the Philippines. Within 30 days of receiving the Certificate of Registration from the Securities and Exchange Commission, the company must present to the Securities and Exchange Commission a certificate of inward remittance from a local bank of at least $30,000 U.S. (or equivalent). Thereafter, within 30 days of the anniversary date of the establishment of

the regional office, the company must present to the Securities and Exchange Commission a certificate of inward remittance of at least $50,000 U.S. or equivalent. The currency used must be converted to Philippine currency.

Furthermore, the Philippine office will be permitted to operate only at the discretion of the Bureau of Internal Revenue that judges on such matters as the source of income, and functions of the branch office.

If the regional office meets the qualifications, it receives the following tax exemptions:

1.   It is exempt from Section 191 -- 3% tax on gross receipts of contractors, proprietors or operations of dockyards and other activates.

2.   It has 100% exemption from all income tax in the Philippines.

3.   It is exempt from all licenses, fees, local taxes, etc.

4.   Its executive personnel qualify for a reduction of the normal withholding tax that is applicable to their wages. The normal tax is 30%, which is reduced to 15%.

5.   There are no import duties on equipment necessary to maintain the local office, or on household items of foreign personnel who manage the office. Furthermore, normal immigration requirements are relaxed so that foreign personnel may have free movement into the Philippines.

The normal corporate tax rate of the Philippines is 35% on taxable income, with foreign branches and resident corporations paying an additional 20% on profits remitted abroad. The income tax rate on Philippine individuals is graduated on a progressive scale, beginning at 3% and going to 70%, with fixed amount exemptions for single persons and dependent children, as well as a standard 10% deduction. Corresponding amounts in U.S. dollar equivalencies are somewhat lower than in the U.S., reflecting the lower per capital income of the Philippines.

A VARIETY OF OTHER

SMALLER HAVENS

These are brief summaries of some of the new tax haven candidates which are just getting started.

Labuan

A Malaysian island, Labuan is receiving strong support from the Malaysian government, but still has limited infrastructure. It is one of the many Pacific area havens hoping to capture flight business from Hong Kong. Which, if any, of these havens will do so is an open question at this time, particularly considering that Hong Kong works not just because it is a tax haven, but because of a superb commercial infrastructure. Since most of the jurisdictions hoping to replace Hong Kong are not willing to allow the immigration of the several million Hong Kong residents it would require to replicate the infrastructure, it is doubtful that any of these havens will ever achieve the same results. In late 1992, the Philippines passed legislation making **Subic Bay** a free port and tax haven.

Cook Island

The Cook Islands, a dependency of New Zealand, has been aggressive in seeking company formation and trust business. It has been especially heavily promoted by certain American law firms, but there are serious questions about the advisability of using the jurisdiction.

Mauritius

Mauritius, may become a significant regional haven. An island in the Indian Ocean, about 500 miles east of Madagascar, Mauritius is today one of the burgeoning economies of the Indian Ocean region. A British colony until 1968, it has now passed tax haven and offshore banking legislation. Unlike many of the tropical island tax havens, unemployment in Mauritius is so low that it is forced to import labor, has a trade surplus, and the budget deficit is only about 2% of gross national product. Both health care and education are free.

Situated in the middle of nowhere, Mauritius has virtually no pollution. Still undiscovered by the world's tourists, it is free of their trappings. The island is a trade center that serves the Indian subcontinent, Oceania, South Africa, and East Africa. It is a free port for the shipment of goods across the Indian Ocean. The island's offshore legislation guarantees that offshore bank accounts are kept secret, and has laws providing for the formation of tax haven banks, corporations, and trusts.

A great deal of the Mauritius business has involved holding companies for investments in India, with which it has a double taxation treaty.

Madeira

The island of **Madeira**, an autonomous region in Portugal — and therefore part of the EU — is situated 625 miles from Lisbon and more than 500 miles from the African coast. The politically-stable island is perhaps best known to foreigners for its fortified wine and for Reid's Hotel in Funchal, the capital, a hotel where afternoon tea on the terrace survives, even into the 1990s.

But Madeira is now making a determined bid to become a major offshore financial center. It is only in recent years that Madeira has made a conscious effort to diversify away from its traditional reliance on up-market tourism. The Madeira Development Company which plays a pivotal role in the island's offshore ambitions says the aim is to offer international companies access to Europe as well as to Africa and North and South America.

Madeira's developing offshore activities can be grouped into four distinct categories: a free trade zone, financial services, offshore services of a non-financial nature such as trusts, and a shipping registry.

The development authority says all four are of equal importance. If one activity is to be more equal than the others, it could well be the free trade zone. Unlike many other offshore centers, Madeira has space to spare.

Its free trade zone is located on a 120-hectare site, half an hour's drive from Funchal and five miles from the airport. The companies which have already set up in the free trade zone are from countries as diverse as Brazil and Lebanon, as well as from Portugal. They are engaged in activities as wide-ranging as textiles, foodstuffs, marble, tobacco, minerals, wood products and electrical appliances.

A long tax holiday, until 2011, is the obvious incentive.

The United Kingdom

As of July 1, 1994, the United Kingdom ended its 25% "advance corporation tax" on dividends funneled through holding companies in the U.K. to non-U.K. parent corporations from non-U.K. subsidiaries. Multinational parent companies typically get home-country tax credits for such foreign levies, but many have more credits than they can use, year after year.

Companies taking advantage of the U.K. change would also benefit from an existing European Union pact on dividends. Under that agreement, dividends passing through a holding company in one

EU country from a subsidiary in another can generally duck a withholding tax of 5% to 25% that is otherwise due on dividends paid to parents outside the EU. Some EU countries may impose a waiting period for new subsidiaries, however.

The U.K. may outbid the Netherlands for new holding companies.

SOME USEFUL HAVENS FOR PERSONAL RESIDENCE

Although the primary use of a tax haven is a place to base entities, such as a corporation or trust, to serve as an interface between yourself and the bureaucratic world, there may come a time when you will find that having personal residence in a tax haven country confers additional benefits. This is particularly the case if you have built up accummulated earnings in a business or in a tax-deferred annuity, and now need to receive those earnings in a residential tax haven in order to maximize the benefit.

Campione: Little Known Tax-free Backdoor to Switzerland

Campione, on the shores of Lake Lugano, is distinguished by its very uniqueness. It is a little piece of Italian soil, completely surrounded by Switzerland. There are no border controls so there is complete freedom to pass in and out of Campione. It is located in the Swiss Canton of Ticino, about 16 miles from the Italian border, and 5 miles from Lugano by road. It has about 2000 inhabitants.

Campione belongs economically to Switzerland, and uses Swiss banks and governmental facilities such as post office, telephone, telegraph, and traffic laws. Cars registered in Campione bear Swiss license plates.

Unlike Switzerland, there is no problem for foreigners in obtaining residence rights in Campione, so the enclave is enjoying a sudden

303

popularity with people looking for a way to obtain Swiss residence. Having a house or apartment in Campione is all that is necessary to obtain a residence permit in Campione, although the local authorities do require that registered residents spend at least some time in Campione.

The lack of border controls gives Campione residents totally unrestricted access to all of Switzerland and Liechtenstein, so it can be a most valuable European executive base.

Besides its residence attraction, the enclave is also gaining in popularity because it has a unique tax haven status. Although part of Italy and subject to Italian law, there are special tax requirements for Campione. There is no personal income tax and no municipal tax as all of Campione's income is raised from the operation of a municipal casino. Campione residents are not subject to Switzerland's many double taxation agreements with such countries as Canada, the U.S. and most of western Europe.

Companies formed in Campione have many advantages over Swiss companies, as they are able to use Swiss banking facilities, have a mailing address that appears Swiss, but not be subject to Switzerland's relatively high income and withholding taxes. Company law is the same as in Italy, and a corporation can be formed with a minimum capitalization of about $1000. Company formation takes longer than in Switzerland, but unlike Switzerland, a Campione company can be entirely owned and directed by foreigners. The formation work is usually handled by Italian lawyers in Milan, and the fees are modest, since this is not a special or complex matter. The personal and company tax exemptions do not apply if the resident is doing business with Italy, but business with Italy can readily be done through a Swiss or Liechtenstein corporation as an intermediary.

Foreigners may buy real estate in Campione without restrictions, unlike Switzerland, so acquisition of a site in Campione for a European regional headquarters is readily carried out with minimal red tape. Demand for real estate in Campione has pushed prices well above the level or surrounding Ticino. As a part of Italy, the European Union regulations apply to businesses, and this includes such things as the right to establish a business and residence by any citizen of another EU country.

The official language is of course Italian, and the enclave is in the Italian speaking portion of Switzerland. Many international schools are located in Switzerland, so school arrangements for children of transferred executives can be easily made.

The recent referendum in which Swiss voters rejected an affiliation with the European Union means that Campione will continue to have its special value for sometime to come. Without the free access to Switzerland that EU affiliation would have provided, the backdoor route via Campione will continue.

There are many recreation facilities in the immediate area, including golf, ski resorts, and water sports. Milan, and all of its cultural attractions, is only an hour away.

Campione's unique status has its origins in the Thirteenth Century when the village and its territory were presented by the Lord of Campione to the Church of St. Ambrosius of Milan. This feudal property survived European upheavals and remained secure to the end of the 18th Century, and then joined the new Cisalpine Republic. Afterwards Campione fell into Austria's hands for a short period and was finally incorporated into the new Kingdom of Italy.

It is one of the world's most unique, and least-known, tax havens, and a most attractive base for companies looking for a regional headquarters in Europe. It is also one of the most expensive tax havens for real estate, because there is so little of it. Apartments will range from $2500 to $3500 per square yard, and you usually pay the broker a 3% buying commission on top of that (the seller also pays 3%).

Getting started in Campione is much more difficult than in other tax havens, because the enclave is not promoting itself, and there is no central office of information to which one can turn for instant literature. You are not unwelcome, but nobody is going to go out of their way to let you in on this secret haven. So there are no promoters or agents that you can write to in advance to send you packets of nice brochures.

The only effective way to establish in Campione is to make a personal visit and spend time talking to people.

Ceuta and Melilla: Reduced Tax Rates for Residents

Two very small enclaves on the coast of Morocco are practically unknown, but may be very appealing for some purposes. The cities are Spanish, and although Spanish taxes do apply, they apply at only half the rate imposed in Spain, so they aren't pure tax havens. Both cities are completely duty-free ports as well, making them particularly useful land bases for keeping a yacht on the Mediterranean and not spending enough months in the house to be deemed resident by the Spanish tax authorities. There is also no VAT.

On the other hand, there can be an advantage to becoming a legal resident of one of the enclaves, since the cost of maintaining an apartment is low, and it provides a visible tax residence to satisfy the authorities in jurisdictions with higher taxes. Since the enclave is your declared legal residence, and you are voluntarily paying Spanish taxes (admittedly at a 50% discount) nobody is monitoring where you spend your time. As a Spanish resident, you certainly are entitled to use your town house in Madrid for business visits (perhaps five days a week), or spend time in your vacation villa in the Canary Islands. The enclave address on your tax return and your residence card is what gets you the tax break, not your physical presence.

Citizens of EU countries can establish residence automatically, because of the treaty rights to live and work anywhere in the EU. All Spanish double taxation treaties apply to the enclaves, since they are legally part of Spain. Thus, to your home country authorities, you are not residing in a tax haven. (They are unlikely to even know that you are getting a discount on your Spanish taxes.)

Between the years 1497 and 1848, Spain acquired two enclave cities and three garrison enclaves on the coast of North Africa. The combined area of these Spanish enclaves is 14 square miles. According to the Spaniards, this area, with over 100,000 Spanish citizens, represents a legal part of metropolitan Spain.

Ceuta and Melilla have about 80,000 people each. In addition to the large civilian populace in both Ceuta and Melilla, there are large garrisons of soldiers.

Both cities are situated between 35 and 36 degrees north latitude. This places them roughly on the same latitude as Cape Hatteras, Memphis, Albuquerque, and San Luis Obispo in the United States; and Malta, Crete, Cyprus, Tehran, Kabul, Pusan and Tokyo in Europe and Asia. Both of the enclaves are located on the Mediterranean side of the Strait of Gibraltar.

The city of Ceuta is directly across the Strait of Gibraltar, twelve nautical miles south of the Rock. Mount Hacho, a 636 foot high mountain on the eastern extreme end of the cape, one mile east of the center of Ceuta, and Gibraltar (elevation 1398 feet), constitute the "Pillars of Hercules" of antiquity.

The city of Melilla lies 155 nautical miles east of Ceuta, on a large cape which juts 15 miles out from the coast.

An overnight ferry goes between Ceuta and Melilla weekly, with the eastern run being Monday/Tuesday, and the western return Thursday/Friday.

Land connection is by Morocco's route P-39 — a distance of about 190 miles. Much of it is winding mountain road, so a trip by car takes about nine hours.

Melilla has a 3,000 foot runway. Normal service for Melilla airport is approximately five flights daily to Malaga. Ceuta has a military heliport. Tangier has a 9,000 foot runway and connecting flights to Casablanca, Madrid, Malaga, and Paris.

Ceuta is about nine square miles, Melilla is four square miles. By comparison, Gibraltar is only 2.4 square miles.

Ceuta and Melilla are characterized by a mild Mediterranean subtropical climate with summer drought and winter rain.

The population in each enclave is about 80% Spanish and 20% Moroccan. This Moroccan percentage can be a bit misleading however, as it refers to actual population. There are between eight and ten thousand Moroccans from the surrounding countryside who cross the borders daily, either to work or to shop. There are also several hundred shop owners from India in the enclaves, although that is still less than 1% of the population, but Indian commercial influence in the duty-free shopping industry is considered to be significant.

In practice there is little concern by the Spanish border authorities to inspect anything carried into Ceuta, either by car or on one's person. On the other hand, Moroccan customs police frequently strip search young European backpackers as they leave Morocco for Ceuta, on the assumption that they may be carrying drugs. The arrest rate on the Moroccan side has been fairly high.

Ceuta has a civil government, and the city is administered as a municipality of the Cadiz Province, and Melilla is administered by Malaga Province. But the cities also have a somewhat special status, in that they each have one Deputy and two Senators in the Spanish Parliament. For practical purposes, the city administration is the government, and there are no functions for the provincial government to carry out.

Ceuta has an excellent natural harbor, and is nearly as busy as Bilbao, the second busiest port in mainland Spain. This isn't some quiet backwater, but a booming freeport that can be a very useful and inconspicuous base. The Melilla port is also modern, but is considerably smaller than Ceuta.

Upon entering the port, Ceuta appears to have many more tall, new buildings than Melilla. This gives Ceuta a more modern look. There is much more useable pier space in Ceuta than in Melilla because much of Melilla's inner harbor is taken up by its beautiful recreational beach.

Ceuta's location at the busy strait contributes greatly to its traffic, whereas Melilla gets little traffic that is not directly destined for the port itself. For a yachtsman, this gives some edge to Ceuta for an ability to disappear in the crowd. Melilla is known for its excellent seafood, and has a small fishing fleet.

The port facility at Ceuta has many sport and recreation boats. There are rows and rows of pleasure craft, compared to a fairly small nautical club at Melilla which includes mostly small sailboats.

Ceuta is only a one-hour ferry ride from Algeciras, Spain. Since it is a shorter journey than the Algeciras-Tangier connection, it rivals Tangier as an easy entry to Morocco from Spain. The ferries carry both passengers and automobiles, and there are at least eight round trips daily — up to fifteen in tourist season. Ceuta newspapers cover happenings across the Strait in the towns around Algeciras bay, and there is close contact with the area for entertainment and visiting.

Since the mid-1960s, Ceuta has been a designated duty-free port of entry for Spain. There are about 500 small appliance stores in Ceuta, selling radios, stereos, cameras, small appliances and watches. All this commerce makes the city's economy quite strong. Other industries are fishing, tourism, and smuggling.

Melilla is much less accessible than Ceuta. Daily round trip ferry service connects Melilla with Malaga, eight hours away, although as mentioned previously, there are five flights daily that connect Melilla with Malaga.

A resident of the enclaves can buy a car duty-free, but must drive it in the enclave for one year before he can take it back to mainland Spain duty-free. In this way, one can buy a Mercedes, for example, at a price that is below even the price of the car in Germany.

Monaco: Traditional Haven of the Wealthy

There are many places where you could live and be free of income taxes, inheritance and estate taxes and real estate taxes. But most are isolated, too cold, too hot, or too distant. Monaco is the only tax haven located a short drive from several truly major cities, and at the same time in a resort area well known for its glitter and the non-stop action of major gambling casinos. It boasts fine beaches, golf and tennis clubs.

Contrary to popular belief, it is possible to live in a hotel, eat regularly, and have a pleasant month in Monaco on a budget of US$30 a day. But as a practical matter, a liveable apartment with a sea-view will cost about US$1000 a month — considerably less than half the price of similar accommodation in New York or London. And the weather is far better!

Monaco is in a slightly different league, offering banking and investment services to a wealthier clientele of tax exiles; the Monagasque financial center is less dependent on fiscal nomads and expatriates than on the international untaxed ranks of the supremely rich.

There is no shortage of heavyweight financial names represented in Monaco.

Among the 40-plus banks are American Express, Chase, Citibank, Credit Suisse, Grindlays and NatWest. They all rub shoulders with each other in and around Monte-Carlo's boulevard des Moulins. Mostly they offer discreet private banking services for Gucci-heeled lotus eaters on the Cote d'Azur. The principality is trying to balance its image as a playground for the rich by promoting itself more strongly as a serious offshore financial center.

While there is no personal income tax in Monaco (except for French nationals in certain circumstances), on the face of it corporations established in Monaco are taxed at a rate of 35 per cent. However, the taxable base to which the 35 per cent rate applies can often be significantly reduced through negotiation with the tax authorities. There are no withholding taxes in Monaco.

There are three other areas in which Monaco may have something to offer as an "offshore" financial center:

The first is mutual funds. Legislation introduced in 1988 means that neither the Monegasque fund, nor its investors, are subject to any tax in Monaco on income or gains.

There are no exchange control limits.

Secondly, Monaco is a popular center for internationally operating companies to set up a co-ordination center or 'bureau administratif.'

Finally, Monaco can be an ideal location for the locally tax-free administration of personal or closely-held investment trusts.

The United Kingdom and Ireland

While both of these would appear at first glance to be high tax countries, both have a concept of "resident but not domiciled" in their tax laws. This concept separates domicile — ones permanent home — from ones current residence. Domicile is a vague concept, since it does not necessarily require having a residence in one's domicile. Thus, a person born in Canada may be considered domiciled in Canada, even though they are living in London, and paying U.K. taxes as a resident.

That would not usually be a good position to be in, but in the case of "resident but not domiciled," one is only taxed on income actually brought into the United Kingdom (or into Ireland). Income earned abroad can continue to accumulate in offshore accounts and not be taxed. Some people reduce the tax exposure even further by setting up two accounts with their investment manager — a capital account and an income account. All income from both accounts is paid into the income account; withdrawals of U.K. (or Irish) living expenses are made only from the capital account, thus proving that one is living on capital and not on income. Hence a zero tax.

This strategy won't work forever, since one would eventually be deemed to have changed ones domicile, and it needs good hand-holding from an experienced tax practitioner, but the technique works well for many. Provided appropriate action is taken, foreign nationals living in the U.K. can often retain their foreign domiciles for many years. It's how those Arab oil sheikhs can live so well in London without being taxed.

It should be noted that the Labor Party has threatened to end this tax break, and tax the worldwide income of all U.K. residents, so if they win an election one should be prepared for a quick change of residence.

The first step is to bring capital rather than income into the U.K. (or Ireland). The capital must be "clean" capital — that is, it must not contain capital gains or income accruing while a resident in the U.K. This is not difficult to arrange. One simple way is to put cash into one offshore bank account (the capital account) before becoming a U.K. resident, and open a separate, initially empty, offshore account to which the interest earned on the cash would be credited. You would then draw on the capital account only.

So long as you are domiciled outside the U.K., only income and gains brought into the U.K. are subject to tax, and as the capital account contains neither, money paid from it to the U.K. is tax free (and the account itself provides the documentation and proof to support this position to the tax inspector).

To get even more sophisticated, if you exhaust the capital account and have to draw on the income account you would become liable to income tax on the income brought into the U.K. But this tax can still be avoided if, before drawing on the income account, it is restructured by closing it down and opening new accounts. It requires timing and planning, but it can be used to wash out the income tax liability and create a new "clean" capital account, which can be drawn on free of tax.

The last step is to put the non-U.K. assets into a suitable offshore trust. This insures that the U.K. inheritance tax on the cash is avoided on death. For inheritance tax purposes, foreign assets are only free of inheritance tax if their owner has been resident in the UK. for tax purposes for less than 17 of the last 20 tax years, so the trust must be established before the 17-year period elapses. So long as the trust assets are kept out of the U.K., no inheritance tax is payable.

If the trustees are resident and the trust is run outside the U.K., it can be used to avoid capital gains tax in the long term, and to defer income tax. (This works best if it is done before becoming a resident of the U.K., but that isn't essential for all purposes.)

The offshore trust strategy can work if it is created before taking up residence in a great many countries, since it separates legal and beneficial ownership of the assets.

The strategy also works in most (but not all) countries which have inherited their tax laws from the U.K., so if you are contemplating residence in an ex-British jurisdiction, it is worth exploring this concept with a local tax advisor.

The concept has even been carried to Israel (which obtained much of its commercial law from the U.K. during the years of the

British mandate over Palestine). New immigrants are granted exemptions on foreign-source-income for up to 30 years, thus putting a huge loophole in the normal perception of Israel as a high-tax country.

Malta and Cyprus

Malta and Cyprus have both passed legislation giving special tax benefits to foreign residents, in each case taxing only a small percentage on the amount brought into the country for living expenses. This results in a nominal tax payment, combined with the ability to claim benefits under the network of double-taxation agreements which each of these countries has. See the sections on these countries in the *Foreign-Source-Income Havens* chapter of this book for more details.

The Americas: A Variety of Residential Havens

Many Central and South American countries do not tax foreign source income. Thus living in Costa Rica, Honduras, Panama, Argentina, Uruguay, and other inexpensive but appealing countries is very practical for anyone who is not earning a local income in the country.

START YOUR OWN TAX HAVEN? THE MEN WHO WOULD BE KINGS

Two people in recent years have become so fed up with taxes that they declared independence.

Sealand

The first was Roy Bates, a former pirate radio station operator in England. He laid claim to an abandoned fort in the English channel, just outside the three mile territorial limit. He declared it to the Principality of Sealand.

Subsequent litigation in the British courts established that the fort was indeed outside of the British jurisdiction, and that the British Crown had in fact abandoned it.

No country has ever diplomatically recognized his independence, but since the only sovereign with a competing claim, Her Majesty Queen Elizabeth II has been found by one of her own courts not to be the sovereign of Sealand, Roy Bates has achieved his legal independence.

The lack of diplomatic recognition is not necessarily a handicap. There are several very real countries with little or no diplomatic recognition. The "homelands" that were granted "independence" by South Africa are recognized only by South Africa. Politicians elsewhere may treat their independence as a joke, but international treaties don't apply to them.

The Turkish Republic of Northern Cyprus is recognized only by Turkey. But it is quite obviously there, well populated, and occupying nearly half of the island of Cyprus.

Andorra has been an independent state for hundreds of years, has its own passports, and approximately 200 square miles of land (depending upon which way you measure the mountainsides). Until very recently it did not have diplomatic relations with anyone — not even the two neighbors, France and Spain, that surround it. Until 1991 it had never been a party to any international treaty — but it is a very real country, and a very popular tourist destination. In 1991 it entered a customs union agreement with the European Union, and in 1993 it joined the United Nations. But for many centuries before that it saw no need for such relationships. Andorra is a terrific residential tax haven, but does not allow company or trust formation.

Hutt River Province

More recently, an enterprising Australian has been trying to make the idea work. Leonard Castley, a Western Australian farmer, seceded from the Commonwealth of Australia in 1970.

He then proceeded to crown himself sovereign of his own principality, and stopped paying taxes to Australia.

He calls it the Hutt River Principality, and it has become something of a tourist destination, with busloads of Japanese tourists stopping to buy souvenirs. Recently the Hutt River Principality issued the world's first palladium coin, which was minted in the United States, and sold by coin dealers in various countries.

In square miles, Hutt River Province Principality dwarfs both Vatican City and Monaco.

Like most of Western Australia, however, it is sparsely populated. For most of the year, the population stands at about 30 (most of whom are royal family members); during peak harvest period, it is about twice that.

The Hutt River Province Principality issues passports and visas to visitors and mints currency embossed with an image of the prince. Stamps are sold as collector's items. About 10,000 people around the globe have become citizens of Hutt River, although the passports do not have legal recognition anywhere (yet).

The outcome of the legal battle with Australia is still undetermined, and they have not recognized the claims to independence.

These approaches may not work, but we pass them along for inspiration. With creativity you may find your own unique and successful solution, and create your own personal tax haven.

BE A PT ... DON'T LIVE

ANYWHERE AT ALL!

Do you want to escape the control over your life and property now held by modern governments? The PT concept could have been called Individual Sovereignty, because PTs look after themselves. PTs don't want or need authorities dominating every aspect of their existence from cradle to grave. The PT concept is one way to break free.

In a nutshell, a PT merely arranges his or her "paperwork" in such a way that all governments consider him a tourist — a person who is just "passing through." The advantage is that being thought of by government officials as a person who is merely "parked temporarily", a PT is not subjected to taxes, military service, lawsuits, or persecution for partaking in innocent but forbidden pursuits or pleasures. Unlike most citizens or subjects, the PT will not be persecuted for his beliefs or lack of them. PT stands for many things: a PT can be a "prior taxpayer," "perpetual tourist," "practically transparent," "privacy trained," or "permanent traveler" if he or she wants to be. The individual who is a PT can stay in one place most of the time. Or all of the time. PT is a concept, a way of life, a way of perceiving the universe and your place in it. One can be a full-time PT or a part-time PT. Some may not want to break out all at once, or become a PT at all. They just want to be aware of the possibilities, and be prepared to modify their lifestyle in the event of a crisis. Knowledge will make you sort of a PT — a "possibility thinker" who is "prepared thoroughly" for the future.

The PT concept was created by Harry Schultz, the financial consultant and author of a number of books on investing that were best sellers in the 1970s.

PT is elegant, simple, and requires no accountants, lawyers, offshore corporations, nor other complex arrangements. Since the income of most PTs is immediately doubled, and most frustrations of life with Big Brother are instantly eliminated, the logical question is only: **"Can you afford not to become a PT?"**

The PT, once properly equipped, operates outside of the usual rules, gaining mobility and a full slate of human rights. The value of these rights cannot even be perceived by people who have never experienced them. Tax havens become an important tool of the PT, because the tax haven corporations and trusts provide an interface to the more permanently settled world, just as a flag of convenience does for a ship.

The message of PT is not, however, to encourage greed, lust, irresponsibility, immorality or any of the other seven deadly sins. The effect of PT being popularized will be to release creative souls from the many burdens of coping with Big Brother.

You don't need to found a new country or displace someone else to make yourself a sovereign. The PT need not dominate other people. He or she must only be willing to break out of a parochial way of thinking: the PT must be superior only in that small area located between the ears. We speak of the potential PT now in terms of wealth, talent, intelligence and creativity. Who is this PT in the upper minuscule of the population? It might well be you...

Why A PT Needs A Tax Haven

A tax haven is an important flag in a PT entrepreneur's arsenal. Just as a PT uses a passport as his personal flag of convenience, a tax haven is his link to the bureaucratic world of business/government relations.

A PT who has only passive personal investments — bank accounts, mutual funds, unit trusts, annuities, etc. — may not need a tax haven at all. But even for the passive investor, there may be great advantages in creating a personal or family trust in a tax haven. Having all of ones finances managed from a tax haven provides a great deal of privacy, combined with professional management, and the ability to have somebody qualified and able to act on your behalf immediately in case of an emergency. Another reason is that the PT's assets can pass privately to his heirs without the interference of government probate systems, or forced inheritance laws in the country where the bank accounts or investment portfolios are held.

Tax havens truly become an important key for a PT who has any form of active business involvement — from something as limited as collecting copyright or patent royalties all the way up to a very active business. A tax haven company provides the permanent base that any company needs to deal with the world at large, since a company cannot effectively become a PT and continue to do business. The tax haven company becomes the PT's interface between his personal lifestyle and the need to anchor the business somewhere and have it appear conventional to those it does business with.

The royalty earning PT may use a tax haven company to take advantage of treaties that eliminate the withholding taxes in the high-tax countries, and then the tax haven company can funnel the money tax free to the PT.

A PT with more active business involvements may use a company in a different type of tax haven — perhaps to publish a newsletter sold on a worldwide basis, or to own a fishing trawler working the high seas, or just as a place to register his personal yacht.

GETTING STARTED AND
DOING IT RIGHT

One of the greatest problems in global investing is the naive fool who breaks laws without thinking through the consequences.

For citizens of many countries (perhaps especially for Americans), there is no such thing as a "secret" bank account, because it is a criminal offense to fail to immediately notify their government of the existence of a foreign account. This isn't only an American problem — citizens of many countries with exchange controls share this onerous legal situation. One bribed bank clerk (perhaps for a mere $100) in a so-called secrecy jurisdiction could put the client in prison for 10 to 15 years under new mandatory minimum sentencing laws.

There are so many legitimate ways that a person can make global investments without running afoul of these draconian laws, as this book has shown you, that nobody needs to do illegally what they can do legally. Proper structuring of trusts and corporations can protect one from the legal obligation to report foreign holdings.

Global investing is a legal, wonderful, profitable, activity that can diversify your investments — and provide a great deal of asset protection as an extra fringe benefit. This asset protection is a major added benefit for the global investor. Everybody has fire insurance, yet the risk of losing your assets to an unfriendly government (or in a lawsuit or divorce) is far higher than the risk of losing your house in a fire.

Global investing is where the world's wealth is flowing. If you are not internationally diversified, you are in imminent danger of losing much of your current wealth. In a recent year the Dow Jones industrial stock average turned in a 13.7% return, while the Philippine market was up 154%, Hong Kong up 116%, Peru up 140%, and Chile and Taiwan "chugged along" with 72% and 80% respectively. Of course, there was Brazil, which posted a 275% return! Many other markets returned 30% to 60%.

As an active investor, this information isn't news to you. These figures only confirm the importance of diversification and asset allocation.

The information in this book has shown you how to diversify and protect your investments overseas, profitably and safely.

The purpose of this book has been to explore the vast array of advantages available in tax havens for shrewd investors who are seriously interested in minimizing their tax burdens. How these advantages may be put to use is up to the individual, and the possible approaches are very nearly as many as the number of people who will read these words.

Seekers of a quick route to a tax haven are often enticed by newspaper advertisements or directories purporting to list purveyors of services. Some are good and some are worse than bad (worse than bad meaning that they not only steal your money but then turn you in to your home country's government, since incarcerated and broke ex-clients can't make problems.) That's why you won't find a list of instant sources in this book, and the only names and addresses given are ones of unquestioned legitimacy that I won't be embarrassed to have readers ask me about some years in the future. (Despite which, you should be aware that they are my personal recommendations, and not necessarily those of my publisher.)

The services I mention can serve every legitimate and legal need. Those looking to find an accomplice for tax evasion, money laundering, or other illicit activity should not even bother to contact them, as they'll see through it immediately. And don't expect "cookie-cutter" solutions". Every situation is unique.

It has not been my intention to recommend any particular course of action. To do so without personal consultation and very careful consideration of individual circumstances would be irresponsible and ineffective. The only way an intelligent investor can make sound decisions on putting tax havens to work for himself is by consulting expert tax advisors, considering carefully all the ins and outs, and then and only then choosing and carrying out a careful program.